# WHERE

# WARS

## GO TO

# DIE

## Other Books by W. D. Wetherell

*Souvenirs (1981)*
*Vermont River (1984)*
*The Man Who Loved Levittown (1985)*
*Hyannis Boat and Other Stories (1989)*
*Chekhov's Sister (1990)*
*Upland Stream (1991)*
*The Wisest Man in America (1995)*
*The Smithsonian Guide to Northern New England (1995)*
*Wherever That Great Heart May Be (1996)*
*North of Now (1998)*
*One River More (1998)*
*Small Mountains (2000)*
*Morning (2001)*
*This American River (2002)*
*A Century of November (2004)*
*Soccer Dad (2008)*
*Yellowstone Autumn (2009)*
*Hills Like White Hills (2009)*
*On Admiration (2010)*
*The Writing on the Wall (2012)*
*Summer of the Bass (2015)*

# WHERE

# WARS

## *GO TO*

# DIE

### The Forgotten Literature of World War I

## W. D. Wetherell

Skyhorse Publishing

Skyhorse Publishing books may be purchased in bulk at special discounts for sales promotion, corporate gifts, fund-raising, or educational purposes. Special editions can also be created to specifications. For details, contact the Special Sales Department, Skyhorse Publishing, 307 West 36th Street, 11th Floor, New York, NY 10018 or info@skyhorsepublishing.com.

Skyhorse® and Skyhorse Publishing® are registered trademarks of Skyhorse Publishing, Inc.®, a Delaware corporation.

Visit our website at www.skyhorsepublishing.com.

10 9 8 7 6 5 4 3 2 1

Library of Congress Cataloging-in-Publication Data is available on file.

Cover design by Anthony Morais

Print ISBN: 978-1-63450-246-7
Ebook ISBN: 978-1-5107-0075-8

Printed in the United States of America

*Dedication*

For Joe Medlicott
Corporal 82nd Airborne Division 1943–45

# Contents

"Some men are trained to fight, and others to write."

—Richard Harding Davis

# Introduction

It's the kind of bookstore where wars go to die, there on the lowest, dustiest, most morgue-like shelves—at least in this country. The books will rest on slightly higher, easier-to-reach shelves in Canada, Australia, Scotland, and England, where the Great War lasted longer, killed more, went deeper into the national memory. In the United States, World War I is a bottom-shelf memory, well below World War II and the Civil War, slightly below Korea and Vietnam, and only one shelf higher than the Spanish-American conflict, though the two collections often bleed into one.

A cranky, chain-smoking, opinionated old guy owns the bookstore, because that's who owns good used bookstores—cranky old guys whose only virtue is their love of books. If you're lucky, he'll have a friendly, endearingly nerdish teenager manning the cash register, and he or she will point you to the basement when you ask about books on war. The light switch will be hard to locate, there will be piles of bound *National Geographics* to edge your way around, the sump pump will still struggle with last week's soaking, and, when you do find the right shelf, you will have to get down on your knees in the muck and twist your head sideways to see what they have.

You'll sometimes smell them before you see them—books published between 1914 and 1918 are a hundred years old now, and they've taken on a distinct aroma. Bananas gone soft is what you think of first, with hints of garlic and mildew, then something that somehow manages to combine a vulgar dampness with an acrid dust. A trench might have smelled that way—a flooded trench outside Ypres circa 1916, only in place of bananas would have been much worse smells.

A bookish boy, I spent a good part of my tenth and eleventh summers leafing through my grandparents' encyclopedia, which had been passed on to my parents in the hope it would contribute to my and my sister's educations. It was old and out of date even then; published in the 1920s, it had represented a serious investment on the part of a family with little in the way of disposable income. When I leafed through the volumes, they exuded the sweet, cloying smell characteristic of a book's old age—and so the smell became forever linked in my mind with my favorite section, the one on the World War, with its old black-and-white illustrations of soldiers, cannon, tanks.

They didn't look like any soldiers I'd ever seen pictures of, which confused me greatly. The only World War known to me was the one that ended ten years before, my parents' war, the one I watched movies about, the war against Tojo and Hitler. You mean to tell me, I asked myself, there was an *earlier* World War? The soldiers in the encyclopedia wore helmets that looked like inverted pie plates and had their legs wrapped in what looked to be bandages; the tanks were rhomboid-shaped, as harmless-looking as hippos; the airplanes had doubled or even tripled wings. Fascinating—and when I pressed the pictures in toward my eyes, the pages smelled like bananas.

So it caught my attention early, World War I. I remember, a few years later, playing touch football with my pals in a grassy, doo-doo-covered park near the Long Island Rail Road station. We used jackets to mark one corner of the end zone and a twenty-foot-high monument mounted on a plinth for the other. I liked showing off my vocabulary in those days. "Go out to the plinth and cut right. Hut, two, three!" I told my receivers during the huddle, but none of them knew what I meant.

And none of them ever read what was written on the monument, much less pondered its implications—though, already the writer-in-embryo, I did both. It commemorated the 42nd Division, the famous "Rainbow" Division, which before going overseas in 1918 had been stationed in the camp that had once covered our little park. The division was called "Rainbow" because it was made up of National Guard units from thirty different states; among its famous members were Douglas MacArthur, Wild Bill Donovan, and Joyce Kilmer, who had not only written a famous two-line poem about trees but had a rest stop named after him on the New Jersey Turnpike. Even F. Scott Fitzgerald had been stationed there.

So, when our game finished and my pals all left, I scuffed my way through the fallen oak leaves and stood by the monument, peering up. It was carved out of something called "rainbow granite"—gray and smooth as it seemed from the distance, its graininess sparkled when you got up close. Engraved on the side was a tall, very grave-looking doughboy presenting arms with his rifle, his legs wrapped in what I prided myself on knowing were called "puttees."

He seemed taller and straighter than the soldiers in my grandparents' encyclopedia, or the ones in the World War II movies; he was wasp-waisted, as if the puttees continued under his uniform up his middle. I put my face up close to his legs, inhaled deeply. But no. He didn't smell like old encyclopedias. He smelled like warm stone, with a bittersweet tincture of autumn.

(I read later that two out of three soldiers who served in the Rainbow Division were wounded or killed in France, so my senses weren't making up the bitter half.)

Years later, visiting Edinburgh, still a young man, I happened upon a ceremony marking Remembrance Sunday, the British version of what in this country used to be called Armistice Day; this was 1976, so the Great War had ended fifty-eight years before. There in the square outside St. Giles Cathedral, the historic center of the Scots' world, a vast congregation was assembled, one that was composed largely of the same aging men I had noticed walking up from the New Town beside me, many with decorations and campaign ribbons on their lapels, or shilling-sized red poppies.

They now formed themselves in three long ranks on the north side of the square; on my side, troops were lined up at parade rest, staring with fixed attention toward the distant cathedral steps, where men in black and scarlet robes moved in ways that made no sense to me, but obviously had something to do with the flags and battle flags gathered there, the honor guard of young soldiers, sailors and cadets who now, at a single barked command, went rigidly to attention.

A bit slow on the uptake, it took me a while to realize this was connected to the poppies, the medals, the fixed concentration on the faces of those aging men. Remembrance Sunday—well, here was the remembrance all right, the Brits at their ceremonial best, complete with an army band playing the slow march from Holst's *The Planets*. No more poignantly martial music, given the echoes it had there, has ever been composed.

Just before the music became unbearable in that mingled note of victory and sorrow it so perfectly conveyed, it stopped, and in the silence where it had been came the high, lonely toll of the cathedral's bells striking off the hour. The eleventh hour of the eleventh day of the eleventh month. Again came that hoarse shouted command, again the hell's drumming in two separate raps against the paving stones, the rifle butts slamming down as every soldier in the square came to attention.

The old soldiers stood at attention, too, trembling, they stood so still, trembling with the rusty skill of rigidity, trembling with what they remembered. Men in their sixties, most of them, but at least a dozen were much older—men who remembered being boys, not in the Western Desert or Dunkirk, but on the Somme, or at Loos, or Cambrai. Watching them, scanning their faces, I realized it wasn't something old and vanished that was being commemorated here, as with the

Rainbow Division monument—not the memory of the Great War, but the actual event still in progress . . . that the war's pain, sorrow, and pride were right there in the square, as tangible and solid and alive as it's possible for anything to be.

I studied them very carefully, these men, their expressions. These were the soldiers in my encyclopedia come to life. These were the soldiers on my monument come to life. In their eyes, in their postures, was a war, a world, a time, I must be very careful to remember and preserve.

And so, thirty-five years now from that Sunday morning, a hundred years now from their war, I spend many hours on my hands and knees in dark bookstore basements, searching for what I can find to bring it all back. Many stores will have nothing whatsoever on World War I; others, in the shelf marked WORLD WAR II, will have mistakenly stacked books from World War I, as indeed, in future generations, the two wars may come to be conflated. But some bookstores, the best ones, will have a dozen or more books on the Great War, though, even on these rare occasions, most of the volumes I only glance at and immediately put back.

It's not because they're bad. Quite the opposite—many of these are splendidly written accounts that combine original historical research with deep human insight, allowing us to understand the events of the war with a perspective totally impossible for participants at the time. Barbara Tuchman's *The Guns of August*. Leon Woolf's *In Flanders Field*. *Death's Men* by Denis Winter. *The Face of Battle* by John Keegan. *The Danger Tree* by David Macfarlane. Martin Middlebrook's *The First Day on the Somme*. Lyn Macdonald's oral histories. Gene Smith's small classic, *Still Quiet on the Western Front*. Written fifty years and more after the war ended, these are the famous secondary sources referenced in almost every new history that comes out. I've read them all, learned lots, but when I find them on the bookstore shelf, I respectfully put them back.

And books written for the buffs, the reenactors, the military enthusiasts. There'll be two or three of these, regimental histories, or tactical analyses published quite recently, so it seems they went directly from the publisher to the remainder bin to the basement. I include in this category the memoirs, the justifications, the apologies (well, not apologies—no generals apologized) written by the primary actors in the immediate aftermath of the war. Ian Hamilton was among the most sensitive Great War generals, a skilled writer and classicist, and yet he butchered men through his incompetence at Gallipoli, and after leafing through the two fat volumes of his *Gallipoli Diary*, I respectfully put it back.

A third category holds the famous classics that form the canon of World War I literature; it will be a rare bookstore that doesn't have a copy of at least one of these memoirs or novels, though you'll be lucky to find a first edition.

Sassoon's *The Memoirs of George Sherston*. Edmund Blunden's *Undertones of War*. *Seven Pillars of Wisdom* by T. E. Lawrence. Remarque's *All Quiet on the Western Front*. Vera Brittain's *Testament of Youth*. *The Good Soldier Svejk* by Jaroslav Hasek. E. E. Cummings's *The Enormous Room*. Hemingway's *A Farewell to Arms*. *Paths of Glory* by Humphrey Cobb. *Goodbye to All That* by Robert Graves. Arnold Zweig's *The Case of Sergeant Grisha*. David Jones's *In Parentheses*. John Dos Passos's *Three Soldiers*. *Death of a Hero* by Richard Aldington. *Her Privates We* by Frederic Manning. Written by survivors of the trenches, published in the 1920s in the hangover of disenchantment left by the war, these are the books everyone knows, the books that are constantly reprinted, studied, and taught, the ones that form *the* literature of World War I, dwarfing by their power and influence almost all the books written earlier. I've read them all, been moved by their passion, surprised by their humor, amazed at their honesty— but when I find them on the shelf I respectfully put them back.

The books I'm searching for are so forgotten, so unknown, they can be easier to find than you would think. No one wants them—books published *during* the war, in the years 1914–18, not written with the hindsight that came later, but in the white heat of the conflict, when none of the authors knew which countries would be victorious or whether Western civilization would survive. These are the books I'm looking for, and when I find one, I take it to where the light is better so I can examine what I've got.

Much of it will be wretched. Blatant propaganda written by hacks, tales of Hun atrocities, books written for children where the Kaiser is shot down as he flies a Fokker across the Somme, war correspondent accounts where the Tommy, doughboy, or *poilu* (French soldier) is always cheerful, and a hundred-yard advance is scored as a great victory. Wretched—though I find even the worst to be interesting and evocative. This isn't history written fifty years after the fact, but the actual event in progress, so what you're holding in your hand has a lot more life in it than most hundred-year-old artifacts. For the time being, I'll put anything with a publication date of 1914–18 into my box as a potential keeper.

For instance—this one.

Its color draws me first. It's red, terra-cotta red—there's an appealing earthiness about the tone. On the front, slightly embossed, is a shield with inter-draped flags, though it's hard to say of which countries. But one must be of France, because, studying the spine (there is no dust cover to peel back; none of these books ever have surviving dust covers), the title becomes plain, *Fighting France,* and below that is the name "Wharton."

Could this be Edith Wharton, *the* Edith Wharton? I open the covers. The endpapers are a map of the French countryside between Varennes and Verdun, and then, turning to the title page, all becomes clear.

*The War on All Fronts*
*FIGHTING FRANCE*
*From Dunkerque to Belport*
*By*
*Edith Wharton*
*Chevalier of the Legion of Honor*
*Illustrated*
*New York*
*Charles Scribner's Sons*
*1915*

It's her all right, the famous American novelist, the pioneering woman writer, the pal of Henry James, the grande dame of American letters. What's more, here's her photo to the left of the title page, posing outside what the caption says is a "French palisade," which, in the black-and-white fuzziness, looks like five or six wicker hampers piled on top of each other, with a protective hood through which two dapper French officers peer toward what you assume are the distant German trenches.

Mrs. Wharton ignores them and faces the camera, leaning on an umbrella. She wears a long black dress, furled around her legs as the umbrella is furled; around her neck is a white bib that makes her upper half look like a pilgrim; on her head is a rakish hat. It's the kind of snapshot a husband or lover would take with his Brownie in the course of a Sunday drive—but there is that palisade behind her, those peering French officers, so it's clear that this isn't a pleasure jaunt, but a visit to the western front.

Edith Wharton—the author of *Ethan Frome*, *The Age of Innocence*, *The House of Mirth*—wrote a book on World War I? How did *that* come about? How close did she get to the actual fighting? What did this woman of supreme sensibility and refinement, this novelist with real insight into the human condition, make of the tragedy?

Yes, definitely—a keeper, to be read as soon as I get home.

Here's another, though the cover is funereal black and the lettering on the spine is hard to decipher. *The German War* by Arthur Conan Doyle, creator of Sherlock Holmes. "The German War"—is that what it was called at first? The book was printed in 1914, so it wasn't "World War I" yet, nor even the "Great War," but some bloody mess concocted by the Germans.

What was Doyle doing, publishing a book so early, when the fighting had barely started? A quick glance at the preface helps explain.

> "These essays, upon different phases of the wonderful world-drama which has made our lifetime memorable, would be unworthy of publication were it not that at such a time every smallest thing which may help to clear up a doubt, to elucidate the justice of our cause, or to accentuate the desperate need of national effort, should be thrown into the scale."

On the shelf next to Doyle, as if taking part in a chin-to-chin debate, is *Justice in War-Time* by Bertrand Russell. Russell the famous philosopher, Russell the mathematician, Russell the great popularizer of abstract thought—Russell who was one of the very few public intellectuals who dared speak out against the war while it was still in progress.

It was printed in Chicago by the Open Court Publishing Company in 1916—so maybe it was only in a still-neutral America that his anti-war writing could get published? There's an old-fashioned bookplate pasted in front showing books arranged against a window, with the marvelous name "Kenneth Glendower Darling," and a little epigraph: "Who hath a book hath but to read/And he may be a king indeed/His kingdom is his ingle-nook."

Like any old book, it implicitly asks a question. Who was Mr. Darling, and why, in a world flooded with propaganda like Doyle's, was he interested in Bertrand Russell?

Here is another book, a hundred-year-old version of a paperback, with covers so tattered and peeling it's as if the book is drawing its last breaths in my hand: *The German Terror; an historical record* by Arnold J. Toynbee.

Toynbee? Wasn't he a famous, highly respected British historian? The cover is gray around the edges, black within, with a garish German imperial eagle surrounded by jagged red flames—it seems to be rising from hell or sinking back again. There's a map in front that needs care in unfolding, but is in perfect shape after that. "The invaded country," it says, with bold red shadings showing the successive stages of the German advance through Belgium and France. The owner's name doesn't appear, but he or she, obviously an American, has scribbled something in pencil just above the publishing date MCMXVII. "We fought for freedom for ourselves in 1776, and we now fight for freedom of the world."

There's another book next to it (a really good day at the bookstore, this, but I'm compacting dozens of visits, dozens of stores, into one miraculous one), the slimmest of the four. *Treat 'em Rough: Letters from Jack the Kaiser Killer* is the title, by Ring W. Lardner.

Lardner was the great American story writer and humorist—but what was he doing writing about war? The cover shows a caricature of a baseball player—small legs and torso, thick bat, big grinning face topped by a doughboy's campaign hat—and he's following through after walloping a baseball, only the baseball is the Kaiser's mustachioed face tucked into a spiked *pickelhaube* helmet.

These books, after being published to what you assume was at least modest interest and receptivity, have gone on to hibernate through the next century, so it's natural to wonder where they've spent the interval—what care or what luck resulted in their surviving long enough for someone like me to find them.

Take the one I have open on the desk, *Essays in War-Time* by Havelock Ellis, published by Constable and Co. in London in 1917. Ellis is remembered as a pioneering researcher into human sexuality, and is usually given credit for coining the terms "homosexual" and "narcissism." He was an important name in his day, and it's understandable that he would bring his far-ranging perspective, his eye for the big picture, to the war that was tearing apart the civilization that had made his career possible.

It's easier to trace this book's history than with most. Published in London, it obviously crossed the Atlantic to the States on a ship, perhaps as a kind of literary ballast to go along with British gold for American munitions. There's a plate pasted on the endpapers, "The Gardner-Harvey Library of Miami University Middletown, Ohio," while on the opposite page is handwritten "F. B. Amato, 26th June 1928," and, below that, "From Mortimer and Daddy," so it must have been on the family's bookshelf until the 1930s. Did someone die then? Was the book then donated to the college library, which may have been interested because of Ellis's reputation?

There's a "Date Due" slip pasted on the back, but it only shows the book being checked out once, on Halloween 1960, with no dates stamped below it. The library, seeing the poor checkout record, must have discarded it at some point, probably in the 1970s, possibly offering it in a campus book sale, where some book lover found it and brought it home.

After that, it's harder to guess. Whoever bought it could have died, and his or her heirs probably donated it to yet another book sale, this one perhaps a fund-raiser at the local library or school. Someone thought well enough of it to load it in their car and drive it across the country, but then it must have ended up in the possession of someone who had no use for it whatsoever. It was somehow transferred to the Whatley Antiquarian Book Center in Whatley, Massachusetts, where (stopping to use their restroom on the way back to New Hampshire) I found it in 2009, and, taking it home, became probably only the third or fourth person to read it cover to cover in a hundred years— and found it to be informative and fascinating, with a perspective on the war far beyond what you would think that anyone writing in the midst of it could possibly achieve.

But here's the remarkable thing. As little read as these books are today, as thoroughly forgotten, there are *lots* of them—books and essays written on the Great War, during the Great War, by the best writers of the day, the greatest novelists, dramatists, poets, and philosophers. List the names and you're listing the literary giants, the Nobel Prize winners, the ones who are still read, studied, and reverenced today. James, Conrad, Shaw, Bergson, Chesterton, Wells, Yeats, Rebecca West, Edmond Rostand, Romain Rolland, Hardy, Masefield, Mann, Cocteau, Gorky, Niebuhr, Dewey, and a dozen others of comparable rank.

Add to these the books written during the war by writers who later became important (Henry Beston, for instance, who, after publishing a totally neglected book called *A Volunteer Poilu,* went on to become the best nature writer in America), the ones written by writers who should have been better known (like Mildred Aldrich, who spent four years living and writing just behind the front lines), and the books written during the war by authors, famous then, who are now totally forgotten (like the novelist Winston Churchill, the *American* Winston Churchill), and you have an entire literature of World War I that hardly anyone has paid attention to in the 100 years since it was produced.

This neglect is almost total. A recent bestselling history of the war cites 216 separate books in the "Notes" section at the end, and yet only nine of these books were published during the war itself, and none were written by the great writers listed above; in an earlier history, this one by the renowned John Keegan, 193 books are cited, but only six that were published 1914–18, and none by the above writers. In *The Penguin Book of First World War Prose*, published in 1990, the emphasis is almost entirely on books written *after* the war, and the same is true of Paul Fussell's landmark study, *The Great War and Modern Memory*, which concentrates on the postwar canon written by ex-soldiers. Hardly any mention is made of the literary giants who wrote while the war was still going on.

You need to read individual biographies of the authors to find any information about their World War I writings, and even here the record is skimpy. One otherwise excellent biography of Ring Lardner devotes no more than five or six sentences to his writings on the war, though Lardner devoted three books to the subject, managing to do the seemingly impossible—make the war humorous in a way that can still be appreciated 100 years later.

Why critics and historians have neglected these books is hard to fathom; why the general reading public forgot them is perfectly understandable. When the war ended, the very *last* thing anyone wanted to read about was the horror they had just experienced, especially when so much of the war writing—the mood having shifted—now seemed shrilly propagandistic. When war books did come back into fashion, it was the 1920s, and the mood was somber, repentant, disenchanted, so the books written back while the war was in progress, even the ones that went far beyond propaganda, now seemed hopelessly idealistic. Hemingway's heroes distrusted "big" words and abstractions—and there were lots of big words in these earlier books.

But the main reason they became forgotten was that another, even greater war came along, producing so many books on its own that the literature from the earlier war was literally pushed from the shelves. Who wanted to read about Kaiser Wilhelm when Hitler was coming to power? Who cared about Sarajevo when Pearl Harbor was under attack? Twenty years after the Armistice, World War I was now ancient history, at least to the reading public, and sympathy for poor gallant Belgium, which had moved so many readers in 1914, now seemed, in the face of fresher horrors, little more than quaint.

And something else was happening—the visual world was taking over from the world of print. When you think of World War I, no iconic photographs spring to mind; when you think of World War II, you picture a whole gallery, from the Marines raising the flag on Mount Suribachi to Mussolini hanging like cold meat at that gas station in Milan to the face of Dachau survivors as they're liberated to the sailor sweeping the girl off her feet on V-E Day in New York. People now wanted their wars photographed or newsreeled, and the few grainy black-and-white illustrations found in the World War I books, added to them as after-thoughts, hardly measured up to the dramatic images they became used to seeing in *The March of Time* or *British Pathe.*

Even without these special cultural circumstances, most of these books would have faded from view, dying the natural death almost every book eventually suffers. Cyril Connolly, writing in 1938, said that the overriding goal for an author is to write a book that will still be read ten years after it's published—and that if a book accomplishes this, then it deserves to be termed "immortal." (Shelf life being what it is today, ten weeks is the new immortal.) To survive that long, Connolly said, a book must have some "quality that improves with time."

The forgotten literature of World War I has this quality, at least the best of it. It's precisely because it *was* written on the other side of a great divide—before the visual age, before the digital age—that it has become so evocative when we try to look back. The writers who produced it were, at least potentially, the men and women whose minds were best equipped to understand what the world was going through, the ones whose hearts could most deeply feel the enormous human tragedy. "War is the most deadly earnest thing," Arthur Conan Doyle wrote, a generalization there is still no arguing with. "This war is the most tragic thing that has ever happened to mankind," added H. G. Wells, speaking more specifically—and at the time there was no question but that he was right, too.

What writers like these had to say about the war not only gives us a clearer idea of what their era was like, but speaks in terms that we can still read with profit; a hundred years is a long time, but not *that* long, not when the war ushered in a modern era that isn't done with us yet. And if the war does indeed mark the divide between what seems, on the far side, the almost ancient, and, on this side, the all-too-painfully modern, then it's in the books written from 1914 to 1918 where we can see the change happening.

(A novelist I know tells me he finds it relatively easy to imagine and write about any event from 1914 onwards, including the Great War, but impossible to contemplate a novel set in 1913 or earlier, since it would be like writing about men in armor or ladies in hooped skirts; he couldn't possibly understand them.)

"In 1914," the Bloomsbury writer Leonard Woolf wrote, "in the background of one's life and one's mind there was light and hope; by 1918, one had accepted a perpetual public menace and darkness, and had admitted into the privacy of one's soul an acquiescence in insecurity and barbarism."

Writer after writer testifies to this change. "Like a band of scorched earth dividing that time from ours," is the way Barbara Tuchman sums up the war. "In pre-war days," L. P. Hartley adds, "hope took for granted what in post-war days fear takes for granted." "A vast age of transition," Vera Brittain calls it, looking back on a war that saw the death of her brother, her fiancé, her best friend, "which carried the nineteenth century into the twentieth; the changes were apocalyptic and fundamental, and mankind was never the same again." "Much that was then taken to be fairly noble now looks pretty mean," C. F. Montague says; "Much that seemed reassuringly stable is now seen to be shaky. Civilization itself wears a strange new air of precariousness." And the American essayist Agnes Repplier worries that "The standard of evil has been forever changed."

The writers anthologized here came to maturity in that prewar world; they were a generation that believed in reason, in civilization, in art, in progress, in a human destiny that was full of hope. These were the qualities that made them the great artists they were, but it did not equip them to deal with the tragic experience of the modern, postwar world— or did it? One of the surprises in reading their work is the amount of cynicism, irony, and "modernism" that you find, even in 1914, so maybe the change wasn't quite as dramatic as later studies like to claim.

Still, the task of interpreting the war was soon given over to a younger generation of writers, particularly those who had served in the trenches and seen the obscenities of war—and thus the modern age— up close. They saw a lot, these writers, but by the same token there was much they didn't understand or care to understand; they were, as most were quick to admit, primarily focused on the little patch of No Man's Land they could see through their trench periscopes, never mind what was happening in the larger world. But it was their writings that became the war's canonical literature, their novels and memoirs that still color our view of the war, while the civilian literary response is largely ignored.

To state the obvious, middle-aged writers like Hardy, Yeats, Rolland, Mann, and Conrad never served in the trenches. They escaped the filth, the carnage, the mud, but that doesn't mean they weren't alive to it, weren't struggling to take in what was going on. Writers like Wharton understood the soldiers' agony, but also understood the pain of the refugees, the widowed, the bereaved, and the tragic implications of what was being destroyed.

These writers had an importance that wasn't confined to the world of ideas. Poets, novelists, and dramatists enjoyed a status and influence in 1914 that writers of today can only dream of; they weren't just ivory-tower intellectuals read by a harmless coterie, but celebrities, opinion makers, movers and shakers, forces for good and sometimes for evil; it's no exaggeration to say that the words of Doyle, Kipling, and Toynbee sent young men to their deaths.

The writer Russell Miller emphasizes this point. "This was an age, before radio, movies and television, when writers wielded huge social as well as literary influence, were quoted as authorities on a whole range of subjects, and were looked upon to provide a moral view of the world."

(Many of the books I find were widely read when first published. Mildred Aldrich's accounts of her life near the trenches were best-sellers in America; John Buchan's novels were the ones soldiers carried with them in the trenches; Edgar Guest's flag-and-motherhood poems appeared in most American newspapers and were read out loud at the supper table.)

And while a modern-day writer, op-editing on the latest war half a world away, will almost certainly not have a friend or relative involved in the fighting, nor gone anywhere near it him- or herself, many of these writers managed to find their way to Flanders to see for themselves what was going on. Many allowed themselves to be taken on well-organized, smoothly-run "trench tours," with a little dollop of danger at the end to make it all seem authentic, but others served in the ambulance corps, worked as nurses, or cared for refugees.

And while jingoistic, bellicose writers like Doyle and Kipling may have influenced young boys to enlist, their own sons were killed in the war, so they can't be accused of blatant hypocrisy. Other writers suffered personally as well. Conrad's son was gassed; Katherine Mansfield's brother was killed; Russell was thrown into prison; Shaw's reputation was destroyed; James, nursing the wounded, died of a broken heart.

One more point to keep in mind when it comes to these books. The authors were working in 1914, when books as physical *objects* were at the peak of their influence and power, but by 1918 had begun their long slow decline, to the point where, in our own day, books as objects have an increasingly tenuous existence, as covers, binding, flaps all disappear and words go electronic . . . and so it's a miracle that books from a hundred years ago even survive at all, let alone the great insights that, if we search them out in old bookstores, still live within those nostalgically familiar cardboard covers.

It is not sufficiently recognized that 100 years after it officially ended, with the last surviving combatants all having died, the Great War is still very much a living memory. People continue to be impacted by its pain, though it's muted now, buffered, but not yet erased. The usual simile is to a boulder being dropped into a still pond, with an explosion, then a wave, then a ripple—and more ripples, each one wider than the next, but softer, spreading a lot farther, if you study the pond carefully, than anyone would expect.

Havelock Ellis understood this as far back as 1916.

> "All these bald estimates of the number of direct victims to war give no clue to the moral and material damage done by the sudden destruction of so large a proportion of the young manhood of the world, the ever widening circles of anguish and misery and destitution which every fatal bullet imposes on humanity, for it is probably true that for every ten million soldiers who fall on the field, fifty million other persons at home are plunged into grief or poverty or some form of life-diminishing trouble."

This is well said—and Ellis could have multiplied his fifty million by a factor of ten if he drew his "ever widening circles" out across the next century.

A few examples.

After writing a novel set in Flanders in 1918, I was interviewed on public radio. The host of the program, a man named John, asked me why I had mentioned, just in passing, the "Bois de Fere" as the place where a minor character's husband has been killed.

"No particular reason," I said. "I found it footnoted in a book. The Americans fought there, a small action, not really a battle."

"Small?" He shook his head. "My grandfather was killed there. Shot through the shoulder and bled to death three hours later."

He said this matter-of-factly, but still, it hit home. It's not that John was actively grieving over his grandfather—a man my age, he had been born long after his grandfather's death—but he had a gap in his life that memories of his grandfather should have filled. I had wonderful experiences with my own grandfather (exempted from the war as a New York City fireman), he taught me many valuable things—but John had never had this, and so it's right to say he suffered from "some form of life-diminishing trouble."

Just recently, visiting a dear friend who is about to turn ninety-six, she asked me what I was working on, and I told her about this book.

"My father was in that awful war. Served with the French. My mother was terribly cross with him, going off when he didn't have to, and she was alone when I was born in 1918."

Jane told me the story—not so much about the war, which of course she doesn't remember, but a trip eight years afterward, when her father took the family over to France to see where he had fought. They went to Verdun first, and Jane described the powerful impression all the spiky, broken trees made on her little girl imagination; they then went on to Chateau-Thierry, where they visited the grave of her father's best friend, killed in the battle there.

"That's why I go to Veterans Day service in town every November," she said. "To remember Norman Williams, my father's best friend."

My wife, daughter, and I made our own pilgrimage to the Flanders battlefields a few years ago. Our guide, Annette, was a self-taught expert on the war—she lived in one of the few houses in Ypres that survived four years of fighting. On our first day, she got us up early, loaded us in her van, and off we drove toward the Somme. Along with us were a couple from Australia, a man and woman in their fifties.

Later, after touring the battlefield proper, we stopped somewhat south of it on a country lane running through the middle of rolling farmland.

"Right here," Annette announced. She got out, held the door open for the Australian woman, took her hand and led her to a grassy knoll.

The woman's great-uncle had died here in 1918, fighting with the Australians in the battle for Villers-Bretonneux. Annette, as part of her guide service, will research where your ancestor was stationed, where his unit was engaged, where he was wounded or killed. The Australian woman had never known her great-uncle, of course, but she had always been very close to her grandmother, her great-uncle's sister. Her grandmother had never been able to afford to come to France to visit her brother's grave, but, before dying, she begged her granddaughter to go visit it for her. And so, a little later, when we came to the cemetery and found the grave with his name on it, the moment—ninety-six years after he had been buried there—was almost unbearably poignant . . . and not just for the great-niece.

If you visit the Flanders battlefields or the ones along the Somme, walk the rows in the well-kept cemeteries managed by the Commonwealth War Graves Commission, stare up at the plaques to the missing and their endless names, visit Ypres, go that night to the Last Post ceremony at the Menin Gate ("We will remember them," intone the onlookers as the ceremony ends)—if you do these things, do them solemnly, you will end up thinking that one of the central purposes of the world is to remember World War I. This is Remembrance with a capital R, with many people, even now, earning their livelihood from it; thousands of pilgrims still come to the fields of the western front to see where their ancestors died.

But if you visit Kobarid in Slovenia as I have, on a very different front of the Great War, you will come to the exact opposite conclusion. Here, the war is almost totally forgotten by the larger world, though this is the epicenter of its most infamous battle. It's not Remembrance that is capitalized here, but Forgetting.

Before Kobarid was a Slovenian market town, before it was a Yugoslavian market town, before it was, briefly, an American market town (in the zone of occupation in 1945), before it was a German market town, before it was an Austrian market town, it was an Italian market town, not "Kobarid" but "Caporetto."

Caporetto was the scene of the catastrophic Italian defeat of 1917, when hundreds of thousands of Italian soldiers, poorly led, cold and weary, homesick, fled before the Austrian-German attack in the nightmarish retreat described in *A Farewell to Arms*; it's Caporetto where the Italian army got the reputation for cowardice it's never shed since.

The Italians don't want to remember Caporetto, despite Mussolini having erected, on a hill above the town, a "Charnel House" for the dead. The Austrians, victors in the battle, went on to lose the war, so they don't visit either. A few military buffs, West Point or Sandhurst types, come with their maps, and they can hire mountaineering guides to take them to where the fighting raged on improbably high Alpine peaks, but other than that, the Great War is forgotten—at least until you go for a walk in the woods.

Walk almost anywhere, especially above the beautiful Soca River (called the "Isonzo" in 1917, scene of a dozen named battles), and you'll soon come upon old dugouts, trenches, pillboxes, latrines, tunnels which the falling autumn leaves, the erosive hand of time, have blended with ruins dating from the Roman era, so sometimes—with no signage to help explain—you don't know which earthwork was raised in 1917 by Italian *Alpini* and which in 217 by Roman legionnaires. And yet, looking at these remains, climbing up the hidden stairways, knowing a little something of what happened here in 1916–17, the tragedy comes alive in an even stronger way than it does in Flanders, just because the memory isn't served to you all prettied up, but raw, so to grasp it you have to reach.

Flanders with its commemorative sites on one side of Remembrance; Caporetto and its hidden ruins on the other. It's exactly this difference that divides the familiar literary canon of World War I and the forgotten literature included here.

In the years leading up to the ninety-fifth anniversary of the war, the media kept an eye on the last known surviving veterans, and noted with sadness when each died. One of the liveliest, right to the end, was 111-year-old Harry Patch, the last known survivor of trench warfare, having been wounded in the groin at Passchendaele while serving with the Duke of Cornwall's Light Infantry in 1917. You can go online and watch an interview with Private Patch recorded shortly before his death in 2009, and it's fascinating—not just his stories of the trenches, but the wobbly yet strong voice he tells them in. It could be the voice of the Great War itself, the inflection, the tone, coming out of the mouth of the only man left who could speak to what it was like.

Now they're all gone, not only the soldiers, sailors, and nurses, but anyone who can tell us what that pre-1914 world was like. In their place, we have grainy black-and-white photographs, newspapers rotting away in museum attics, a few jumpy newsreels, and—strongest witnesses—the books written and published during the war, the ones I so assiduously seek out. Old veterans, as compelling as their stories were, tended to have their reflections shaded by everything that happened in the world since, or the expectations of the people interviewing them. The surviving books are immune to this shading. When you read them, you're getting 1914–18 pure.

On our tour of the Somme battlefield, Annette drove us to a place that is usually off-limits to most visitors. Mouquet Farm, on a slight rise behind Thiepval, was the scene of some of the heaviest fighting during the battle, the German trench line there holding out long after every other position around it had been captured; there can't have been many spots on the western front that received such concentrated shelling, nor had so many young men killed trying to take it. "Moo Cow Farm," they called it, or sometimes "Mucky Farm."

Annette had made friends with the farmer who lives there now, thanks to a gift of fine Belgian chocolates delivered every Christmas. He was on his tractor spreading manure over his fields when we got there (the fields that still show chalk white stripes where the old trenches were), but he climbed down and came over to greet us. He spoke only French, so I didn't catch all that he said, but at the end, stooping, he picked something up from the ground and handed to me as a souvenir.

It was shrapnel—three rusted, marble-sized balls of it, plus a little pretzel-like twist of rusty barbed wire. He didn't have to search hard for this—his fields are composed of scraps of old metal. It staggered me, holding these; I had enough time to wonder if it was "good" shrapnel, having exploded and gone flying directly into the earth, or whether it was "bad" shrapnel, having been intercepted by a young man's arm, leg, or heart on its way. I carefully wrapped the metal up when we got back to Annette's house and carried it with me across the Atlantic; it's been on my shelf ever since.

It brings much back, when I take it out to hold it again; it gets me thinking. But when I hold these books, the ones manufactured during the war like shrapnel was manufactured, I feel it even stronger—the last faint pulse of the past, with no rust, no tarnish, no diminution.

In almost every instance, the books from which the excerpts are drawn are ones I found through the process described above—by searching as many used bookstores as I could, near home and on my travels. Almost every book cost less than a dollar—further proof that this literature is forgotten, even by collectors.

Once, in an old bookstore in Chicago, in a locked, glassed-in case, I came across a volume that Edith Wharton put together to raise money for Belgian refugees. Published by Scribner's in 1916, it's called *The Book of the Homeless (Les Livres des San-Foyer)*. Wharton recruited her friends in the art world to contribute, so not only are there essays by Joseph Conrad and Henry James, poems by W. B. Yeats, Thomas Hardy, and Jean Cocteau; not only are there little exhortative paragraphs by Teddy Roosevelt, General Joffre, and Sarah Bernhardt; not only are there musical score excerpts from Vincent d'Indy and Igor Stravinsky (*Souvenir d'une marche boche*) . . . not only are there all these, but plates drawn by, among others, John Singer Sargent, Auguste Rodin, Claude Monet, Charles Dana Gibson, and Pierre-Auguste Renoir.

Great geniuses pitting their art against the horrors of war. Who wouldn't want to bring a book like that home? My hands were trembling when I turned to the price. $7,500. I almost cried.

But, as with every other aspect of life now, dusty old bookstores have gone online, so you can search the world with your computer for an affordable copy of a book you're longing to have. A bookstore in Pittsburgh listed a 1916 first edition of *The Book of the Homeless* for $65; some of the plates have been pilfered, but other than that it's perfect—and so one of the most interesting survivors is now mine.

While probably no one cares about the distinction but me, this is not an "anthology," not in the old sense, where writings are dumped higgledy-piggledy into a book like old clothes into a trunk, with little sorting. A "compilation" might be a better word, or, in 1914 phrasing, a "reader," a transformative reader, where the compiler shares a personal selection, with lots of comments along the way, trying to give the sense of reading and exploring together. It's also a book of literary criticism and comparison, a historical record, and not least of all a personal narrative by someone who, just when the world seems to be abandoning them, is still in love with printed books.

As much as I've learned from reading the books in their entireties, almost all of them benefit from being shortened and abridged, so there will be no shortage of editorial ellipses. As for the whys and wherefores of the passages selected, I had several considerations in mind.

Excerpts that vividly reflect the mood of the time caught my eye, as did, conversely, writings that speak to our era across the years. Some passages were chosen primarily because of who wrote them. Henry James, writing of visiting the wounded in London hospitals, uses his most impenetrable late-Jamesian style—but Henry James is, well, Henry James. Other excerpts were chosen because they contribute to telling a story, or rather two stories—one about the larger tragedy of a civilization in the process of destroying itself, the other about the individual tragedies of the souls caught up in it. (The older writers tend to be better on the first, the younger writers on the second.) Empathy is important—I was always looking for writers who rose above their nationality and remembered their humanity. Several were chosen because they are outstandingly bad, but revealing in their wretchedness, giving us insight into what people of the time, ordinary people, were reading.

It's hard to generalize about the overall mood of these writings when you have, on one hand, the radical originality of Randolph Bourne and, on the other, the cheery rhythms of the (then) world's most popular poet, Robert W. Service. But decades after the war ended, Philip Larkin, looking back on the assumptions and beliefs of the prewar era, wrote his famous line about "never such innocence again."

Innocence? Yes, perhaps—but writers like Shaw, Wells, Conrad, Mann, and Rolland, whatever else they were, were certainly not innocents.

Or were they? There was little in human nature that would have surprised fifty-year-old Nobel Prize–winning novelists, but the organized, mechanical butchery of the first truly "total" war—yes, this would have surprised them, shaken them, staggered them . . . and it's this response of brutalized innocence that colors many of the passages quoted here.

To stress a point made earlier—one of the surprises I had in compiling this book was how so many of the attitudes characteristic of what we now term the "modern" age were on display even while the war was in progress. No historian, looking back on the Great War from the cynical vantage point of the 1960s, managed more irony than George Bernard Shaw did writing in 1914; no one, writing today, had a larger, broader sense of war's human tragedy than the classicist Gilbert Murray writing in 1917. Chauvinism, jingoism, hate—there's plenty of these in the writers' responses, but there is also objectivity, generosity, forgiveness.

Murray, who understood war's awfulness better than most, still thought it was worth fighting.

"I desperately desire to hear of German dreadnoughts sunk in the North Sea," he wrote, marveling at his own bloodthirstiness. "Mines are treacherous engines of death, but I should be only too glad to help lay one of them. When I see that 20,000 Germans have been killed in such-and-such an engagement, and next day that it was only 2,000, I am sorry."

Almost all the writers included here shared this opinion, and the courage of the ones who didn't, writers like Bertrand Russell, Jane Addams, and the all-but-forgotten G. F. Nicolai, still compels our admiration 100 years later.

If I were to choose one word to describe the characteristic quality in all these writings, it would be not "innocence" but "wonder"— wonder in the old, prewar sense, meaning "to feel astonishment." The British writers in particular use the word "wonderful" surprisingly often, applying it to what in our view is the exact opposite of "wonderful"—to heavy artillery barrages or the towns those barrages destroyed. This kind of astonishment, this incapacity to believe man is capable of doing what he was then in the process of doing, this "wonder" that it isn't all a nightmare but real, colors almost every word included here. It's a response that wouldn't survive the war; after 1918, bloodlettings and butcheries wouldn't surprise us again.

There's another note that colors much of the writing: guilt. These were middle-aged or older men and women, and many of them felt ashamed and embarrassed that they were only writing about the war, not fighting it. Maurice Maeterlinck lamented, "At these moments of tragedy, none should be allowed to speak who cannot shoulder a rifle, for the written word seems so monstrously useless and so overwhelmingly trivial in the face of this mighty drama." Even a raving jingoist like Kipling, when visiting the trenches, could write, "The soldiers stared, with justified contempt I thought, upon the civilian who scuttled through their life for a few emotional minutes in order to make words out of their blood."

With the guilt came doubt—were their talents up to describing what they witnessed? Even the supremely confident Edith Wharton could speak of "those strange and contradictory scenes of war that bring home to the bewildered on-looker the utter impossibility of figuring out how the thing *really happens.*" And, assuming they could find the right words, would it even matter? H. G. Wells has his thinly disguised alter ego, Mr. Britling (in his forgotten classic, *Mr. Britling*

*Sees It Through*), penning articles about the war, worry, "If he wrote such things, would they be noted or would they just vanish indistinguishably into the general tumult? Would they be audible and helpful shouts, or just waste of shouting?"

The writers worry about understanding the war, but in the end, they all give it a try. Even as Mr. Britling frets about his son in the trenches, tries to balance this with his own involvement, he realizes, "He could find no real point of contact with the war except the point of his pen. Only at his writing desk were the great presences of the conflict his."

Most writers, while feeling those doubts, probably, in the end, consoled themselves with a reflection similar to that made by Richard Harding Davis, the great American war correspondent:

"Some men are born to fight, and others to write."

There's an important final point. This book will have much to say about war, but even more to say about literature. For it was a literary challenge each of these authors faced—how to write about something that (unlike love and hate, friendship and loneliness, hope and despair, and all the "normal" human emotions) they had never experienced before: the end of the world. For this is what they honestly thought they were faced with—the destruction of the civilization of which they were among the primary creators, and the loss of everything they held dear.

What kind of moral, ethical, and imaginative forces do you find in yourself to pit against this? In total war, writers would be expected to "enlist" like everyone else; writers in 1914 were more influential than they ever were before or ever would be afterwards; print remained the dominant means of communication. How writers used print, how they responded to the catastrophe, tells us much about the power—and lack of power—literature had at its height. The writers included here argued about the war, moralized about it, witnessed it, prevaricated and lied about it, pitied those caught up in it, mourned the dead, sought—some of them—to amuse and entertain, and, in the end, exhausted, reflected on what it all meant—and the chapters will be organized accordingly.

The books excerpted here were written with passion, sincerity, and belief, and they deserve to be read one last time, to see what's worth remembering in them and worth preserving. Taken as a whole, they should help widen and deepen the narrow literary canon of the war that has ossified into place.

So. It's the summer of 1914—to outward appearances, a time of peace and unprecedented prosperity right across the European continent. The heir to the tottering Austrian-Hungarian throne makes a foolish, ill-advised trip to the city of Sarajevo and is shot along with his wife by an amateurish Bosnian-Serbian assassin. Ordinary people hardly notice, so caught up are they in their peaceful lives, until, without warning, the thing happens, the long-dreaded *thing*, and these same people, with no quarrel against each other or conceivable interest in the fate of the silly archduke, are joining armies in their millions as if, demented, they have caught a common, lemming-like impulse of mutual extermination, an evil death wish that will all too soon come true.

The nations look to their great novelists, poets, and dramatists as they look to their statesmen and generals, desperate for guidance. A telegram arrives, the maid brings it into the parlor. It's an editor asking for a quick 1,500 words on the developing struggle, and already talking about a visit to the war zone and a possible book. (A book? Well, that's *some* good news at any rate; our writer, like other breadwinners, worries about the war robbing him of his livelihood.) The author scans it again, nods—he or she has been expecting just this—and immediately goes up to the study and starts work, determined to prove, in the unfolding crisis, that writers can do their part.

# Chapter One:

# **Argue**

Patriotism may be the last refuge of the scoundrel, but as war broke out in 1914 it was the first response of the mystery writers, the playwrights, the Nobel Prize winners. Events happened so fast that writers hardly had time for anything more nuanced than reflexive chauvinism. The archduke was shot in Sarajevo on June 28. On August 2, near the small border town of Jonchery, a French corporal named Jules Andre Peugeot shot a German lieutenant named Camille Mayer as he fired back; both died, thereby becoming the first casualties of the First World War— and eerily prefiguring the tit-for-tat stalemate of the next four years.

Four weeks later, forty thousand French soldiers had been killed and over two hundred thousand wounded, with German casualties just as high. The unstoppable inertia of mobilization, the secret treaties that compelled nations to fight, the speed of the German advance through Belgium. Writers could respond to this *fait accompli,* but they couldn't get out ahead of it, or have the luxury of arguing whether or not their country should get involved.

They argued anyway, inspired not so much by the ethos of "my country right or wrong" as by "my country *is* right—and here's why." England had only a small standing army and no conscription, so to fill up the ranks they needed volunteers and they needed them fast—many of these writers' arguments are intended to drive young men to the recruiting offices. Then, too, all eyes were already fixed on the neutral United States, the world's greatest industrial power—it was important to convince Americans that right was entirely on the Allies' side.

And posterity was an issue, right from the start. Much of the writing excerpted here, English, French, and German, seems like arguments made to future generations, an attempt to set the record straight, or rather to slant it in favor of whichever country the writer lived in, primarily by framing it as a "just war," a war of national defense.

Almost all the excerpts (Shaw's is the exception, but he had his own argumentative fish to fry) are arguments prompted by one or more of these motives. What immediately stands out is how the writers tend to treat countries as individuals, with an individual's code of morality; this could be a bitter family quarrel we're reading about, which of course in many respects it was. (H. G. Wells: "One writes 'Germany' as though it had a single brain and single purpose.") And, as in family fights, the argument quickly descends into name-calling, the French writers calling the Germans "barbarians," while the Germans—prickly proud of their *kultur*— hurl the epithet right back.

You get the sense that this vitriol was a kind of defensive transference. Maybe, in their deepest hearts, men like Galsworthy, Bergson, and Chesterton sensed that they themselves were the barbarians, and the only way to fight this realization off was to accuse the other side of being worse.

From our own cynical vantage point, most of these writers seemed easily shocked—this is one of the great differences between our era and theirs—and this adds an old-fashioned soundness to their moral outrage, so that the dropping of a tiny bomb on a Belgian town from a primitive aeroplane seems the ultimate in newfangled horror, an unspeakable outrage, a criminal brutalization of all civilized values.

And while the younger generation who would actually do the fighting eventually looked back in anger at the shrillness and chauvinism of these writers, a reader today will be struck at how *well* it's all written, never mind the tone. These were men and women who, whatever their opinions, used language with power, economy, and grace. The purple floridity of the nineteenth century was already a thing of the past; newspapers—and a large, educated reading public—had tautened up everyone's prose style.

When I first read these books, I detected something I thought at first was vanity, then realized was something deeper and more essential—supreme self-confidence. These men and women wrote believing that they were the equals of the soldiers and statesmen, and that their words would carry enormous weight.

Writers, editors, publishers, the reading public. They all seemed terribly aware of participating in "history," and wanted not only to set the record straight, but to rush into print as soon as possible. *The New Statesman,* founded in Britain by Sidney and Beatrice Webb just before the war started, commissioned essays from most of the leading writers of the day; after first appearing there, the essays were stapled together and issued as "Special War Supplements" that, tattered and faded now, diligent readers can still find in British used bookstores, complete with the original advertisements.

The more solemn and established *New York Times,* adding their own specially commissioned essays, reprinted these in the United States, binding them into book-sized, chocolate-colored volumes under the general title *Current History; the European War.* These are massive dreadnoughts of literature, ranging upwards of 1,200 pages—and that's just for Volume One, covering December 1914 to March 1915. It includes photos of the contributing writers, printed the same size and with the same prominence as kings, field marshals, and generals. My copy has a beautifully written name, "Erik Achorn," and a bookplate from "Georgia Southern College Library." Someone has stamped *Withdrawn* over it in black ink—the epitaph for a whole literature.

One of the most stridently bellicose writers of any combatant nation was Arthur Conan Doyle, fifty-five at the start of the war, and the wildly popular creator of Sherlock Holmes. He had seen war's suffering up close serving as a doctor in South Africa during the Boer War, but this didn't stop him from doing everything in his power to make sure British manhood joined wholeheartedly in this latest, more perilous fight. Before the war had even started, he organized a local rifle detachment that trained in his village; once the fighting began, he was full of war-winning ideas, ranging from the futuristic (a Channel tunnel) to the immediately practical (lifebelts for Tommies crossing to France).

He wrote *The German War* to help speed recruiting. Some of the book's anger may come from a sense of personal betrayal, since Doyle, before the war started, had been one of the leading lights of the Anglo-German Friendship Society. ("I did everything I could to avoid the war," he wrote plaintively, "and I realized that I had been wrong.")

His nephew died in the fighting, his brother-in-law, many family friends. His son Kingsley was badly wounded on the Somme, then died of the Spanish flu just weeks before the Armistice, as did Innes Doyle, the brother Conan Doyle worshipped, dying of exhaustion while serving with the army in Belgium.

With all these deaths in his own family, it's not entirely surprising that the postwar years would see Doyle putting all his considerable energy into promoting the cause of Spiritualism, hosting séances, photographing fairies, talking knowledgeably about ectoplasm. At one séance in the family parlor, Kingsley materialized, laid a hand on Doyle's shoulder, and said his wounds had healed now and he was happy. Doyle was always more like Watson than Holmes—a bluff, sports-loving pillar of the establishment—but the Great War totally unhinged him.

He came to feel the war was part of a "Divine plan" that would cleanse and purify the world before the emergence of a utopian state. After doing so much to make sure they fought, he had the courage— or effrontery—to go before the newsreel cameras in 1928 and tell British mothers still mourning their sons that they weren't really dead at all, but happy in an afterlife they could communicate with if they attended the right séance.

Europe couldn't have contained two more different sensibilities than Arthur Conan Doyle's and Maurice Maeterlinck's, yet they both hated Germany with similar passion, in the latter's case with perhaps more justification, since he was a native of the invaded Belgium. His reputation as the "Belgian Shakespeare" came from writing plays like *Pelléas and Mélisande*, adapted by Debussy into the opera that is still performed today. He was an exponent of art for art's sake, which was the exact opposite of Doyle's view of a writer's task. Yet like Doyle he had a mystical side, and became one of the leading lights of the *fin de siècle* Symbolists. He won the Nobel Prize for Literature in 1911.

At the outbreak of the war, it is said that he tried to enlist in the French Foreign Legion, though many fifty-two-year-old men would later claim they had "tried" to enlist. His hatred of the Hun led him to write a play, *The Mayor of Stillmonde*, about the occupation of Belgium. This ruined his reputation in Germany, and in 1940 he had to flee the advancing *Wehrmacht* and move to America. He wrote a classic of natural history, *The Life of the Bee*, from which Winston Churchill liked to recite to his generals.

He was considered a great sage in his day, and his essays on world events were much in demand. *Current History; the European War* includes his photo; he looks like a banker who aspires to be a poet, with a *vie de Boheme* cravat above the wide lapels of his dining jacket, and, loftily above it, a sensitive face swept by a boyish cowlick.

G. K. Chesterton, forty-four at the outbreak of the war, had the reputation of being an astute literary critic, a lover of paradox, and an eloquent apologist for the Catholic Church. Like Doyle, he wrote mysteries, with his priest-detective Father Brown solving cases through spiritual intuition.

Of all the writers in this book, Chesterton may have the largest fan base today; a search of his name on the Internet brings up three million entries. The American Chesterton Society, with over sixty local chapters, has as its goal "raising Chesterton's profile and bringing his common sense, his profound Christian faith, and his joy to a new generation so desperately in need of hope." And it has an even more ambitious goal now—getting Chesterton canonized as a Catholic saint.

His brother Cecil, also a writer, enlisted in the army and was wounded three times, dying in a hospital after the Armistice. Chesterton, who remained convinced all his life that the war was a righteous moral crusade, wrote of him, "He lived long enough to march to victory which was for him a supreme vision of liberty and the light."

Henri Bergson was much more than a public intellectual in France—he was the nation's favorite philosopher, and his lectures drew enormous crowds. He was famous for stressing the importance of what he termed *élan vital,* or "living energy"; his metaphysical worldview emphasized becoming, process, flux, over mechanistic determinism.

A bastardized version of this philosophy was taken up by the intellectually inclined in the military, particularly General Ferdinand Foch, who, long before he became the Allies' Supreme Commander, translated Bergson's *élan vital* into the "doctrine of the offensive," stressing how an army's spirit (and its bayonets) would always triumph over an army whose strength was merely in cannon. The government adopted this as its official strategy in the years just before the war, with new field regulations ordering that "The French army, returning to its traditions, henceforth admits no law but the offensive," a law that led to those 250,000 casualties in the war's first month.

Bergson was no ivory-tower intellectual. With a big reputation in America, he was sent to Washington to help negotiate the terms of the United States' joining the war; he was said to get on famously with his fellow professor Woodrow Wilson.

He was fifty-five years old at the outbreak of the war, and was married to Marcel Proust's cousin. He would receive his Nobel Prize in 1927.

When the war started, George Bernard Shaw, at fifty-eight, was at the height of his power and influence, not only as a popular playwright, but as England's most prominent iconoclast, contrarian, and gadfly. He was Protestant Irish, and saw himself as an outsider who could deliver bitter home truths to the British public. ("I retain my Irish capacity for criticizing England with something of the detachment of a foreigner, and with a slightly malicious taste for taking the conceit out of her.") He published a long, deliberately provocative pamphlet in 1914, *Common Sense About the War*, which generated as much controversy as anything he ever wrote.

He was immediately attacked on all sides—there was even talk of prosecuting him for treason. It wasn't until 1923 and his enormously popular *St. Joan* that he managed to restore his popularity. *Heartbreak House*, written during the war, reflects his bitterness about British society and his disillusionment with a world at war.

Shaw was no pacifist, and when you read his writings on the war, it's clear that he is basically in favor of it; what he objects to is the way it's being considered and approached—he believes that if the Great War were run *his* way, England would be better off. As one writer puts it, "Shaw seemed to be one of the belligerents himself, enjoying the use of his verbal firepower in his pugnacious campaign against politicians' ineptitude and his audience's fatal misunderstanding of what is going on."

Despite—or because of—his iconoclastic stance, Shaw became friends with one of the war's great heroes, T. E. Lawrence; when Lawrence joined the Royal Air Force as an enlisted man after the war, he used the pseudonym "Shaw." Shaw himself published a hard-to-find story during the war to raise money for Belgian children, "The Emperor and the Little Girl," wherein the Kaiser encounters an innocent child on a corpse-ridden battlefield.

He won his Nobel in 1925, and died, age ninety-four, from a fall while trimming a tree.

It's not surprising that the British establishment immediately hit back at Shaw for his views; what's surprising is who one of the counterattackers turned out to be.

The thirty-four-year-old Christabel Pankhurst along with her mother and sister were the most prominent suffragettes in England, the founders of the influential Women's Social and Political Union; their militant campaign for women's rights made them detested by some, worshipped by others. Pankhurst had been imprisoned for assault after interrupting a Liberal Party meeting in 1905. She fled to Paris to avoid being imprisoned again, returning to England only when war broke out.

And now something strange happened. Pankhurst turned all her considerable passion and energy to supporting the war. Not just supporting it—demanding that it be fought as ruthlessly as possible. Primed with a generous (and secret) grant from the government, she changed the name of her paper from *The Suffragette* to *Britannia,* and traveled the country making speeches that urged the introduction of conscription and the immediate replacement of those politicians whose attitudes toward Germany weren't sufficiently hawkish.

Famous before the war for her "anti-male" stance, she now seemed obsessed (a cynic might say) with getting as many young males killed as possible. Her supporters were said to be the ones who handed white feathers to men of military age not in uniform. While this has the feel of an urban legend transformed into history, Pankhurst was a past master of such attention-grabbing tactics, so she may have indeed been behind it.

In 1936, for her services to England during the war, she was made a Dame Commander of the Order of the British Empire.

By the time John Galsworthy was forty-seven, he had achieved a reputation as one of England's most important novelists and playwrights, with a special talent for dissecting the lives of the prosperous upper middle class.

He tried his best to contribute to the war effort, working as a hospital orderly in France, letting his house be used as a rest center for wounded soldiers, and writing articles and essays for England's official War Propaganda Bureau. By the end of the war, he had gained a reputation as a strong advocate for disabled veterans, but felt guilty over his early propaganda work.

> "I have often thought during these past years, what an ironical eye Providence must have been turning on National Propaganda—on all the disingenuous breath which has been issued to order, and all those miles of patriotic writings dutifully produced in each country, to prove to the other countries that they are its inferiors! A very little wind will blow these ephemeral sheets into the limbo of thin air. Already they are decomposing, soon they will be dust."

His linked novels, *The Forsyte Saga,* got a new life in later years when, like so many other British novels from that era, it was filmed as a BBC miniseries. He won the Nobel Prize in 1932.

Arnold Bennett was another big prewar name in England, thanks to his bestselling 1908 novel about the industrial Midlands, *The Old Wives' Tale,* though many critics dismissed him as an unapologetic hack (he liked to brag about churning out half a million words a year). "He was a merchant of words," one summary puts it, "frankly writing for money, but writing with extraordinary facility and keen observation."

He lived in France for eight years prior to the war (he was forty-seven when it broke out), and had married a French actress—so it was no surprise when, after writing suitably jingoistic articles for the secret War Propaganda Bureau, he was made Director of Propaganda in France for the Ministry of Information.

In 1915, he toured the western front, and his shock at the conditions in the trenches, it is said, caused him to be physically ill for several weeks afterwards.

> "A great nation assailed by war has not only its frontiers to protect; it must also protect its good sense. It must protect itself from the hallucinations, injustices, and follies which the plague lets loose. To each his part: to the armies the protection of the soil of their native land; to the thinkers the defense of its thoughts."

No one did more to protect "good sense" during the war than the man who wrote these lines: the French novelist Romain Rolland, author of the ten-volume *Jean-Christophe,* which brought him the Nobel Prize in 1915. He had an immense reputation across Europe, but that didn't save him from being savagely excoriated from all sides when he published a book called *Above the Battle* in 1915, laying out with impeccable logic and passion the insanity of Germans, French, and English alike.

The uproar forced him to leave France for Switzerland, where he spent the war years doing his best to help combatants of all armies through his *Agence internationale des prisonniers de guerre,* and reading and rereading his beloved Tolstoy.

He was forty-eight when the war started, well up in middle age, but he was and remained a fierce defender of the rights of the young against the evil of the old: "Young men," he implored, "do not bother about old people. Make a stepping-stone of our bodies and go forward."

*Jean-Christophe* had been one of the very few novels predicting the war, which lent even more authority to Rolland's antiwar stance. Despite the abuse, he was a writer more than capable of standing up for himself.

"For a year I have been rich in enemies," he wrote in 1915 in the preface to his book. "Let me say this to them: they can hate me, but they will not teach me to hate. I have no concern with them. My business is to say what I believe to be fair and humane. Whether this pleases or irritates them is not my business. I know that words once uttered make their way of themselves. Hopefully I sow them in the bloody soil. The harvest will come."

The writer that Rolland is addressing, Gerhart Hauptmann, largely forgotten now, once enjoyed a reputation equal to Rolland's own. He won the Nobel Prize in 1912 for naturalistic plays in the Ibsen style, like *The Weavers,* which brought him world fame. Fifty-two when the war broke out, he was considered by the German authorities as suspiciously radical, possibly a pacifist, though it's clear from this entry that he could defend German actions as fiercely as the most rabid patriot.

Hauptmann's reputation had its ups and downs after the war. The Weimar Republic anointed him as one of the great German immortals, but his reputation suffered abroad; he remained in Germany under the Nazis and this was held against him, though his posthumously produced play, *The Darkness,* was one of the first German works to try to come to terms with guilt toward the Jews.

It wasn't just novelists, playwrights, and poets that were commissioned to write about the war as it broke out. Jerome K. Jerome, at fifty-five, was England's most popular humorist thanks to his still highly readable account of a trip down the Thames, *Three Men in a Boat,* which sold over a million copies worldwide. During the war, he gave up writing and served as an ambulance driver for the French. Forgotten now, he managed to sound like the adult in the room at a time when writers with more serious reputations were responding semi-hysterically.

He's in Bartlett's for a one-liner more than a little applicable to wartime propaganda.

"It is always the best policy to speak the truth, unless, of course, you are an exceptionally good liar."

American writers, when war approached their own country, would respond like their German, French, and English colleagues, turning out articles and essays for the leading magazines and newspapers; Americans, though, could afford to argue in comparative leisure, with their country maintaining a precarious neutrality for the war's first three years. Writerly arguments in America could potentially affect policymakers in a way they couldn't over in Europe.

Booth Tarkington was almost unique in American literary history, being a novelist who enjoyed both a high critical reputation and enormous public popularity. His *Penrod* remains a classic account of a Midwestern boyhood, while his *Alice Adams* and *The Magnificent Ambersons* both won Pulitzer Prizes, the latter being turned into one of Orson Welles's best movies. Forty-seven when America joined the war, he would publish, under the "National Security League" imprint, an impossible-to-find book with the provocative title *The Rich Man's War.*

## The Most Desperately Earnest Thing
### —Arthur Conan Doyle

When one writes with a hot heart upon events which are still recent one is apt to lose one's sense of proportion. At every step one should check oneself by the reflection as to how this may appear ten years hence, and how far events which seem shocking and abnormal may prove themselves to be a necessary accompaniment of every condition of war. But a time has now come when in cold blood, with every possible restraint, one is justified in saying that since the most barbarous campaigns of the Thirty Years War there has been so such deliberate policy of murder as has been adopted in this struggle by the German forces. This is the more terrible since these forces are not bands of turbulent mercenary soldiers, but they are the nation itself, and their deeds are condoned or even applauded by the entire national Press. It is not on the chiefs of the army that the whole guilt of this terrible crime must rest, but it is upon the whole German nation, which for generations to come must stand condemned before the civilised world for this reversion to those barbarous practices from which Christianity, civilisation, and chivalry had gradually rescued the human race. They may, and do, plead the excuse they are "earnest" in war, but all nations are earnest in war, which is the most desperately earnest thing of which we have any knowledge. How earnest we are will be shown when the question of endurance begins to tell. But no earnestness can condone the crimes of the nation which deliberately breaks those laws which had been endorsed by the common consent of humanity.

War may have a beautiful as well as a terrible side, and be full of touches of human sympathy and restraint which mitigates its unavoidable horror. Such have been the characteristics always of the secular wars between the British and the French. Could one imagine Germans making war in such a spirit? Think of their destruction of the University of Louvain and the Cathedral of Reims. What a gap between them—the gap that separates civilisation from the savage!

Can any possible term save a policy of murder be applied to the use of aircraft by the Germans? It has always been a principle of warfare that unfortified towns should not be bombarded. What is to be said, then, for the continual use of bombs by the Germans, which have usually been wasted in the destruction of cats or dogs, but which have occasionally torn to pieces some woman or child? If bombs were dropped on the forts of Paris as part of a scheme for reducing the place, then nothing could be said in objection, but how are we to describe the action of men who fly over a crowded city dropping bombs promiscuously which can have no military effect whatever, and are entirely aimed at the destruction of innocent civilians? These men have been obliging enough to drop their cards as well as their bombs on several occasions. I see no reason why these should not be used in evidence against them, or why they should not be hanged as murderers when they fall into the hands of the Allies. It is a murderous innovation in the laws of war, and unless it is sternly repressed it will establish a most sinister precedent for the future.

If the words of one humble individual could reach across the sea, there are two things upon which I should wish to speak earnestly to a German: the one, our own character, the other, the future which he is deliberately preparing for the Fatherland which he loves. Our papers do get over there, even as theirs come over here, so one may hope it is not impossible that some German may give a thought to what I say, if he is not so bemused by the atmosphere of lies in which his Press has enveloped him that he cannot recognise cold truth when he sees it.

First as to ourselves: we have never been a nation who fought with hatred. It is our ideal to fight in a sporting spirit. It is not that we are less in earnest, but it is that the sporting spirit itself is a thing very largely evolved by us and is a natural expression of our character. We fight as hard as we can, and we like and admire those who fight hard against us so long as they keep within the rules of the game. All British prize-fights end with the shaking of hands. Though the men could no longer see each other, they were led up and their hands were joined. When a combatant refuses to do this, it has always been looked upon as unmanly, and we say that bad blood has been left behind. So in war we have always wished to fight to a finish and then be friends, whether we had won or lost.

Now, this is just what we should wish to do with Germany, and it is what Germany is rapidly making impossible. She has, in our opinion, fought a brave but thoroughly foul fight. And now she uses every means to excite a bitter hatred which shall survive the war. The Briton is tolerant and easy-going in times of peace—too careless, perhaps, of the opinion of other nations. But at present he is in a most alert and receptive mood, noting and remembering very carefully every word that comes to him as to the temper of the German people and the prospects of the future. He is by no means disposed to pass over all these announcements of permanent hatred. On the contrary, he is evidently beginning, for the first time since Napoleon's era, to show something approaching hatred in return. He—and "he" stands for every Briton across the seas as well as for the men of the Islands—makes a practical note of it all, and it will not be forgotten, but will certainly bear very definite fruits. The national thoughts do not come forth in wild poems of hate, but they none the less are gloomy and resentful, with the deep, steady resentment of a nation which is slow to anger.

But the pity of it all! We might have had a straight, honest fight, but all this has been rendered impossible by all these hysterical scream-ers of hate, and by those methods of murder on land, sea, and in the air with which the war has been conducted.

It is understood that this is a fight to the end. That is what we desire. Our grandchildren will thrill as they read of the days that we endure.

From *The German War* by Arthur Conan Doyle; Hodder and Stoughton, London, 1914.

## *They Must Be Destroyed*
### —Maurice Maeterlinck

At these moments of tragedy none should be allowed to speak who cannot shoulder a rifle, for the written word seems so monstrously use-less and so overwhelmingly trivial in face of this mighty drama that will for a long time and maybe forever free mankind from the scourge of war—the one scourge among all that cannot be excused and that can-not be explained, since alone among all scourges it issues entirely from the hands of man.

This is the moment for us to frame our inexorable resolution. After the final victory, when the enemy is crushed—as crushed he will be—efforts will be made to enlist our sympathy. We shall be told that the unfortunate German people are merely the victims of their mon-arch and their feudal caste; that no blame attaches to the Germany we know that is so sympathetic and cordial—the Germany of quaint old houses and open-hearted greetings; the Germany that sits under its lime trees beneath the clear light of the moon—but only to Prussia; that homely, peace-loving Bavaria, the genial, hospitable dwellers on the banks of the Rhine, the Silesians and Saxon—I know not who besides—have merely obeyed and been compelled to obey orders they detested, but were unable to resist.

We are in the face of reality now. Let us look at it well and pronounce our sentence, for this is the moment when we hold the proofs in our hands; when the elements of the crime are hot before us and should out—the truth that will soon fade from our memory. Let us tell ourselves now therefore that all we shall be told thereafter will be false. Let us unflinchingly adhere to what we decide at this moment when the glare of the horror is upon us.

It is not true that in this gigantic crime there are innocent and guilty or degrees of guilt. They stand on one level, all who have taken part. The German from the north has no more especial craving for blood than the German from the south has especial tenderness and pity. It is very simple. It is the German from one end of the country to the other who stands revealed as a beast of prey. We have here no wretched slaves dragged along by a tyrant King who alone is responsible. Nations have the governments they deserve, or rather the Government they have is truly no more than a magnified public projection of the private morality and mentality of a nation.

No nation can be deceived that does not want to be deceived.

We have forces here quite different than those on the surface—forces that are secret, irresistible, profound. It is these we must judge, must crush under heel once for all, for they are the only ones that will not be improved, softened, or brought into line by experience, progress, or even the bitterest lessons. Their springs lie far beneath hope or influence. They must be destroyed as we destroy a nest of wasps.

Even though individually and singly Germans are all innocent and merely led astray, they are none the less guilty in mass. This is the guilt that counts—that alone is actual and real, because it lays bare underneath their superficial innocence, the subconscious criminality of it all. No influence can prevail on the unconscious or subconscious. It never evolves. Let there come a thousand years of civilization, a thousand years of peace, with all possible refinements, art, and education, the German spirit which is its underlying element will remain absolutely the same as today and would declare itself when the opportunity came under the same aspect with the same infamy.

Through the whole course of history two distinct will-powers have been noticed that would seem to be the opposing elemental manifestations of the spirit of our globe, one seeking only evil, injustice, tyranny, suffering, the other strives for liberty, right, radiance, joy. These two powers stand once again face to face. Our opportunity is to annihilate the one that comes from below. Let us know how to be pitiless that we have no more need for pity. It is essential that the modern world should stamp out Prussian militarism as it would stamp out a poisonous fungus that for half a century had poisoned its days. The health of our planet is the question. Tomorrow the United States and Europe will have to take measures for the convalescence of the earth.

From *Current History; the European War;* The New York Times Company, New York, 1915.

## *The Most Sincere War*
### —G. K. Chesterton

Unless we are all mad, there is at the back of the most bewildering business a story; and if we are all mad, there is no such thing as madness. If I set a house on fire, it is quite true that I may illuminate many other people's weaknesses as well as my own. It may be that the master of the house was burned because he was drunk; it may be that the mistress of the house was burned because she was stingy, and perished arguing about the expense of the fire-escape. It is, nevertheless, broadly true that they both were burned because I set fire to their

house. That is the story of the thing. The mere facts of the story about
the present European conflagration are quite as easy to tell.

Before we go on to the deeper things which make this war the
most sincere war of human history, it is easy to answer a question of
why England came to be in it at all; as one asks how a man fell down
a coal hole, or failed to keep an appointment. Facts are not the whole
truth. But facts are facts, and in this case the facts are few and simple.

Prussia, France, and England had all promised not to invade
Belgium, because it was the safest way of invading France. But Prussia
promised that if she might break in through her own broken promise
she would break in and not steal. In other words, we were offered at
the same instant a promise of faith in the future and a proposal of
perjury in the present.

Upon the immediate logical and legal origin of the English interest
there can be no rational debate. There are some things so simple that
one can almost prove them with plans and diagrams, as in Euclid.
No; upon the cold facts of the final negotiations, as told by any of
the diplomatists in any of the documents, there is no doubt about the
story. And no doubt about the villain of the story . . . .

It will be noted that this ultimate test applies in the same way
to Serbia as to Belgium and Britain. The Serbians may not be very
peaceful people; but on the occasion under discussion it was certainly
they who wanted peace. You may choose to think of the Serb as a sort
of born robber; but on this occasion it was certainly the Austrians
who were trying to rob. Similarly, you may call England perfidious as
a sort of historical summary, and declare your private belief that Mr.
Asquith was vowed from infancy to the ruin of the German Empire.
But when all is said, it is nonsense to call a man perfidious because he
keeps his promise.

Lastly, there is an attitude not unknown in the crisis against which I
should particularly like to protest. I should address my protest especially
to those lovers and pursuers of peace who, very shortsightedly, have

occasionally adopted it. I mean the attitude which is impatient of these preliminary details about who did this or that and whether it was right or wrong. They are satisfied with saying that an enormous calamity called war has been begun by some or all of us, and should be ended by some or all of us. To these people this preliminary chapter about the precise happenings must appear not only dry, but essentially needless and barren. I wish to tell these people that they are wrong; that they are wrong upon all principles of human justice and historic continuity; but that they are especially and supremely wrong upon their own principles of arbitration and international peace.

We keep the peace in private life by asking for the facts of the provocation and the proper object of punishment. We do not go into the dull details; we do inquire into the origins; we do emphatically inquire who it was that hit first.

Given this, it is indeed true that behind these facts are the truths—truths of a terrible, of a spiritual sort. In mere fact the Germanic power has been wrong about Servia, wrong about Russia, wrong about Belgium, wrong about England, wrong about Italy. But there was a reason for its being wrong everywhere, and that root reason, which has moved half the world against it, is nothing less than the locating, after more than a hundred years of recriminations and wrong explanations, of the modern European evil—the finding of the fountain from which poison has flowed upon all the nations of the earth . . . .

The Prussian begins all his culture by that act which is the destruction of all creative thought and constructive action. He breaks that mirror in the mind in which a man can see the face of his friend or foe. The truth is that they are breaking up the whole house of the human intellect that they may abscond in any direction. There is an ominous and almost monstrous parallel between the position of their overrated philosophers and of their underrated soldiers. For what their professors call roads of progress are really routes of escape.

From *Current History; the Euopean War*; The New York Times Company, New York, 1915.

# *The Moral Energy of Nations*
## —Henri Bergson

The issue of the war is not doubtful: Germany will succumb. Material force and moral force, all that sustains her, will end by failing her because she lives on provisions garnered once for all, because she wastes them and will not know how to renew them.

Everything has been said about her material resources. She has money, but her credit is sinking, and it is not apparent where she can borrow. She needs nitrates for her explosives, oil for her motors, bread for her sixty-five millions of inhabitants. For all this she has made provision, but the day will come when her granaries will be empty and her reservoirs dry. How will she fill them? War as she practices it consumes a frightful number of her men, and here, too, all revitalization is impossible; no aid will come from without, since an enterprise launched to impose German domination, German "culture," German products, does not and never will interest those who are not Germans.

But it is not merely a question of material force, of visible force. What of the moral force that cannot be seen and that is more important than the other, since without it nothing avails?

The moral energy of nations, like that of individuals, can only be sustained by some ideal superior to themselves, stronger than they are, to which they can cling with a strong grip when they feel their courage vacillate. Where lies the ideal of contemporary Germany? The time has passed when her philosophers proclaimed the inviolability of justice, the eminent dignity of the individual, the obligation laid upon nations to respect one another. Germany militarized by Prussia has thrust far from her those noble ideas which came to her for the most part from the France of the eighteenth century and the Revolution.

The Germany of the present worships brute force. And as she believes herself strongest she is entirely absorbed in adoration of herself. Her energy has its origins in this pride. Her moral force is only the confidence by which her material force inspires her. That is to say, that here also she lives on her reserves, that she has no means of revitalization. Long before England was blockading her coasts she had blockaded herself morally by isolating herself from all ideals capable of revivifying her.

Therefore she will see her strength and her courage worn out. But the energy of our French soldiers is linked to something which cannot be worn out, to an ideal of justice and liberty. Time has no hold on us. To a force nourished only by its own brutality we oppose one that seeks outside of itself, above itself, a principle of life and renewal. While the former is little by little exhausted, the latter is constantly revived. The former already is tottering, the latter remains unshaken. Be without fear; the one will be destroyed by the other.

From *Current History; the European War;* The New York Times Company, New York, 1915.

## *I Do Not Hold My Tongue Easily*
### —George Bernard Shaw

The time has now come to pluck up courage and begin to talk and write soberly about the war. At first the mere horror of it stunned the more thoughtful of us; and even now only those who are not in actual contact with or bereaved relation to its heartbreaking wreckage can think sanely about it, or endure to hear others discuss it cooly. As to the thoughtless, well, not for a moment dare I suggest that for the first few weeks they were all scared out of their wits. But they certainly were— shall I say a little upset? They felt in that solemn hour that England was lost if only one single traitor in their midst let slip the truth about anything in the universe. It was a perilous time for me. I do not hold my tongue easily; and my inborn dramatic faculty and professional habit as a playwright prevent me from taking a one-sided view even when the most probably result of taking a many-sided one is prompt lynching.

Having thus frankly confessed my bias, which you can allow for as a rifleman allows for the wind, I give my views for what they are worth. They will be of some use; because, however blinded I may be by prejudice or perversity, my prejudices in this matter are not those which blind the British patriot, and therefore I am fairly sure to see some things that have not yet struck him.

And first, I do not see this war as one which has welded Governments and peoples into complete and sympathetic solidarity against the common enemy. I see the people of England united in a fierce detestation and defiance of the views and acts of Prussian Junkerism. (What is a Junker? Is it a German officer of twenty-three, with offensive manners, and a habit of cutting down innocent civilians with his sabre? Something like this—but he is by no means peculiar to Prussia; we may claim to produce the article in a perfection that may well make German despair; our governing classes are overwhelmingly Junker.) And I see the German people stirred to the depths of a similar antipathy to English Junkerism, and anger at the apparent treachery and duplicity of the attack made on them by us in their extremest peril from France and Russia. I see both nations duped, but alas! not quite unwillingly duped, by their Junkers and Militarists into wreaking on one another the wrath they should have spent in destroying Junkerism and Militarism in their own country. And I see the Junkers and Militarists of England and Germany jumping at the chance they have longed for in vain for many years of smashing one another and establishing their own oligarchy as the dominant military power in the world.

No doubt the heroic remedy for this tragic misunderstanding is that both armies should shoot their officers and go home to gather in their harvests in the villages and make a revolution in the towns; and though this is not at present a practical solution, it must be frankly mentioned, because it or something like it is always a possibility in a defeated conscript army if its commanders push it beyond human endurance when its eyes are opening to the fact that in murdering its neighbors it is biting off its nose to vex its face, beside riveting the intolerable yoke of Militarism more tightly than ever around its own neck.

But there is no chance—or, as our Junkers would put it, no danger—of our soldiers yielding to such an ecstasy of common sense. They have enlisted voluntarily; they are not defeated nor likely to be; their communications are intact and their meals reasonably punctual; they are as pugnacious as their officers; and in fighting Prussia they are fighting a more deliberately, conscious, tyrannical, personally insolent, and dangerous Militarism than their own. Still, even for a voluntary professional army, that possibility exists.

I mention all this, not to make myself disagreeable, but because military persons are now talking of this war as likely to become a permanent institution like the Chamber of Horrors at Madame Tussaud's . . . .

What has made Germany formidable in this war? Obviously her overwhelmingly superior numbers. That was how she rushed us back almost to the gates of Paris. The organization, the readiness, the sixteen-inch howitzer helped; but it was the multitudinous *kanonnen-futter* that nearly snowed us under. The British soldier at Cambrai and Le Cateau killed and killed until his rifle was too hot to hold and his hand was paralyzed with slayer's cramp; but still they came and came.

Well, there is no obscurity about that problem. The Germans who took but an instant to kill had taken the travail of a woman for three-quarters of a year to breed, and eighteen years to ripen for the slaughter. All we have to do is to kill, say, 75 per cent. of all the women in Germany under 60. Then we may leave Germany her fleet and her money, and say "Much good may they do you." Why not, if you are really going in to be what you call a Nietzschean Superman? War is not an affair of sentiment. It is not more cowardly to kill a woman than it is to kill a wounded man. And there is only one reason why it is a greater crime to kill a woman than a man, and why women have to be spared and protected when men are exposed and sacrificed. That reason is that the destruction of the women is the destruction of the

community. Men are comparatively of no account; kill 90 per cent.
of the German men, and the remaining 10 per cent. can repeople her.
But kill the women, and *Delenda est Carthago.* Now this is exactly
what our militarists want to happen to Germany. Therefore the objection to killing women becomes in this case the reason for doing it . . .

Supermen! Nonsense! O, my brother journalists, if you revile the
Prussians, call them sheep led by snobs, call them beggars on horseback,
call them sausage eaters, depict them in the good old English fashion
in spectacles and comforter, seedy overcoat buttoned over paunchy
figure, playing the contrabass tuba in a street band; but do not flatter
them with the heroic title of Superman, and hold up as magnificent
villainies worthy of Milton's Lucifer these common crimes of violence
and lust that any drunken blackguard can commit when the police
are away, and that no mere multiplication can justify. As to Nietzsche,
with his Polish hatred of Prussia, when did he ever tell the Germans to
allow themselves to be driven like sheep to the slaughter in millions by
mischievous dolts who, being for the most part incapable of reading
ten sentences of a philosophic treatise without falling asleep, allow
journalists as illiterate as themselves to persuade them that he got his
great reputation by writing a cheap gospel for bullies? . . . .

Prussia's ruler, with the kid gloves he called mailed fists and the high
class tailoring he called shining armor, is in practice a most peaceful
teetotaller, as many men with their imaginations full of the romance
of war are. He had a hereditary craze for playing at soldiers; and he
was and is a naive suburban snob, as the son of The Englishwoman
would naturally be, talking about "the Hohenzollerns" exactly as my
father's people in Dublin used to talk about "the Shaws." His stage
walk, familiar through the cinematograph, is the delight of romantic boys, and betrays his own boyish love of the parade ground. It is
frightful to think of the powers which Europe, in its own snobbery,
left in the hands of this Peter Pan. His victory over British and French
democracy would be a victory for Militarism over civilization; it would
literally shut the gates of mercy on mankind. Let Thomas Atkins,

Patrick Murphy, Sandy McAlister, and Pitou Dupont fight him under what leadership they can get, until honour is satisfied, simply because if St. George does not slay the dragon the world will be, as a friend of mine said of Europe the other day, "no place for a gentleman." . . .

The one danger before us that nothing can avert but a general raising of the human character through the deliberate cultivation and endowment of democratic virtue without consideration of property and class, is the danger created by inventing weapons capable of destroying civilization faster than we produce men who can be trusted to use them wisely. At present we are handling them like children. Now children are very pretty, very lovable, very affectionate creatures (sometimes); and a child can make nitroglycerine or chloride of nitrogen as well as a man if it is taught to do so. We have sense enough not to teach it; but we do teach the grown-up children. We actually accompany that dangerous technical training with solemn moral lessons in which the most destructive use of these forces at the command of kings and capitalists is inculcated as heroism, patriotism, glory and all the rest of it. It is all very well to fire cannons at the Kaiser for doing this; but we do it ourselves. It is therefore undeniably possible that a diabolical rhythm may be set up in which civilization will rise periodically to the point at which explosives powerful enough to destroy it are discovered, and will then be shattered and thrown back to a fresh start with a few starving and ruined survivors . . .

To sum up, we must remember that if this war does not make an end of war in the west, our allies of to-day may be our enemies of to-morrow, as they are of yesterday, and our enemies of to-day our allies of to-morrow as they are of yesterday; so that if we aim merely at a fresh balance of power, we are as likely as not to negotiate our own destruction. We must use the war to give the *coup de grace* to medieval diplomacy, medieval autocracy, and anarchic export of capital, and make its conclusion convince the world that Democracy is invincible, and Militarism a rusty sword that breaks in the hand. We must free our soldiers, and give them homes worth fighting for. And we must, as the old phrase goes, discard the filthy rags of our righteousness, and fight like men with everything, even a good name, to win, inspiring and encouraging ourselves with definite noble purposes (abstract nobility butters no parsnips) to face whatever may be the price of proving that war cannot conquer us, and that he who dares not appeal to our conscience has nothing to hope from our terrors.

From *Current History; the European War,* The New York Times Company; New York, 1915.

## *Mere Wordmonger to Shame*
### —Christabel Pankhurst

His reputation for perversity and contrariety is full maintained by George Bernard Shaw in the ineptly-named "Common Sense About the War." At home in Britain we all know that it is Mr. Shaw's habit to oppose where he might be expected to support, and vice versa. He sees himself as the critic of everything and everybody—the one and only man who knows what to do and how to do it.

Mr. Shaw charges his compatriots with intellectual laziness, but they are not so lazy as to leave him to do their thinking for them. That he sometimes—and oftener in the past than now—says illuminating things is true, but firm reliance cannot be placed on his freakish mental processes, exemplified in his writings about the war. He has played with effect the part of jester to the British public, but when, as now, his jests are empty of the kernel of good sense, the matter gets beyond a joke.

The truth is that in face of this great and tragic reality of war the men of mere words, the literary theorists, are in danger of missing their way. Certainly women of deeds are more likely to see things aright than are men of words, and it is as a woman of deeds that I, a suffragette, make answer to my irresponsible compatriot, Mr. Bernard Shaw. And yet not a compatriot, for Mr. Shaw disclaims those feelings of loyalty and enthusiasm for the national cause that fills the mass of us who live under the British flag!

The suffragettes, who have fought and suffered for their cause as no living man reformer in the British Isles has fought and suffered for his, have during the present crisis subordinated their claim to the urgent claims of national honor and safety. So Mr. Shaw, whose campaigning is done generally in the armchair, and never in any place more dangerous than the rostrum, ought surely to refrain from his frivolous, inconsistent, destructive and unprofitable criticism of our country.

As for the question of lynching, Mr. Shaw is, the American public may be assured, in no danger whatsoever of being lynched. He is in far more danger of having the Iron Cross conferred upon him by the Kaiser. The only retribution that will come upon this man, who exploits the freedom of speech and pen that England gives him, is that his words will lose now and henceforth the weight they used to have. Oh, the conceit of the man, who in this dark hour, when the English are dying on the battlefield, writes of "taking the conceits out of England" by a stroke of his inconsequential pen! . . .

The spirit of national freedom, which is as precious to humanity as is the spirit of individual freedom, cannot be driven out by words any more than it can be driven out by blows. The most unlettered Belgian soldier, fighting for a truth that is at the very heart and depth of all things true, puts the mere wordmonger to shame. We fight for the all-sufficient reason of self-defense.

From *Current History; the European War*, The New York Times Company, New York, 1915.

## *The God of Force*
—John Galsworthy

I believe in peace with all my heart. I believe that war is outrage—a black stain on the humanity and fame of man. I hate militarism and the god of force. I would go to any length to avoid war for material interests, war that involved no principles, distrusting profoundly the common meaning of the phrase "national honor."

But I believe there is a national honor charged with the future happiness of man, that loyalty is due from those living to those that will come after; that civilization can only wax and flourish in a world where faith is kept; that for nations, as for individuals, there are laws of duty, whose violation harms the whole human race; in sum, that stars of conduct shine for peoples, as for private men.

And so I hold that without tarnishing true honor, endangering civilization present and to come, and ruining all hope of future tranquility, my country could not have refused to take up arms for the defense of Belgium's outraged neutrality, solemnly guaranteed by herself and France . . .

I do not believe that jealous, frightened jingoism has ever been more than the dirty fringe of England's peace-loving temper, and I profess my sacred faith that my country has gone to war not from fear, not from hope of aggrandizement, but because she must—for honor, for democracy, and for the future of mankind.

From *Current History; the European War;* The New York Times Company; New York, 1915.

## *I Am a Professional Observer*
### —Arnold Bennett

To come at the truth by observation about a foreign country is immensely, overpoweringly difficult. I am a professional observer: I have lived in Paris and the French provinces for nine years; I am fairly familiar with French literature and very familiar with the French language—and I honestly would not trust myself to write even a shilling handbook about French character and life.

Still, I do myself believe that the heart of the German people is in the war, and that the heart is governed by two motives—the motive of self-defense against Russia and the motive of overbearing self-aggrandizement. I do not base my opinion on phenomena which I have observed. Beyond an automobile journey through Schleswig-Holstein, which was formidably tedious, and a yacht journey through the Kiel Canal which was somewhat impressive, I have never traveled in Germany at all. I base my opinion on general principles. In a highly educated and civilized country such as Germany (the word "civilized" must soon take on a new significance!) it is impossible that an autocracy, even a military autocracy, could exist uprooted in the people. Prussian militarism may annoy many Germans, but it pleases more than it annoys, and there can be few Germans who are not flattered by it. That the lower classes have an even more tremendous grievance against the upper classes in Germany than in England or France is a certitude. But the existence and power of the army are their reward, their sole reward, for all that they have suffered in hardship and humiliation at the hands of the autocracy. It is the autocracy's bribe and sweetmeat to them.

The Germans are a great nation; they have admirable qualities, but they have also defects, and among their defects is a clumsy arrogance, which may be noticed in any international hotel frequented by Germans. The war may be autocratic, dynastic, what you will; but it is also national, and it symbolizes the national defect.

From *Current History; the European War*, The New York Times Company, New York, 1915.

## *The Children of Attila*
### —Romain Rolland

I am not, Gerhart Hauptmann, one of those Frenchmen who regard Germany as a nation of barbarians. I know the intellectual and moral greatness of your mighty race. I know all that I owe to the thinkers of old Germany; and even now, at this hour, I recall the example and words of *our* Goethe—for he belongs to the whole of humanity—repudiating all national hatreds and preserving the calmness of his soul on those heights "where we feel the happiness and misfortunes of other people as our own." I have labored all my life to bring together the minds of our two nations; and the atrocities of this impious war in which, to the ruin of European civilization, they are involved, will never lead me to soil my spirit with hatred.

Whatever pain, then, your Germany may give me, whatever reasons I have to stigmatize as criminal German policy and the means it employs, I do not attach responsibility for it to the people which is burdened with it and is used as its blind instrument. It is not that I regard, as you do, war as a fatality. A Frenchman does not believe in fatality. Fatality is the excuse of souls without a will. War springs from the weakness and stupidity of nations. One cannot feel resentment against them for it; one can only pity them. I do reproach you with our miseries; for yours will be no less. If France is ruined, Germany will be ruined too. I did not even raise my voice when I saw your armies violating the neutrality of noble Belgium.

But when I see the fury with which you are treating that magnanimous nation whose only crime has been to defend its independence and the cause of justice to the last . . . that is too much! The world is revolted by it. Keep those savageries for us, Frenchmen, your true enemies! But to wreak them against your victims, this small, unhappy, innocent Belgium people . . . how shameful this is!

And not content to fling yourselves on living Belgium, you wage war on the dead, on the glories of past ages. You bombard Maines, you burn Rubens, and Louvain is now more than a heap of ashes—Louvain with its treasures of art and of science, the sacred town! What are you, then, Hauptmann, and by what name do you want us to call you now, since you repudiate the title of barbarians? Are you the grandsons of Goethe or of Attila? Are you making war on enemies or on the human spirit? Kill men if you like, but respect masterpieces. They are the patrimony of the human race. You, like all the rest of us, are its depositories; in pillaging it, as you do, you show yourselves unworthy of our great heritage, unworthy to take your place in that little European army which is civilization's guard of honor.

It is not the opinion of the rest of the world that I address myself in challenging you, Hauptmann. In the name of our Europe, of which you have hitherto been one of the most illustrious champions, in the name of the civilization for which the greatest of men have striven all down the ages, in the name of the very honor of your Germanic race, Gerhart Hauptmann, I abjure you, I challenge you, you and the intellectuals of Germany, among whom I reckon so many friends, to protest with all your energy against this crime which is recoiling upon you.

If you fail to do this, you will prove one of two things: either that you approve what has been done—and in that case may the opinion of mankind crush you—or else that you are powerless to raise a protest against the Huns who command you. If this be so, by what title can you still claim, as you have claimed, that you fight for the cause of liberty and human progress? You are giving the world a proof that, incapable of defending the liberty of the world, you are even incapable of defending your own, and that the best of Germany is helpless beneath a vile despotism which mutilates masterpieces and murders the spirit of man.

I am expecting an answer from you, Hauptmann, an answer that may be an act. The opinion of Europe awaits as I do. Think about it: at such a time silence itself is an act.

From *Above the Battle*; The Open Court Publishing Company, Chicago, 1916.

## *Are We Barbarians?*
### —Gerhart Hauptmann

You address me, Herr Rolland, in public words which breathe the pain over this war (forced by England, Russia and France), pain over the endangering of European culture and the destruction of hallowed memorials of ancient art. Your beautiful novel *Jean-Christophe* will remain immortal among us Germans. But France became your adopted fatherland; therefore your heart must now be torn and your judgement confused. You have labored zealously for the reconciliations of both peoples. In spite of all this when the present bloody conflict destroys your fair concept of peace, as it has done for so many others, you see our nation and our people through French eyes, and every attempt to make you see clearly and as a German is absolutely sure to be in vain.

Naturally everything which you say of our Government, of our army and our people, is distorted, everything is false, so false that in this respect your open letter to me appears as an empty black surface.

War is war. You may lament war, but you should not wonder at the things that are inseparable from the elementary fact itself. Assuredly it is deplorable that in the conflict an irreplaceable Rubens is destroyed, but—with all honor to Rubens!—I am among those in whom the shattered breast of his fellow-man compels far deeper pain.

And, Herr Rolland, it is not exactly fitting that you should adopt a tone implying that the people of your land, the French, are coming out to meet us with palm branches, when in reality they are plentifully supplied with cannon, with cartridges, yes, even with dumdum bullets. It is apparent that you have grown pretty fearful of our brave troops! That is to the glory of a power which is invincible through the justice of its cause. The German soldier has nothing whatsoever in common with the loathsome and puerile were-wolf tales which your lying French press so zealously publishes abroad, that press which the French and the Belgium people have to thank for their misfortune.

Let the idle Englishmen call us Huns; you may, for all I care, characterize the warriors of our splendid *Landwehr* as sons of Attila; it is enough for us if this *Landwehr* can shatter into a thousand pieces the ring of our merciless enemies. Far better that you call us sons of Attila, cross yourselves in fear and remain outside our borders, than that you should indict tender inscriptions upon the tomb of our German nation, calling us the beloved descendants of Goethe. The epithet Huns is coined by people who, themselves Huns, are experiencing disappointment in their criminal attacks on the life of a sound and virtuous race, because it knows the trick of parrying a fearful blow with still more fearful force. In their impotence, they take refuge in curses.

I say nothing against the Belgian people. The peaceful passage of the German troops, a question of life for Germany, was refused by Belgium because the Government had made itself a tool of England and France. This same Government then organized an unparalleled guerrilla warfare in order to support a lost cause, and by that act—Herr Rolland, you are a musician!—struck the horrible keynote of conflict . . . .

The barbarian Germany has, as is well known, led the way among other nations with her great institutions for social reform. A victory would oblige us to go forward on this path and to make the blessings of such institutions general. Our victory would, furthermore, secure the future existence of the Teutonic race for the welfare of the world . . . .

I hear that abroad an enormous number of lying tales are being fabricated to the detriment of our honor, our culture, and our strength. Well, those who create these idle tales should reflect that the momentous hour is not favorable for fiction. On three frontiers our own blood bears witness. I myself have sent out two of my sons. All our intrepid German soldiers know why they are going to war. There are no illiterates to be found among them; all the more, however, of those who, beside their rifle, have their Goethe's *Faust,* their *Zarathustra,* a work of Schopenhauer's, the Bible, or their Homer in their knapsack. And even those who have no book in their knapsack know they are fighting for a hearth at which every guest is welcome.

On the frontier stands our blood testimony; the Socialist stands side by side with the bourgeois, the peasant beside the man of learning, the Prince beside the workman; and they all fight for German freedom, for German domestic life, for German art, German science, German progress; they fight with the full, clear consciousness of a noble and rich national possession, for internal and external goods, all of which serve for the general progress and development of mankind.

From *Current History; the European War*, The New York Times Company, New York, 1915.

## *The Man Who Does His Fighting with His Mouth*
### —Jerome K. Jerome

There is a certain noisy and, to me, particularly offensive man (and with him, I am sorry to say, one or two women) very much to the fore just now with whose services the country could very well dispense. He is the man who does his fighting with his mouth. Unable for reasons of his own to get at the foe in the field, he thirsts for the blood of the unfortunate unarmed and helpless Germans that the fortunes of war have stranded in England. He writes to the paper thoughtfully suggesting plans that have occurred to him for making their existence more miserable than it must be. He generally concludes his letter with a short homily directed against the Prussian Military staff for their lack of the higher Christian principles.

Our weapons have to be hard blows, not hard words. We are tearing at each other's throats; it has got to be done. It is not a time for yelping.

Jack Johnson as a boxer I respect. The thing I do not like about him is his habit of gibing and jeering at his opponent while he is fighting him. It isn't gentlemanly and it isn't sporting. The soldiers are fighting in grim silence. When one of them does talk, it is generally to express admiration of German bravery. It is our valiant stay-at-homes, our valiant clamorers for everybody else to enlist but themselves, who would have us fight like some drunken fish hag, shrieking and spitting while she claws . . .

Half of these stories of atrocities I do not believe. The truth is bad enough, God knows. There is no sense in making things out worse than they are. War puts a premium on brutality and senselessness. Men with the intelligence and instincts of an ape suddenly find themselves possessed of the powers of a god. And we are astonished that they do not display the wisdom of a god!

When this war is over we will have to forget it. To build up barriers of hatred that shall stand between our children and our foeman's children is a crime against the future.

From *Current History; the European War*, The New York Times Company, New York, 1915.

## *All Normal Americans*
### —Booth Tarkington

All normal and educated Americans have been from the beginning "pro-ally." There are no exceptions. A few "prominent" citizens, not a dozen, have been entertained and personally enlightened by the Kaiser, or by his close adherents, and are "pro-Germans"; but that sort of enlightenment, of course, is destructive to education, and these troubled gentlemen have had no visible influence, though one hears that two or three of them have been able to convert their wives to the German view. There are also, here and there, a few "pro-German" oddities, quirk-brained persons and tender hearted souls, who are "for Germany" because everybody else is cursing Germany. They are of no consequence and may fairly be classed as not normal . . .

We were the onlookers from the beginning, and we saw that the Germans made the war. We saw that the German Nation went into the war with a patriotic stupidity, magnificent and horrible; that the German Nation was wholly in the grip of a herd instinct which had been used by manipulators; and that these manipulators, having made the Germans into a loyal, warlike tribe, brought on the war in the approved manner employed by all war chiefs desiring a war. Their unblemished hypocrisy was of an old, old model always employed by war chiefs—and absolutely obvious to any mind not under the sway of herd instinct. The Germans saw what happened here. They understood that an impartial national mind had judged them; so they naturally organized a stupendous campaign attacking our judgement. For their purpose, their propaganda accomplished precisely nothing.

Their descendants, who will probably become civilized over the course of time, will be dishonored by this crime, but the barbarians who committed it will naturally never comprehend the shame of it . . .

And about our getting rich through the sale of munitions to the Allies. I am sorry if that sale is what causes our prosperity. It is a horrible way to make money. It is absolutely necessary that we furnish munitions to the Allies; and we shall not tolerate interference with our manufacture and shipping of these munitions, but I wish there was no profit-taking. However, under any circumstances, the Allies must be supplied with munitions—*for they must win!*

That is the American thought.

From *Current History; the European War,* The New York Times Company, New York, 1916.

# Chapter Two:

# Moralize

After the initial war hysteria ran its course, a slightly more measured, nuanced, and thoughtful response became possible, especially by the prominent older writers who had hitherto remained silent. Compared to the likes of Doyle and Arnold Bennett, they were the literary heavy hitters, writers with real insight into the human condition. Their motives differed from the jingoists and apologists; they weren't trying to justify the war (though most of them supported it) as much as they were trying to understand it, and understand in particular the complex moral issues at stake.

Implicit in their writings is a difficult question—literature never faced a tougher one, at least not until the Holocaust. Can an elegant prose style, a flexible syntax, talent with simile, an ear for rhythm and cadence, parenthetical phrasings, a huge vocabulary be brought to bear on the horrors of total war?

Well, they would give it a try—and they would do this without any illusions about the enormity of the task.

While the mood temporarily brightened in September 1914, when the Battle of the Marne saved Paris, the elation was soon sobered by the stalemate of trench warfare. Christmas that year featured the spontaneous, short-lived truce on the western front, but 1915 saw disaster after disaster, including the first use of poison gas at Ypres, the butchery at Loos (forty-eight thousand British casualties), the sinking of the *Lusitania,* the spread of fighting to Africa and the Middle East, the fiasco of Gallipoli, brutal "wastage" on the eastern front (by early 1915, Austria-Hungary had lost 1,268,000 men), and the massacres of the Armenians in Turkey.

The enormous trench system fronted by barbed wire on both the western and eastern fronts came to symbolize the war's futility. By 1917, measured from Memel on the Baltic to Czernowitz in the Carpathians, and from Nieuport in Belgium to the Swiss border near Freiburg, the trenches stretched for over 1,200 miles.

"You could get to Switzerland along this trench," an officer explained to Rudyard Kipling when he visited the front.

> "And from here to the other end you will find the same mess. This isn't war. It's worse. It's an entire people who are being engulfed and swallowed up. They arrive here, fill up the trenches, and then die here. They die and they die and then watch others who die just as they will die."

While soldiers facing no man's land could still fool themselves into thinking that the war would soon be over, this was harder to do for the well-connected, well-informed writers trying to take in the larger picture. Conrad, James, Hardy, Wells. They tried to be the adults in the room, detached from the politics, but fully engaged with the enormous tragedy their civilization was facing.

Should they have done more? Toward the end of the war, Romain Rolland, writing from his refuge in Switzerland, judged them very harshly.

> "The war has disordered our ranks. Most of the intellectuals placed their art, their reason, at the service of the government. Let us point out the disasters that have resulted from the almost complete abdication

of intelligence throughout the world, and from its voluntary enslavement to the unchained forces. Thinkers, artists, have added an incalculable quantity of envenomed hate to the plague which devours the flesh and spirit of Europe. They have worked to destroy mutual understanding and mutual love among men. So doing, they have disfigured, defiled, debased, degraded thought, of which they were the representatives."

It would be hard to argue with Rolland's verdict, looking back on these writers now. In writing history, it's best not to judge using hindsight, but in assessing literature we do it all the time—and it's difficult to understand why the literary giants, who saw and understood so much, didn't make the extra moral effort to condemn their own side as much as they did the opposing one. A brave few did—we will read their work later—but the giants excerpted here wrote nothing that risked their enormous reputations.

The best of them, the ones whose writings still resonate a hundred years later, were at least honest enough to admit that they found the war a torturous and tragic reversal of all they held dear. The one book that captures this best—the struggle of a sensitive writer to understand the Great War—is H. G. Wells's *Mr. Britling Sees It Through*, which, though forgotten now, is *the* classic novel of World War I, or rather, the classic *civilian* novel of World War I.

My copy is the May 1917 edition published by Macmillan in New York. On the title page is listed the twenty-two reprintings the novel had had since it was published the previous September—an astonishing tribute to its popularity. "Gladys Stinnaman" is the name elegantly penciled in the front, and she added the date, "July 1917." In the back, testifying further to Wells's enormous influence, are advertisements for his earlier novels, including *The War in the Air*, published in 1907, which accurately predicted the battles that were now taking place between Fokkers and Spads in the skies over France.

The binding is the deep red that publishers of the day favored for their big names, with proud gold lettering for the title. It has just one illustration, a color frontispiece, with a handsome young man (he turns out to be an American) standing with his arms crossed, staring down at a pretty, redheaded Gibson girl reading a book on a garden bench. They will turn out to be minor characters—Wells needs a naive, well-meaning American to symbolize a naive, well-meaning America—but love and romance sold books even then, never mind the novel's darkly serious themes.

The real hero of *Mr. Britling Sees It Through* is the title character, who is very much Wells himself—a renowned public intellectual who, after writing suitably patriotic articles at war's start, retreats to the countryside and begins having second (and third and fourth) thoughts. It may be the bravest, most honest account of an intellectual dealing with the war that we have—and, by writing frankly about his own tortured sympathies and thoughts, Britling/Wells manages to speak for all those other writers who were trying to find a language suitable for a tragedy whose horrors not a single one of them had foreseen.

Joseph Conrad's short novel *The Heart of Darkness* is such an unsparing depiction of the horrors central to the modern world that it comes as a shock to realize it was written in 1899, fifteen years before the Great War started. Still, if any writer was equipped by temperament and talent to understand the unfolding tragedy, it was surely Conrad, with his pessimism and irony, his empathy for strong men in situations of extreme duress . . . but he wrote very little about the war, and it seems to have caught him by surprise.

Dangerous surprise. Of all times to leave England for a European vacation, he chose the summer of 1914, taking his family to his birthplace in Poland just as the war was breaking out. He was very nearly caught and interned there as an enemy civilian; it was only by some behind-the-scenes diplomatic work that he was allowed to travel to Vienna (now an enemy capital) and on through Italy to home, an experience he chose to write about when Edith Wharton asked him to contribute an essay to *The Book of the Homeless* to raise money for Belgian refugees.

Once this initial adventure was over, he had a hard time settling in, writing to a friend:

> "Fact is I am hard up simply because I haven't been able to write of late to any serious amount. I have been more affected morally and physically by the war than I thought possible. Perhaps if I had been able to lend a hand in some way I would have found the war easier to bear."

Word of this itchiness must have been passed to the Navy, because the veteran sea captain (he was fifty-nine) was invited to go on a twelve-day cruise on the HMS *Ready*, an armed "Q" boat disguised as a merchant vessel to lure German submarines. As his son John noted, the experience cheered Conrad up, changing him "from the gouty individual I knew to an able and energetic seaman almost as soon as his feet hit the deck."

This was the high point of the war for him before things got darker. His son Borys was gassed and shell-shocked near Cambrai in October 1918. This gave Conrad a sardonic view of the Armistice when it came, writing to a friend:

> "The great sacrifice is consummated—and what will come of it to the nations of the earth the future will show. I cannot confess to an easy mind. Great and very blind forces are set catastrophically over all the world."

Conrad is the one writer you wish had written a Great War novel who didn't. Was he too old to take it on? Was the tragedy too vast for him? Was horror a subject he could only write about if it took place not in Flanders, but in the Congo or the South Seas?

Henry James, the great aesthetician and moralist (Conrad called him "the historian of fine consciences") was seventy-one when the war broke out, and not a well man. Various physical ailments were ganging up on him, but even more disturbing was the heart trouble caused by having lived long enough to witness the civilization he wrote about so brilliantly about come crashing down in flames.

For James, World War I was "a nightmare from which there is no waking save by sleep." Shortly after it began, he wrote to some American friends:

> "I write to you under the black cloud of portentous events on this side of the world, horrible, unspeakable, iniquitous things. I mean horrors of war criminally, infamously precipitated . . . Black and hideous to me is the tragedy that gathers and I'm sick beyond cure to have lived to see it. You and I, the ornaments of our generation, should have been spared the wreck of our beliefs that through the long years we had seen civilization grow and the worst become impossible . . . it seems to me to *undo* everything, everything that was ours, in the most horrible retroactive way—but I avert my eyes from the monstrous scene."

He tried his best to help the war effort. He opened his London house to Belgian refugees, accepted the chairmanship of the American Volunteer Motor-Ambulance Corps, took out British citizenship (he listed Prime Minister Asquith as a reference on his application), and visited wounded soldiers at St. Bartholomew's Hospital in London.

"The men probably didn't know who he was," his biographer Leon Edel writes.

"What came through to them was his kindness, his warmth . . . All his life he had preached the thesis of 'living through' and 'infinite doing.' Now he practiced it in full measure. It gave him new reason for existence, and through the rest of 1914 and well into 1915, until recurrent illness slowed him up, he surrendered himself to the soldiers."

He died February 28, 1916, without knowing how the war would end. A year earlier, he had been cajoled by his friend Edith Wharton ("Almost too insistently Olympian," he said of her) to contribute an essay to *The Book of the Homeless,* and the result, "The Long Wards," is one of the last pieces he wrote.

Cyril Connolly would call James's later style a "tyranny of euphonious nothings," but, at least in this context, its intricacies show a refined intelligence trying bravely, via language, to come to terms with war's evil.

Thomas Hardy, seventy-four, could remember as a boy talking to veterans of Wellington's army; his three-part drama in verse, *The Dynasts,* was considered by many critics to be the most memorable literary response to the Napoleonic Wars written by an Englishman.

But perhaps one war is all a writer can be asked to respond to in a lifetime. "Hardy seems to have been aged ten years by this war," his wife wrote in 1914. "I think he feels the horror of it so keenly that he loses all interest in life."

He was nothing if not patriotic, so, when called to the (later) infamous meeting of British writers called by Charles Masterman, head of the War Propaganda Bureau, he not only attended, but tried his best to write poems to order, including the wretched, well-meant "A Call to National Service."

"I now would speed like yester wind and whirred
Through yielding pines; and serve with never a slack

So loud for promptness all around outcries!"

He did better with "Before Marching and After," which was dedicated
to the memory of a favorite nephew killed on the western front.
"But he still only asked the spring starlight, the breeze
What great thing or small thing his history would borrow
From that Game with Death he would play on the morrow"

To Hardy's great credit, he kept an eye out for the young war poets,
including Siegfried Sassoon who, though decorated for his bravery in the
trenches, would soon become famous for his bitterly antiwar poems. "I
do not know how I could stand the suspense of war," the old poet wrote
the younger one, "if it were not for the sustaining power of poetry."

When Edith Wharton came begging for a contribution to her
anthology, he offered a poem that manages to suggest, however tentatively,
that perhaps not *just* Germany was to blame for unleashing the war.

Few British intellectuals wrestled with the moral implications of the
war as assiduously as Gilbert Murray. An Oxford don, he enjoyed a
wide reputation as the leading authority on ancient Greek language
and culture; his translations of Euripides brought him tremendous
acclaim, and there could be few humanists in Europe who understood
more about tragedy than he did.

In 1917, he put together a collection of his talks and speeches,
*Faith, War and Policy,* and had it published in the United States by
Houghton Mifflin. My copy is from the library of Rev. Henry L.
Griffin, D.D., of the Bangor Theological Seminary—just the sort of
person, you feel, who *would* buy the book.

"Such interest as this book may possess," Murray writes in the
introduction,

>"will be in large part historical. Changes have assuredly
>been wrought in the minds of all thoughtful people

throughout Europe by the experiences of these shattering years. And it seems worth while to have a record
of the mind of a fairly representative English Liberal,
standing just outside the circle of official politics."

Murray, then fifty-one, wrote better than he knew. His essays
show the torment of a supremely civilized writer trying to come to
terms with war's horror; much of it reads like a passionate *anti*-war
tract, and yet, when you read closer, it's clear that he supported the
war and thought it should be fought with all necessary rigor.

His great friend Bertrand Russell, who reached just the opposite
conclusion, held his views in contempt, writing, "I naturally expected
that Murray would be on the side of peace, yet he went out of his way
to write about the wickedness of the Germans, and the superhuman
virtues of Sir Edward Gray."

Murray deserved better than this—and when Russell went to
prison for his own antiwar views, Murray tried his best to come
to Russell's aid. Later in the war, he worked with H. G. Wells for a
postwar league of nations, and eventually became one of the founders
of the famine-relief organization Oxfam. His ashes are buried in
Westminster Abbey.

Thomas Mann would come to regret his wartime writings.
*Reflections of a Nonpolitical Man* (written in part to refute his
brother Heinrich's influential essay "Zola" that defended French
culture) stressed the primacy of conservative values over liberal
ones, and pointed to Germany as the supreme defender of the
former and hence the war's righteous party.

"War!" he wrote in November 1914. "We felt purified, liberated;
we felt an enormous hope."

He had already achieved an international reputation as one of the
world's great novelists, and his panegyric to war appalled many who
admired him, including the great German composer Richard Strauss.

"It is sickening," he wrote in a letter, referring to Mann, "to read in the papers of the regeneration of German art . . . to read how the youth of Germany is to emerge cleansed and purified from this 'glorious war,' when in fact one must be thankful if the poor blighters are at least cleansed of their lice and bed-bugs, and cured of their infections, and once more weaned from murder."

Romain Rolland, the conscience of Europe, was if anything even madder than Strauss.

"In an access of delirious pride and exasperated fanaticism, Mann employs his envenomed pen to justify the worst accusations that have been made against Germany. He affirms that *Kultur* and Militarism are brothers—their ideal is the same, their aim the same, their principle the same. Their enemy is peace—war brings out strength."

Mann soon outgrew these views—Nazi Germany would have no more ardent enemy—and he was forced into exile in 1933. Thirty-nine years old when the war broke out, he would go on to win the Nobel Prize for Literature in 1929.

By 1914, Mary Augusta Ward had come to epitomize the values of Victorian England that were already being discredited, including her choice of a byline to write her enormously popular religious-themed novels. It was never "Mary Ward" on the title page, always "Mrs. Humphrey Ward." No surprise, then, that she wasn't popular with suffragettes—she was president of the Women's National *Anti*-Suffrage League—and was seen as a force for reaction, never mind that she had been instrumental in establishing educational settlement houses across England to help the poor.

H. G. Wells even mentions her in his *Mr. Britling Sees It Through,* taking it as a given that his audience would know whom he was referring to.

"When I looked out the train this morning," he has an American character say, "I thought I had come to the England of Washington Irving. I find it is not even the England of Mrs. Humphrey Ward."

A figure of fun to the younger generation—but as the niece of Matthew Arnold, related by marriage to the extraordinary Huxley family, she was too well-connected and successful to pay them much mind. She was six-ty-three when the war broke out, but that didn't keep her from engaging in British propaganda efforts—she would write three books on the war.

Later, we'll see what she was capable of in this line; the excerpt below, written in a more sensitive, measured tone, was her contribution to Edith Wharton's fund-raising effort for Belgian refugees.

Sadly, H. G. Wells is remembered now, at least in the United States, almost solely as the author of the science-fiction novel *The War of the Worlds,* and for the 1938 radio adaptation by Orson Welles that supposedly (this has been debunked now) sent Americans rushing panicked into the streets. Even his famous catchphrase for World War I, "the war to end all wars," is usually attributed to Woodrow Wilson.

This is a shame, for Wells, at forty-eight, was at the height of his power and influence during the Great War, and no writer on any side was more engaged in thinking about the war, writing about the war, and working toward the eventual peace. He even had an influence on the fighting; his 1903 short story, "The Land Ironclads," accurately predicted the development of the tank, and Winston Churchill was always quick to credit Wells with giving him the idea when he set out to find a machine that would break the deadlock of trench warfare.

Wells, who was nothing if not energetic, also spent the war engaged in a number of love affairs, the most notorious of which was with Rebecca West, who—as we'll see later—wrote a classic civilian war novel herself.

*Mr. Britling Sees It Through*, Wells's autobiographical novel detailing his reactions to the war (he had also written an earlier one, *Boon*, dealing with similar themes), enjoyed enormous popularity when it was published—and not just in English-speaking countries. It was immediately translated into German (two of the most sympathetic characters are German), and, via Switzerland, was widely distributed behind enemy lines. Maxim Gorky wrote Wells from Russia, telling him that "*Britling* was without doubt the finest, most courageous, truthful and humane book written in Europe in the course of this accursed war."

The novel begins at Matching Easy, Mr. Britling's home in rural Essex, where a boisterous weekend party is in progress, featuring, among other innocent diversions, a wild game of lawn hockey. Britling—famous for his articles on a whole range of political, cultural, and scientific subjects—is at the center of all this, and Wells pokes gentle fun at his alter ego.

> "No photographer had ever caught a hint of his essential Britlingness and bristlingness. Only the camera could ever induce Mr. Britling to brush his hair, and for the camera alone did he reserve that expression of submissive martyrdom. He was wearing now a very old blue flannel blazer, no hat, and a pair of knickerbockers of a remarkable bagginess, and made of one of those virtuous socialistic homespun tweeds that drag out into wooly knots and strings wherever there is attrition. His face wore the amiable expression of a wire-haired terrier disposed to be friendly . . . He talked about everything, he had ideas about everything; he could no more help having ideas about everything than a dog can resist smelling at your heels. He sniffed at the heels of reality."

The fun and games are interrupted only by worries about unrest in Ireland, at least until word comes of a much more serious development on the opposite side of Europe.

Havelock Ellis, at fifty-five, was famous/infamous for his pioneering writings on human sexuality, but this was only one of the many subjects that he wrote about authoritatively—only Wells among British writers rivaled him in range of interests. Just a list of chapter headings in his *Essays in War-Time* (my copy is a fifth impression from 1917) gives an idea of this breadth.

Evolution and War; War and Eugenics; Morality in Warfare; Is War Diminishing?; War and the Birth-Rate; War and Democracy; Feminism and Masculinism; The White Slave Crusade; The Conquest of Venereal Disease; The Nationalisation of Health; Eugenics and Genius; The Production of Ability; Birth Control.

Ellis was capable of taking the long view, morally and historically, but was this possible in the midst of total war? He would do his best to try.

William Butler Yeats, fifty-eight years old in 1914, had a complicated attitude toward the war. "He saw the conflict as a battle between the ideas of the New and Old Testament (Germany represented the latter), and, more concretely, was struck by the incompetence and 'useless heroism' of British officers."

He wrote to a friend, "England is paying the price for having despised intellect. The war will end in a draw and everybody too poor to fight for another hundred years."

Much of his ambivalence came from his Irish nationalism. When it came time for him to write his great poem about the war, "An Irish Airman Foresees His Death," he was very careful to make him an *Irish* volunteer; "Those that I fight I do not hate/Those who I guard I do not love."

Yeats won the Nobel Prize in 1923, cited "for his always inspired poetry, which in a highly artistic form gives expression to the spirit of a whole nation." No one had to explain that the nation was Ireland, not Britain.

When Edith Wharton called upon him to make a contribution to *The Book of the Homeless,* he responded with wry humor, managing to suggest that writers might have better things to do than comment on war.

## *The Big Guns at Work*
### —Joseph Conrad

I have never believed in political assassination as a means to an end, and least of all if the assassination is of the dynastic order. I don't know how far murder can ever approach the efficiency of a fine art, but looked upon with the cold eye of reason it seems but a crude expedient either of impatient hope or hurried despair. There are few men whose premature death could influence human affairs more than on the surface. The deeper stream of causes depends not on individualities which, like the mass of mankind, are carried on by the destiny which no murder had ever been able to placate, divert or arrest.

In July of 1914, I was a stranger in a strange city and particularly out of touch with the world's politics. Never a very diligent reader of newspapers, there were at that time reasons of a private order which caused me to be even less informed than usual on public affairs as presented from day to day in that particular atmosphere-less, perspective-lessness of the daily paper which somehow for a man with some historic sense robs them of all real interest. I don't think I had looked at a daily paper for a month past.

It was a friend who one morning at breakfast informed me of the murder of the Archduke Ferdinand.

The impression was mediocre. I was barely aware that such a man existed. I remembered only that not long before he had visited London, but that memory was lost in a cloud of insignificant printed words his presence in this country provoked. Various opinions had been expressed of him, but his importance had been archducal, dynastic, purely acci- dental. Can there be in the world of real men anything more shadowy than an archduke? And now he was no more, and with a certain atroc- ity of circumstance which made one more sensible of his humanity than when he was in life. I knew nothing of his journey. I did not connect that crime with Balkanic plots and aspirations. I asked where it had happened. My friend told me it was in Sarajevo, and wondered what would be the consequence of that grave event. He asked me what I thought would happen next.

It was with perfect sincerity that I said "Nothing," and I dismissed the subject, having a great repugnance to consider murder as an engine of politics . . . .

We had received an invitation to spend some weeks in Poland in a country house in the neighborhood of Cracow. The first of the third week in July, while the telegraph wires hummed with the words of enormous import which were to fill blue-books, yellow-books, white-books and rouse the wonder of the world, was taken up with light-hearted preparations for the journey. What was it but just a rush through Germany to get over as quickly as possible?

It is the part of the earth's solid surface of which I know the least. In my life I had been across it only twice. I may well say of it, "Vidi tantum," and that very little I saw through the window of a railway carriage at express speed. Those journeys were more like pilgrimages when one hurries on to the goal without looking to the right or left for the satisfaction of deeper need than curiosity.

Yet in truth, as many others have done, I had "sensed it," that promised land of steel, of chemical dyes, of method, of efficiency; that race planted in the middle of Europe, assuming in grotesque vanity the attitude of Europeans among effete Asiatics or mere nig- gers, and with a feeling of superiority freeing their hands of all moral bonds and anxious to take up, if I may express myself so, the "perfect man's burden." Meantime in a clearing of the Teutonic forest their sages were rearing a Tree of cynical wisdom, a sort of Upas tree, whose shade may be seen lying now over the prostrate body of Belgium. It must be said that they laboured open enough, watering it from the most authentic sources of all evil, and watching with bespectacled eyes the slow ripening of the glorious blood-red fruit. The sincerest words of peace, words of menace, and I verily believe, words of abasement even, if there had been a voice vile enough to utter them, would have been wasted on their ecstasy. For when a fruit ripens on a branch, it must fall. There is nothing on earth that can prevent it . . . .

I let myself be carried through Germany as if it were pure space, without sights, without sounds. No whispers of the war reached my voluntary abstractions. And perhaps not so very voluntary after all! Each of us is a fascinating spectacle to himself, and I had to watch my own personality returning from another world, as it were, to revisit the glimpses of old moons. Considering the condition of humanity, I am, perhaps, not so much to blame for giving myself up to that occupation. We prize the sensation of our continuity, and we can only capture it that way. By watching . . . .

And there we remained among the Poles from all parts of Poland, not officially interned, but simply unable to obtain permission to travel by train or road. It was a wonderful, a poignant two months. This is not the time, and perhaps not the place, to enlarge upon the tragic character of the situation; a whole people seeing the culmination of its misfortunes in a final catastrophe, unable to trust any one, to appeal to any one, to look for help from any quarter; deprived of all hope, and even of its last illusions, and unable in the trouble of minds and the unrest of consciences to take refuge in stoical acceptance. I have seen all this. And I am glad I have not so many years left to me to remember that feeling of inexorable Fate, tangible, palpable, come after so many cruel years, a figure of dread, murmuring with iron lips the final words: "Ruin—and Extinction."

But enough of this. For our little band there was the awful anguish of incertitude as to the real nature of events in the West. It is difficult to give an idea how ugly and dangerous things looked to us over there. Belgium knocked down and trampled out of existence. France giving in under repeated blows, a military collapse like that of 1870, and England involved in that disastrous alliance, her army sacrificed, her people in a panic! Polish papers, of course, had no other than German sources of information. Naturally, we did not believe all we heard, but it was sometimes excessively difficult to react with sufficient firmness. We used to shut our door, and there, away from everybody, we sat weighing the news, hunting up discrepancies, scenting lies, finding reason for hopefulness and generally cheering each other up . . . .

But enough of this, too. Through the unremitting efforts of Polish friends we obtained at last the permission to travel to Vienna. Once there, the wing of the American eagle was extended over our uneasy heads. We cannot be sufficiently grateful to the American Ambassador for his exertions on our behalf. We effected our hair's-breadth escape into Italy, and, reaching Genoa, took passage in a Dutch mail-steamer, homeward bound from Java, with London as a port of call.

On that sea route I might have picked up a memory at every mile if the past had not been eclipsed by the tremendous actuality. We saw the signs of it in the emptiness of the Mediterranean, the aspect of Gibraltar, the misty glimpses in the Bay of Biscay of an outward-bound convoy of transports, in the presence of British submarines in the Channel. Innumerable drifters flying the naval flag dotted the narrow waters, and two naval officers coming on board off the South Foreland piloted the ship through the Downs.

The Downs! There they were, thick with memories of my sea life. But what were to me now the futilities of individual past! As our ship's head swung into the estuary of the Thames a deep, yet faint, concussion passed through the air, a shock rather than a sound, which, missing my ear, found its way straight into my heart. Turning instinctively to look at my boys, I happened to meet my wife's eyes. She also had felt profoundly, coming from far away across the grey distances of the sea, the faint boom of the big guns at work on the coast of Flanders—shaping the future.

From *The Book of the Homeless,* edited by Edith Wharton; Charles Scribner's Sons, New York, 1916.

## *The Abyss of Our Past Delusion*
### —Henry James

There comes back to me out of the distant past an impression of the citizen soldiers at once in his collective grouping and in his impaired, his more or less war-worn state, which was to serve me for long years as the most intimate vision of him that my span of life was likely to disclose. This was a limited affair indeed, I recognise as I try to recover it, but I mention it because I was to find at the end of time that I had kept it in reserve, left it lurking deep down in my sense of things, however shyly and dimly, however confusedly even, as a term of comparison, a glimpse of something by the loss of which I should have been the poorer; such a residuary possession of the spirit, in fine, as only needed darkness to close round it a little from without in order to give forth a vague phosphorescent light. It was early, it must have been very early, in our Civil war, yet not so early but that a large number of those who had answered President Lincoln's first call for an army had had time to put in their short period and reappear again in camp, one of those of their small New England State, under what seemed to me at the hour, that of a splendid autumn afternoon, the thickest mantle of heroic history. If I speak of the impression as confused I certainly justify that mark of it by my failure to be clear at this moment as to how much they were in general the worse for wear—since they can't have been exhibited to me, through their waterside settlement of tents and improvised shanties, in anything like hospital conditions. However, I cherish the rich ambiguity, and have always cherished it, for the sake alone of the general note exhaled, the thing that has most kept remembrance unbroken. I carried away from the place *the* impression, the one that not only was never to fade, but was to show itself suscep-tible to extraordinary mutual enrichment. I may not pretend now to refer it to the most particular sources it drew upon at that summer's end of 1861, or to say why my repatriated warriors were, if not some-how definitely stricken, so largely either lying in apparent helplessness or moving about in confessed languor: it suffices me that I have always thought of them as expressing in themselves at almost every point in the minor key, and that this has been the reason of their interest. What I call the note therefore is the characteristic the most of the essence and the most inspiring—inspiring I mean for consideration of the admirable sincerity that we thus catch in the act: the note of the quite abysmal softness, the exemplary genius for accommodation, that forms the alternative aspect, the passive as distinguished from the active, of the fighting man whose business is in the first instance formi-dably to bristle. This aspect has been produced, I of course recognise, amid the horrors that the German powers had, up to a twelvemonth ago, been for years conspiring to let loose upon the world by such appalling engines and agencies as mankind had never before dreamed of; but just that is the lively interest of the fact unfolded to us now on a scale beside which, and though save indeed for a single restriction, the whole previous illustration of history turns pale. Even if I catch but in a generalising blur that exhibition of the first American levies as a measure of experience had stamped and harrowed them, the signally attaching mark that I refer to is what I most recall; so that if I didn't fear, for the connection, to appear to compare the slighter things with the so much greater, the diminished shadow with the far-spread sub-stance, I should speak of my small old scrap of truth, miserably small in contrast with the immense evidence even then to have been gathered, but in respect to which latter occasion didn't come to me, as having contained possibilities of development that I must have languished well-nigh during a lifetime to crown it with . . . .

The degree was to alter by swift shades, just as one's comprehension of the change grew and grew with it; and thus it was that, to cut short the record of our steps and stages, we have left immeasurably behind us here the question of what might or what should have been. That belonged, with whatever beguiled or amused ways of looking at it, to the abyss of our past delusion, a collective state of mind in which it had literally been possible to certain sophists to argue that, so far from not having soldiers enough, we had more than we were likely to know any respectable public call for. It was in the very fewest weeks that we replaced a pettifogging consciousness by the most splendidly liberal, and, having swept through all the first phases of anxiety and suspense, found no small part of our measure of the matter settle down to an almost luxurious study of our multiplied defenders after the fact, as I may call it, or in the light of that acquaintance with them as products supremely tried and tested which I began by speaking of. We were up to our necks in this relation before we could turn round, and what upwards of a year's experience of it has done in the contributive and enriching way may now well be imagined. I might feel that my marked generalisation, the main hospital impression, steeps the case in too strong or too stupid a synthesis, were it not that to consult my memory, a recollection of countless associative contacts, is to see the emphasis almost absurdly thrown on my quasi-paradox . . .

We after this fashion score our very highest on behalf of a conclusion, I think, in feeling that whether or no the British warrior's good nature has much range of fancy, his imagination, whatever there may be of it, is at least so goodnatured as to show absolutely everything it touches, everything without exception, even the worst machinations of the enemy, in that colour. Variety and diversity of exhibition, in a world virtually divided as now into hospitals and the preparation of subjects for them, are, I accordingly conceive, to be looked for quite away from the question of physical patience, of the general consent to suffering and mutilation, and, instead of that, in this connection of the sort of mind and thought, the sort of moral attitude, that are born of the sufferer's other relations; which I like to think of as being different from country to country, from class to class, and as having their fullest national and circumstantial play.

It would be of the essence of these remarks, could I give them within my space all the particular applications naturally awaiting them, that they pretend to refer here to the British private soldier only—generalisation about his officers would take us so considerably further and so much enlarge our view . . . .

From *The Book of the Homeless,* edited by Edith Wharton; Charles Scribner's Sons, New York, 1916.

## *The Unfurling of the Future*
—Thomas Hardy

Cry of the Homeless

Instigator of the ruin—
Whichsoever thou mayst be
Of the mastering minds of Europe
That contrived our misery—
Hear the wormwood-worded greeting
From each city, shore, and lea
        Of thy victims:
"Enemy, all hail to thee!"
Yea: "All hail!" we grimly shout thee
That wast author, fount and head
Of these wounds, whoever proven
When our times are thoroughly read
"May thy dearest ones be blighted
And forsaken," be it said
        By thy victims,
"And thy children beg their bread!"

Nay: too much the malediction—
Rather let this thing befall
In the unfurling of the future,
On the night when comes thy call:
That compassion dew thy pillow
And absorb thy senses all
          For thy victims,
Till death dark thee with his pall.


From *The Book of the Homeless,* edited by Edith Wharton; Charles Scribner's Sons, NY, 1916.

## *Let Loose These Evil Powers*
### —Gilbert Murray

Thucydides did his best two thousand years ago to explain it to us—that war is not an instrument that can be directed with precision to a perfectly definite aim and turned off and on like a garden hose. It is a flood on which, when once the flood-gates are opened, those who have opened them will be borne away. In August 1914, for the sake of our own rights, of justice and of humanity, we appealed to Force. Force entered and took the centre of the stage. It became a struggle, not of Right against Force, but of one Force against another. The struggle deepened, became closer, more terrible, more fraught with anxiety. It became very nearly a struggle for existence. We gave all our minds to it. Gradually, inevitably, increasingly, the fight began to absorb us. And while the men who guided England and expressed the spirit of England in the early days of the war were men of lofty spirit and a profound sense of responsibility, as the war proceeded, there came a change. England ceased to be occupied with questions of right and wrong; she became occupied with questions of fighting and killing. We turned, so to speak, from the men who could give wise counsel; we called on all who could fight, and we liked best those who could fight hardest.

Do you remember how Sir Francis Drake once had to hang one of his officers; and how before executing the sentence he passed some time in prayer, and then shook hands with the offender? That is the sort of spirit, perhaps the only spirit in which any man of conscience can without inward misery approach the killing and torturing of his fellow creatures. He is ready, if need be, to shed blood; but he must know that he does it for the Right, and because he must. It would sicken him to think that while doing it, he was secretly paying off old scores, or making money out of it, or, still worse, enjoying the cruelty. The slaying of men, if you do it for the right motive, may be a high and austere duty; if you admit any wrong motive, it begins to be murder—and hypocritical murder.

And yet, as soon as you let loose in war the whole of a big nation, you have handed over that high and austere duty to agents who cannot possibly perform it; to masses of very ordinary people, and not only of ordinary people, but of stupid and vulgar and drunken and covetous and dishonest and tricky and cruel and brutal people, who will transform your imagined crusade into a very different reality.

When the war was flung into the midst of all this seething, heterogeneous mass of men who make up Great Britain or the British Empire, it called out naturally those who in their different ways were most akin to it. It called out both the heroes and the ruffians. But in the main, as the war atmosphere deepened among the civilian population, the men who were interested in justice became unimportant; those who were specially interested in humanity were advised to be discreet in their utterances. It is quite others who came to the front: the men—for such exist in all countries—who believe in Force and love Force; who love to wage bloody battles, or at least to read about them and lash their younger neighbors into them; who rage against the "mere lawyers" who care about right and wrong; despise the pulling sentimentalists who have not deadened their hearts to all feeling of human compassion; loathe the doctrinaire politicians who dare to think about the welfare of future generations instead of joining in the carnival of present passion.

We knew we should let loose these evil powers, but we believe we can cling to our duty in spite of them. It was part of the price we had to pay, if we wished to save Europe, to save the small nationalities, so save liberty and civilization. And it is by no means all the price. It is only an extra. It comes as an addition to the long bill of dead and wounded, of the mountains of unatoned and inexplicable suffering, the vista of future famine and poverty, and the beggary of nations. And it is not the only extra. There is something that goes wrong in ourselves . . . .

This is how it happens. You face the beginning of the war with intense feeling. You feel the casualties, you feel the pain of the wounded, you feel the horror of what your friends have to do, as well as what they have to suffer. You feel also the uplifting emotion of sacrifice for a great cause.

But you cannot possibly go on feeling like that. War is a matter of endurance, and if you allow yourself to feel continually in this intense way, you will break down. If mere self-protection a man, whether soldier or civilian, grows an envelope of defensive callousness. Instinctively, by a natural process, you avoid feeling the horrors and you cease to climb the heights of emotion. After all, an average man may be sorry for the Czecho-Slovaks; he may even look them up on a map; but he cannot go on grieving about them year in and year out. He may realize in flashes the actual meaning in terms of human misery of one hour of the war which he is not fighting indeed, but ordering and paying for. But he could not live if he did so steadily.

He proceeds, quite naturally, first to put the enemy's suffering out of account. *He* deserves all he gets, anyhow. Then the suffering of the victim nations; he is very sorry, of course, for Belgium, Poland, Serbia, Rumania, the Armenians. But it is no good being sorry. Better to get on with the war! Then the sufferings of his own people, the young men and middle-aged men who have gone out to France or the East. He cannot quite forget these; he must think about them a good deal and the thought is painful. So he transforms them. When they once put on khaki, they became, he imagines, quite different. They were once James Mitchell the clerk, Thomas Brown the railway porter, John Baxter the Wesleyan carpenter. But now they are "Tommies." And we invent a curious psychology for them, to persuade ourselves somehow that they like the things they do, and do not so very much mind the things they suffer.

And then, in spite of all this protective callousness, in spite of the pretences we build up in order to make ourselves comfortable, there continues underneath the brazen armour of our contentment a secret horror, a raging irritation—how shall I put it? It is the ceaseless, bitter sobbing of all that used once to be recognized as the higher part of our nature, but now is held prisoner, stifled and thrust aside . . . because the need for the world is for other things.

When we remember all this it makes us feel lost and heavy-hearted, like men struggling and unable to move in an evil dream . . . so, it seems, for the time being we must forget it. We modern men are accustomed by the needs of life to this division of feelings. In every war, in every competition almost, there is something of the same difficulty, and we have learned to keep the two sides of our mind apart. We must fight our hardest, indomitably, gallantly, even joyously, forgetting all else while we have to fight. When the fight is over we must remember.

From *Faith, War, and Policy,* by Gilbert Murray; Houghton Mifflin, Boston, 1917.

# *The Will to Power*
## —Thomas Mann

When I have held that democracy, that politics itself, is foreign and poisonous to the German character, when I have doubted or argued against Germany's calling to politics, I have not done so—personally or impersonally—with the laughable purpose of spoiling my nation's will to reality, of shaking its belief in the justice of its international claims. I myself confess that I am deeply convinced that the German people will never be able to love political democracy simply because they cannot love politics itself, and that the much decried "authoritarian state" is and remains the one that is proper and becoming to the German people, and the one they basically want. A certain amount of courage is required today to express this conviction. Nevertheless, in doing so, I not only intend no derogation of the German nation in the intellectual or moral sense—I mean just the opposite—I also believe that its will to power and worldly greatness (which is less a will than a fate and a world necessity) remains completely uncontested in its legitimacy and its prospects. There are highly "political" nations—nations that are never free of political stimulation and excitement, that still, because of a complete lack of ability in authority and governance, have never accomplished anything on earth and never will. The Poles and the Irish, for example.

On the other hand, history has nothing but praise for the organizing and administrative powers of the completely nonpolitical German Nation. When one sees where France has been brought by her politicians, it seems to me that one has the proof in hand that at times things do not work at all with "politics" and this is a sort of proof that things can also work in the end *without* "politics." Therefore no misunderstanding should arise when people like me declare the political spirit to be an alien and impossible spirit in Germany . . . .

It is the "politicization of the intellect," the distortion of the concept of intellect into that of reforming enlightenment, of revolutionary humanitarianism, that works like poison and orpiment on me.

From *Betrachtungen eines Unpolitischen,* by Thomas Mann; S. Fisher, Berlin, 1919.

# *Wordsworth's Valley in War-time*
## —Mrs. Humphrey Ward

August 8th, 1915. It is now four days since, in this village of Grasmere, at my feet, we attended one of those anniversary meetings, marking the first completed year of this appalling war, which were being called on that night over the length and breadth of England. Our meeting was held in the village schoolroom; the farmers, tradesmen, innkeeper and summer visitors of Grasmere were present, and we passed the resolution which all England was passing at the same moment, pledging ourselves, separately and collectively, to help the war and continue the war, till the purposes of England were attained, by the liberation of Belgium and northern France, and the chastisement of Germany.

And I stand to-night on this lovely mountain-side, looking out upon the harvest fields of another August, and soon another evening newspaper sent up from the village below will bring the latest list of our dead and our maimed, for which English mothers and wives have looked in terror, day after day, through this twelve months.

And yet, but for the brooding care in every English mind, how could one dream of war in this peaceful Grasmere?

Is it really true that somewhere in this summer world, beyond those furthest dells, and the Yorkshire moors behind them, beyond the silver sea dashing its waves upon our Eastern coasts, there is still going on the ruin, the agony, the fury, of this hideous struggle into which Germany plunged the world, a year ago? It is past eight o'clock; but the sun which is just dipping behind Silver How is still full on Loughrigg, the beautiful fell which closes in the southern end of the lake. Between me and these illumined shores lies the lake—shadowed and still, broken by its one green island. I can just see the white cups of the water-lilies floating above the mirrored woods and rocks that plunge so deep into the infinity below.

The square tower of the church rises to my left. The ashes of Wordsworth lie just beyond it—of Wordsworth, and that sister with the "wild eyes," who is scarcely less sure of immortality than himself, of Mary Wordsworth, too, the "perfect woman, nobly planned," at whose feet, in her white-haired old age, I myself as a small child of five can remember sitting, nearly sixty years ago. Generally, the tiny house and garden are thronged by Americans in

August, who crowd about the charming place like flies about the milk pails in summer.

But this year there are no Americans, and few visitors. But Grasmere does not distress itself as it would in other years, Wordsworth's village is thinking too much about the war. Last year, within a few months of the outbreak, seventy young men from the village offered themselves to the army; fifty are serving. Their women left behind have been steadily knitting and sewing since they left. Every man from Grasmere got a Christmas present of two pairs of socks. Day after day, women from the village have gone up to the fells to gather the absorbent sphagnum moss, which they dry and clean, and send to a manufacturing chemist to be prepared for hospital use. One old woman gathered the tufts of wool which the sheep leave behind them on the brambles and fern, washed them, and made them into the little pillows which prop wounded limbs in hospital . . . .

One sits and ponders about these things, as the golden light recedes from Loughrigg, and that high crag above Wordsworth's cottage. Little Grasmere has indeed done all she could, and in this lovely valley, the heart of Wordsworth's people, the descendants of those dalesmen and daleswomen whom he brought into literature, is one—passionately one—with the heart of the allies. Lately the war has bitten into the life of the village. Of its fifty young sons, many are now in the thick of the Dardenelles struggle; three are prisoners of war, two are said to have gone down in the *Royal Edward*, one officer has fallen, others are wounded. Grasmere has learned much geography and history this last year; and it has shared in the full in the general deepening and uplifting of the English soul, which the war has brought about. France, that France which Wordsworth loved in his first generous youth, is in all our hearts. And where shall we find nobler words in which to clothe the feeling of England towards a France which has lost Rheims, or a Belgium which has endured Louvain, than those written a hundred years ago in that cottage across the lake?

Air, earth and skies—

There's not a breathing of the common wind
That will forget thee; thou hast great allies;
Thy friends are exultations, agonies,
And love, and man's unconquerable mind!

To Germany, then, the initial weight of big battalions, the initial successes of a murderous science; to the nations leagued against her, the unconquerable power of those moral faiths which fire our clay, and in the end mould the history of men!

Along the mountain-side, the evening wind rises. The swell and beat of it among the rocks and fens, as the crags catch it, echo it, and throw it back reverberate, are as the sound of marching feet.

I hear it in the tread—irresistible, inexorable—of an avenging Humanity. The living and dead are there, and in their hands they bear both Doom and Comforting.

From *The Book of the Homeless,* edited by Edith Wharton; Charles Scribner's Sons; New York, 1916.

## *Men Whispered Together*
### —H. G. Wells

Mr. Britling took up the thread of speech again.

"The psychology of all this recent insubordination and violence is—curious. Exasperating too . . . I don't quite grasp it . . . It's the same thing whether you look at the suffrage business or the labour people or at this Irish muddle. People may be too safe. You see we live at the end of a series of secure generations in which none of the great things of life have changed materially. We've grown up with no sense of danger—that is to say, with no sense of responsibility. None of us, none of us—for though I talk my actions belie me—really believe that life can change very fundamentally any more forever. All this,"—Mr. Britling waved his arm comprehensively—"looks as though it was bound to go on steadily forever. It seems incredible that the system can be smashed . . . We shall go on—until there is a spark right into the magazine. We have lost any belief we ever had that fundamental things happen. We are everlasting children in an everlasting nursery . . . If the world were like a whispering gallery, what whispers might we not hear now—from India, from Africa, from Germany, warnings from the past, intimations of the future . . . We shouldn't heed them."

And indeed at the very moment when Mr. Britling was saying these words, in Sarajevo in Bosnia, where the hour was somewhat later, men whispered together, and one held nervously to a black parcel that had been given him and nodded as they repeated his instructions, a black parcel with certain unstable chemicals and a curious arrangement of detonators therein, a black parcel destined ultimately to shatter nearly every landmark of Mr. Britling's cosmogony . . . .

One writes "Germany." That is how one writes of nations, as though they had single brains and single purposes. But indeed while Mr. Britling lay awake and thought of his son and Lady Frensham and his smashed automobile and of God and evil and a thousand perplexities, a multitude of other brains must also have been busy, lying also in beds or sitting in studies or watching in guard-rooms or chatting belatedly in cafes or smoking-rooms or pacing the bridges of battleships or walking along in city or country, upon this huge possibility the crime of Sarajevo had just opened, and of the state of the world in relation to such possibilities. Few women, one guesses, heeded what was happening, and of the men, the men whose decision to launch that implacable threat turned the destinies of the world to war, there is no reason to believe that a single one of them had anything approaching the imaginative power needed to understand fully what it was they were doing. We have looked for an hour or so into the seething pot of Mr. Britling's brain and marked its multiple strands, its inconsistencies, its irrational transitions. It was but a specimen. Nearly every brain of the select few that counted in this cardinal determination of the world's destinies, had its streak of personal motive, its absurd and petty impulses and deflections. One man decided to say *this* because if he said *that* he would contradict something he had said and printed four or five days ago; another took a certain line because so he saw his best opportunity of putting a rival into a perplexity . . . It would be strange if one could reach out now and recover the states of mind of two such beings as the German Kaiser and his eldest son as Europe stumbled toward her fate through the long days and warm close nights of that July. Here was the occasion for which so much of their lives had been but the large pretentious preparation, coming right into their hands to use or forgo, here was the opportunity that would put them into the very forefront of history forever; this journalist emperor with the paralysed arm; this common-fibred, sly, lascivious son. It is impossible that they did not dream of glory over all the world. And being what they were they must have imagined spectators, and the young man, who was after all a young man of particularly poor quality, imagined no doubt certain women onlookers, certain humiliated and astonished friends, and thought of the clothes he would wear and the gestures he would make. The nickname his English cousins had given this heir to all the glories was the "White Rabbit." He was the backbone of the war party at court. And presently he stole bric-a-brac. This will help posterity to the proper value of things in 1914 . . .

Readers of histories and memoirs as most of this class of men are, they must have composed little eulogistic descriptions of the part themselves were to play in the opening drama, imagined pleasing vindications and interesting documents. Some of them perhaps saw difficulties, but few foresaw failure. For all this set of brains the thing came as a choice to take or reject; they could make war or prevent it. And they chose war.

Thus—a vivid fact as yet only in a few hundred skulls—the vast catastrophe of the Great War gathered behind the idle, dispersed and confused spectacle of an indifferent world, very much as the storms and rains of late September gathered behind the glow and lassitudes of August, and with scarcely more of set human intention.

From *Mr. Britling Sees It Through*, by H. G. Wells; Macmillan, NY, 1917.

# *Scientific Barbarism*
## —Havelock Ellis

Germany, with its ancient genius for warfare, has in the present war taken the decisive step of placing warfare definitely on the basis on scientific barbarism. To do this is, in a sense, we must remember, not a step backwards, but a step forward. It involved the recognition of the fact that war is not a game to be played for its own sake, by a professional caste, in accordance with fixed rules which it would be dishonourable to break, but a method, carried out by the whole organised manhood of the nation, of effectively attaining an end desired by the state, in accordance with the famous statement of Clausewitz that war is State policy continued by a different method. Humane sentiments and civilised traditions, under the moulding hand of Prussian leaders of Kultur, have been slowly but firmly subordinated to a political realism which, in the military sphere, means a masterly efficiency in the aim of crushing the foe by overwhelming force combined with panic-striking "frightfulness." In this conception, that only is moral which served these ends. The horror which this "frightfulness" may be expected to arouse is from the German point of view a tribute of homage.

The military reputation of Germany is so great in the world, and likely to remain so, whatever the issue of the present war, that we are here faced by a grave critical issue which concerns the future of the whole world. The conduct of wars has been transformed before our eyes. In any future war the example of Germany will be held to consecrate the new methods, and the belligerents who are not inclined to accept the supreme authority of Germany may yet be forced in their own interests to act in accordance with it. The mitigating influence of religion over warfare has long ceased to be exercised, for the international Catholic Church no longer possesses the power to exert such influence, while the national Protestant churches are just as bellicose as their flocks. Now we see the influence of morality over warfare similarly tending to disappear. Henceforth, it seems, we have to reckon with a conception of war which accounts it a function of the supreme State, standing above morality and therefore able to wage war independently of morality. Necessity—the necessity of scientific effectiveness—becomes the sole criterion of right and wrong.

The conclusion seems to be that we are to-day entering on an era in which war will not only flourish as vigorously as in the past, but with an altogether new ferocity and ruthlessness, with a vastly increased power of destruction, and on a scale of extent and intensity involving an injury to civilisation and humanity which no wars of the past ever perpetrated.

From *Essays in War-Time,* by Havelock Ellis; Constable and Co., London, 1917.

## *Keep Our Mouths Shut*
—W. B. Yeats

A Reason For Keeping Silent

I think it better that at times like these
We poets keep our mouths shut, for in truth
We have no gift to set a statesman right;
He's had enough of meddling who can please
A young girl in the indolence of her youth
Or an old man upon a winter's night.

From *The Book of the Homeless,* edited by Edith Wharton; Charles Scribner's Sons, New York, 1916.

# Chapter Three:

# Witness

Writers seeking to do more than pontificate from the comfort and safety of their studies could go see for themselves what the war was about. From the ferry terminal at Folkestone to the front lines in Ypres was ninety miles—the distance from Manhattan to Philadelphia—and a good part of the journey would be in the clubby smoking room of a cross-Channel steamer. From Paris to the battlefields on the Marne was thirty miles, so even a leisurely tour would get a writer back to the Ritz in time for cocktails. The cataclysm lay close at hand, and once the stalemate of trench warfare set in, the writer could make the visit in complete safety.

There were several ways civilian writers gained proximity to the war. They could have themselves accredited as war correspondents for one of the numerous daily newspapers, though—after an initial freewheeling period—this meant coming under the control of military censors. Too much control; the correspondents' stream of cheery, optimistic dispatches having nothing to do with actual conditions would eventually contribute to the postwar disillusionment. Even as early as 1915, a favorite catchphrase among soldiers, delivered with a cynical shake of the head, was "Can't believe a word you read."

Writers, if sufficiently famous, would be taken on elaborately choreographed official tours of the war zone. While authors as honest as Edith Wharton could rise above the obvious traps of these chaperoned visits, lesser writers usually couldn't.

Writers, especially younger ones, could join one of the numerous volunteer ambulance brigades or hospitals springing up in all the Allied nations—the American Field Service, the Friends Ambulance Unit, the Norton-Harjes Ambulance Corps, and dozens of similar outfits. Indeed, being a wartime ambulance driver was all but *de rigueur* for postwar writing success; a partial list of those who served includes Hemingway, Dos Passos, E. E. Cummings, Somerset Maugham, Archibald MacLeish, John Masefield, Malcolm Cowley, and, yes, Gertrude Stein.

Some writers didn't have to go to the war—the war came to them. Mildred Aldrich, after a long editorial career in the States, retired to the small hamlet of Huiry, east of Paris, to spend the remainder of her days there tending to her garden and beloved cats. A few months after moving in, the Battle of the Marne erupted all around her, and for the next four years she was never far from the front lines, giving her the material for five bestselling books.

(My small, tidy copy of *A Hilltop on the Marne,* the first in this series, is a sixth impression from December 1915; on the flyleaf, written in pencil, is "Christmas 1915," the initial "J.," and the note "The author is a friend of mine.")

During the war's first three years, the best, most objective witnesses tended to be American. Their country still remained neutral, which gave them more freedom to move around than their British or French counterparts, plus the ability to stand at least somewhat above the fray. Most of them favored the Allies (H. L. Mencken was one exception), but, at least until 1917 and Wilson's declaration of war, they could write honestly and not feel like they were letting down the side.

Their reactions when facing this enormous new fact of total war are of permanent value, if for no other reason than that they *are* new. None of them had seen anything like this before; their moral sense hadn't been jaded, and so, reading them now, we can witness what happens when the nineteenth-century way of looking at the world collides with the twentieth-century way of doing business.

Several things hit the writers hard. Civilian refugees fleeing the fighting—this contradicted all writerly notions of mercy and fair play. The sound of artillery—writers could hear this well back of the front, and it was often the first of war's realities to hit them. Destroyed houses in shelled villages—writer after writer describes the pathos of these homes split in half, exposing the family's secrets.

(If you want to separate the real writers of World War I from the hacks, focus on how they describe the sound of cannon. The hacks like to write, "The guns spoke," which is both as passively bland a description as you could find and, unwittingly, the most telling. Writers who worked harder at their craft always devoted more care to describing the sound of artillery, without resorting to the obvious clichés.)

Many of these writers noted another bizarre aspect of the war. A few miles behind the desolation of no man's land were often scenes of lush pastoral beauty, as if the war were being fought a thousand miles away. This kind of irony added to the writer's sense of unreality, the sense that they were trying to describe something "entirely beyond human experience."

Given that this *was* an experience entirely beyond anything these civilians had ever witnessed before, it's remarkable how well they managed to write about it. Compare their prose style with the earlier writers in this volume, the ones who opined, argued, and pontificated far from the shooting. The eyewitnesses, as they move closer to war's reality, work their way—are forced to work their way—toward a tauter prose style; they replace lazy, bloated adverbs with lean, well-chosen adjectives; purple passages with objective ones; sweeping generalizations with individualized moments and particular scenes.

Few of them bother wasting time on their own personal responses, though these come through implicitly by what they choose to describe and how they choose to describe it; they take their duty as eyewitnesses seriously. Their prose styles, along with the attitudes that shaped them, were changing under the pressure of the enormities their words had to describe, becoming more modern, more tempered.

As Camus wrote after the century's next world war, "When even the simplest words and phrases cost their weight in freedom and blood, the artist must learn to handle them with restraint."

No other writer felt so heartsick over the war as Edith Wharton. A passionate Francophile (she lived in France for over thirty years), she could write in total sincerity that the French were "the most intelligent people in the world," and worried, in novels, essays, poems, and letters, that civilization would fall if France were defeated.

Biographer Hermione Lee describes how deep this identification went.

> "She spoke French immaculately. Her letters and diaries are full of French words and phrases, almost instinctively used. Much of her correspondence—and her conversation—was in French. She was divorced through the French courts. She dealt with every aspect of French bureaucracy, law and administration, particularly in wartime, with tremendous competence. She could write fiction in French. She had numerous French friends, French publishers, French readers. Whether she dreamed in French we do not know."

She was fifty-two when the war began, at the height of her literary talents and her equally impressive organizational ones. As part of her commitment to the war effort (partial list), she raised money for Wharton's American Hostels for Refugees; operated charity grocery and clothing depots in Paris; set up fund-raising committees in America; hosted Christmas parties for hundreds of refugees; opened two sanatoriums for soldiers with tuberculosis;

collared her writer, painter, and composer friends for contributions to *The Book of the Homeless* (which, after her relentless promotion efforts, brought in $9,500 for her hostels); and authored three books on the war herself.

Her *Fighting France* was intended to help sway a still-dithering United States into taking a more active role. She wrote American friends:

> "The German atrocities one hears of are *true*. Spread it abroad as much as you can. It should be known that it is to America's interest to help stem this hideous flood of savagery. No civilized race can remain neutral in feeling now."

The French knew how valuable a champion they had in her; in 1916, she was made a *Chevalier,* and then an *Officier* of the *Legion d'honneur.* Her war work wore her out; she collapsed with heart trouble in 1918, and never totally regained her health. "In more than a manner of speaking, she gave her heart to France."

Mildred Aldrich is one of the most forgotten writers of World War I, and one of the most deserving of rediscovery. Written in epistolary form, as letters to a friend back home in America, her books tell of life in a simple French village just behind the front lines, and combine two literary genres that would seem to be incompatible: a book of simple rural pleasures with a book on war.

She spent her working life in Boston, then—a lifelong Francophile—retired to a peasant's cottage in the small village of Huiry, just in time to be caught up in the Battle of the Marne. She was a close friend of Gertrude Stein (she liked saying that she really didn't understand Stein's work, but was sure Gertrude knew what she was doing), and, at least in her first book, the letters (though she doesn't use salutations) are probably addressed to Stein and Alice B. Toklas.

She was sixty-one when the war broke out—old enough to remember young men going off to fight the Civil War—and the surprising courage she found in herself was her making both as a writer and as a woman.

Though ignored by critics, Aldrich has always had her small band of devotees, many of whom, a hundred years after her books came out, still make the pilgrimage to her cottage in Huiry to see for themselves the village she wrote of so movingly.

*A Hilltop on the Marne* was a bestseller in the States, going into seventeen printings; she used the royalties to help care for Huiry's wounded soldiers. Next to the title page on my copy is a medallion of her profile done by an artist named Theodore Spicer-Simson. If Aldrich was as strong and compassionate in person as the face he depicts, than she would have been a woman well worth meeting.

Richard Harding Davis, at fifty-two, was not only the most famous and highly paid war correspondent in the world—he had all but invented the role. In America, at the turn of the century, his adventurous life, even more than his highly romanticized novels and reportage on war, was a tremendous influence on a whole generation of American writers.

Van Wyk Brooks's summary is worth quoting.

> "These were the times of Richard Harding Davis, a young man who was so dramatic in such a special way that he became the symbol of a young man's epoch. He was one of those magnetic types who establish patterns of living for others of their kind, and the notion of the novelist as war correspondent which prevailed so long in American writing began in the early 1890s undoubtedly with him. It was the result of a personality that brought back in a humdrum business world the adventurous swashbuckling life of another time . . . One of

the most influential of writers, not as a writer but as
a man, Davis was like the reporter who made himself
King; Kipling himself had less personal influence than
this literary soldier of fortune who was all high spirits,
good looks and sporting blood . . . Davis was a man of
generous sympathies, always on the side of the under-
dog; as a correspondent, he was swift and shrewd."

By the time he wrote *With the Allies*, his youthful good looks were
gone, but not his boyish sense of adventure; much of the book involves
his staying one step ahead of the Germans in Belgium who arrested him
and threatened to shoot him as a spy. But it's more than that. Davis had
seen as much of war as any writer, and he brought a steely profession-
alism to bear on scenes of horror that might have overwhelmed a less
experienced man.

Another American caught by the war was Frances Wilson Huard, the
feisty *chatelaine* of the luxurious Chateau de Villiers, sixty miles from
Paris on the Marne. Her husband was Charles Huard, a prominent
French lithographer, etcher, and illustrator, who was mobilized as a
war artist by the government.

"Listen," he tells her, as he's about to leave for the front,

> "Listen—before I forget. My will is at my notary's in
> Paris, and on your table is a letter to your father. If
> anything happens to me you know what to do."

But it's Frances who turns out to be the one in danger. As the
German troops advance on her village of Charly, she evacuates the chateau and the hospital she's begun there for French troops, fleeing with
her maids, cooks, and butlers, one step ahead of the *Uhlans,* until with
the battle over she returns to her home through the desolation described
in her bestselling *My Home in the Field of Honor.*

The book is illustrated with drawings by her husband in the style of Gustave Dore. At the back of my copy is an ad for other books on the war published by Grosset & Dunlap, including *I Accuse!* by A German; "a Scathing Arraignment of the German War Policy," showing "to every patriotic American" how "the German masses were deluded with the idea they were making a defensive war to protect the Fatherland."

Henry Beston's classic account of his life in a beach shack on the dunes of Cape Cod, *The Outermost House,* has been continually in print since first being published in 1928, and is considered one of the masterpieces of American nature writing.

Beston was twenty-six when the war broke out, and he had already spent his student years in France. He volunteered for ambulance duty, and his account of his experience, *A Volunteer Poilu* (published under his real name, Henry Sheahan), is totally different in style and tone than his later books on the natural world. In the latter, he seldom writes about people or world events; it's as if the war permanently soured his interest in humankind, and he turned to celebrating seascapes and landscapes as a relief from the horrors he had witnessed on the western front.

He wrote a second book on the war, *Full Speed Ahead,* about his time aboard Navy destroyers, which is even harder for collectors to find than *A Volunteer Poilu.*

His experience in the trenches seems to add a second level to passages in his nature writing that at first glance seem to have nothing to do with war.

> "Every once and a while, when one lives in the country and observes wild animals, one is sure to come upon dramas and acts of courage which profoundly stir the heart. The tiniest birds fight off the marauder, the mother squirrel returns to the tree

already scorched by the on-coming fire, even the
creatures in the pond face in their own strange fashion the odds and the dark. Surely courage is one of
the foundations on which all life rests! I find it moving to reflect that to man has been given the power
to show courage in so many worlds, and to honor it
in the mind, the spirit, and the flesh."

John Reed was a younger, more radical incarnation of Richard
Harding Davis—a war correspondent with a vivid writing style, an
outsized personality, and tremendous courage. His eyewitness account
of the Russian Revolution, *Ten Days that Shook the World,* has been
considered a classic since the day it was published, and the biopic
movie *Reds* brought him an even larger posthumous reputation. "The
playboy of the revolution," Upton Sinclair called him. When he died
in 1920 he was buried in the Kremlin.

Twenty-eight when the war broke out, he went in search of
something more adventurous (and underreported-on) than the
western front—and found it in Serbia, Bessarabia, Romania, Bulgaria,
and Turkey. *The War in Eastern Europe* is a forgotten minor classic;
here in the introduction he tries to explain what he was striving for.

"The most important thing to know about the war
is how the different peoples live; their environment,
traditions, and the revealing things they do and say.
In times of peace, many human qualities are covered
up which come to the surface in a sharp crisis, but on
the other hand, much of personal and racial quality is
submerged in times of public stress. And in this book,
I have simply tried to give my impressions of human
beings as we found them in the countries of Eastern
Europe, from April to October 1915."

My first edition is wonderfully illustrated with drawings by his companion on his travels, the artist Boardman Robinson. Just the captions alone give you a sense of what they look like.

> "Half-savage giants dressed in the ancient panoply of that curious Slavic people whose main business is war . . . Turcomans from beyond the Caspian . . . Blind for life . . . A glimpse of the Serbian retreat . . . A little avenger of Kosovo."

In the 1890s, if you had asked an educated American, "Who is Winston Churchill?" he or she would have replied, "The bestselling historical novelist, author of *Richard Carvel.* Why did you ask?"

Churchill, a graduate of the U.S. Naval Academy, achieved extraordinary success; *Richard Carvel* sold over two million copies. It made him rich, but he remained a progressive in politics, and ran unsuccessfully for governor of New Hampshire.

There is an amusing exchange of letters between Churchill (the American one), and Churchill (the English one), wherein the latter agrees to use his middle name in his byline.

The American Churchill responds:

> "Mr. Winston Churchill is extremely grateful to Mr. Winston Churchill for bringing forward a subject which has given Mr. Winston Churchill much anxiety. Mr. Winston Churchill appreciates the courtesy of Mr. Winston Churchill in adopting the name of 'Winston Spencer Churchill' in his books, articles, etc. Mr. Winston Churchill makes haste to add that, had he possessed any other names, he would certainly have adopted one of them."

Churchill, forty-six, went to Europe to report on the war. This, for American writers, involved not a short hop across the Channel but a long sea voyage, and the scene he describes appears in many similar wartime books. His *A Traveller in War-Time* also includes a description of a weapon few Americans had yet seen or written about.

Sometimes, driving on an errand, I'll pass Churchill's old mansion in Cornish, New Hampshire. It's deserted now, a house fit for haunting—and you don't have to be a novelist yourself to understand what it says about what time can do to a writer's memory.

## *A Calamity Unheard of in Human Annals*
### —Edith Wharton

It was sunset when we reached the gates of Paris. Under the heights of St. Cloud and Suresnes the reaches of the Seine trembled with the blue-pink lustre of an early Monet. The Bois lay about us in the stillness of a holiday evening, and the lawns of the Bagatelle were as fresh as June. Below the Arc de Triomphe, the Champs Élysées sloped downward in a sun-powdered haze to the mist of fountains and the ethereal obelisk; and the currents of summer life ebbed and flowed with a normal beat under the trees of the radiating avenues. The great city, so made for peace and art and all humanist graces seemed to lie by her river-side like a princess guarded by the watchful giant of the Eiffel Tower.

The next day the air was thundery with rumours. Nobody believed them, everybody repeated them. War? Of course there couldn't be war! The Cabinets, like naughty children were again dangling their feet over the edge; but the whole incalculable weight of things-as-they-were, of the daily necessary business of living, continued calmly and convincingly to assert itself against the bandying of diplomatic words. Paris went on steadily about her mid-summer business of feeding, dressing, and amusing the great army of tourists who were the only invaders she had seen for nearly half a century.

All the while, every one knew that other work was going on also. The whole fabric of the country's seemingly undisturbed routine was threaded with noiseless invisible currents of preparation, the sense of them was in the calm air as the sense of changing weather is in the balminess of a perfect afternoon. Paris counted the minutes until the evening papers came.

At the dressmaker's, the next morning, the tired fitters were preparing to leave for their usual holiday. They looked pale and anxious—decidedly, there was a new weight of apprehension in the air. And in the rue Royale, at the corner of the Place de la Concorde, a few people had stopped to look at a little strip of white paper against the wall of the Ministere de la Marine. "General mobilization" they read—and an armed nation knows what that means. But the group about the paper was small and quiet. Passers by read the notice and went on. There were no cheers, no gesticulations; the dramatic sense of the race had already told them that the event was too great to be dramatized.

That evening, in a restaurant of the rue Royale, we sat at a table in one of the open windows, abreast with the street, and saw the strange new crowds stream by. In an instant we were being shown what mobilization was—a huge break in the normal flow of traffic, like the sudden rupture of a dyke. The street was flooded by the torrent of people sweeping past us to the various railway stations. All were on foot, and carrying their luggage; for since dawn every cab and taxi and motor-omnibus had disappeared. The War Office had thrown out its drag-net and caught them all. The crowd that passed our window was chiefly composed of conscripts, the *mobilisables* of the first day, who were on the way to the station accompanied by their families and friends; but among them were little clusters of bewildered tourists, labouring along with their bags and bundles, and watching their luggage pushed before them on hand-carts—puzzled inarticulate waifs caught in the cross-tides racing to a maelstrom.

In the restaurant, the befrogged and red-coated band poured out patriotic music, and the intervals between the courses that so few waiters were left to serve were broken by the ever-recurring obligation to stand up for the Marseillaise, to stand up for God Save the King, to stand up for the Russian National Anthem, to stand up again for the Marseillaise.

As the evening wore on and the crowd about our window thickened, the loiterers outside began to join in the war-songs. *"Allons, debout!"*—and the loyal round begins again. "Le chanson de depart!" is a frequent demand; and the chorus of spectators chimes in roundly. A sort of quiet humour was the note of the street. Down the rue Royale, toward the Madeleine, the bands of other restaurants were attracting other throngs, and martial refrains were strung along the Boulevard like its garlands of arc-lights.

Meanwhile, beyond the fringe of idlers the steady stream of conscripts still poured along. Wives and families trudged beside them, carrying all kinds of odd improvised bags and bundles. The impression disengaging itself from all this superficial confusion was that of a cheerful steadiness of purpose. The faces ceaselessly streaming by were serious but not sad; nor was there any air of bewilderment—the stare of driven cattle. All these lads and young men seemed to know what they were about and why they were about it. The youngest of them looked suddenly grown up and responsible; they understood their stake in the job, and accepted it . . .

There is another army in Paris. Its dingy streams have percolated through all the currents of Paris life, so that wherever one goes, in every quarter and at every hour, among the busy confident strongly-stepping Parisians one sees these other people, dazed and slowly moving—men and women with sordid bundles on their backs, shuffling along hesitatingly in their tattered shoes, children dragging at their hands and tired-out babies pressed against their shoulders: the great army of the Refugees.

Their faces are unmistakable and unforgettable. No one who has ever caught that stare of dumb bewilderment—or that other look of concentrated horror, full of the reflection of flames and ruins—can shake off the obsession of the Refugees. The look in their eyes is part of the look of Paris.

They were ploughing and sowing, spinning and weaving and minding their business, when suddenly a great darkness full of fire and blood came down on them. And now they are here, in a strange country, among unfamiliar faces and new ways, with nothing left to them in the world but the memory of burning homes and massacred children and young men dragged to slavery, of infants torn from their mothers, old men trampled by drunken heels and priests slain while they prayed beside the dying. These are the people who stand in hundreds every day outside the doors of shelters improvised to rescue them, and who receive, in return for the loss of everything that makes life sweet or intelligible or at least endurable, a cot in a dormitory, a meal-ticket—and perhaps, on lucky days, a pair of shoes.

From *Fighting France,* by Edith Wharton; Charles Scribner's Sons; New York, 1919.

## *I Shall Stay*
### —Mildred Aldrich

September 8, 1914 . . . Oh, the things I have seen and felt since I last wrote to you over two weeks ago. Here I am again cut off from the world, and have been since the first of the month. For a week now I have known nothing of what was going on in the world outside the limits of my own vision. For that matter, since the Germans crossed the frontier our news of the war has been meager. We got the calm, constant reiteration—"Left wing—held by the English—forced to retreat a little." All the same, the general impression was, that in spite of all that, "all was well." I suppose it was wise.

On Sunday week—that was August 30—Amelie walked to Esbly, and came back with the news that they were rushing trains full of wounded soldiers and Belgian *refugies* through toward Paris, and that the ambulance there was quite insufficient for the work it had to do. So Monday and Tuesday we drove down in the donkey cart to carry bread and fruit, water and cigarettes, and to "lend a hand."

It was a pretty terrible sight. There were long trains of wounded soldiers. There was train after train crowded with Belgians—well-dressed women and children—packed on to open trucks, without shelter, covered with dust, hungry and thirsty. The sight set me to doing some hard thinking after I got home that first night. But it was not until Tuesday afternoon that I got my first hint of the truth. That afternoon, while I was standing on the platform, I heard a drum beat in the street, and sent Amelie out to see what was going on. She came back at once to say it was the *garde champetre* calling on all inhabitants to carry all their guns, revolvers, etc. to the *mairie* before sundown. That meant the disarming of our *departement,* and it flashed through my mind that the Germans must be nearer than the official announcements had told us.

While I stood reflecting a moment—it looked serious—I saw approaching from the west side of the track a procession of wagons. Amelie ran down the track to the crossing to see what it meant, and came back at once to tell me that they were evacuating the towns to the north of us.

I handed the basket of fruit I was holding into a coach of the train just pulling into the station, and threw my last package of cigarettes after it; and, without a word, Amelie and I went out into the street, untied the donkey, climbed into the wagon, and started for home.

By the time we got to the road which leads east to Montry, whence there is a road over the hill to the south, it was full of the flying crowd. It was a sad sight. The procession led in both directions as far as we could see. There were huge wagons of grain. There were herds of cattle, flocks of sheep; there were wagons full of household effects, with often as many as twenty people sitting aloft; there were carriages; there were automobiles with the occupants crowded in among bundles done up in sheets; there were women pushing over-loaded handcarts; there were women pushing baby-carriages; there were dogs and cats and goats; there was every sort of vehicle you ever saw, drawn by every sort of beast that can draw, from dogs to oxen, from boys to donkeys.

I asked from where these people had come, and was told that they were evacuating Daumartin and all the towns on the plain between there and Meaux, which meant that Monthyon, Neufmortier, Penchard, Chauconin, Barcy, Chambry—in fact, all the villages visible from my garden were being evacuated by order of the military authorities.

One of the most disquieting things about this was to see the effect of the procession as it passed along the road. All the way from Esbly to Montry people began to pack at once, and the speed with which they fell into the procession was disconcerting.

When we finally escaped from the crowd into the poplar-shaded avenue which leads to the Chateau de Conde, I turned to look at Amelie for the first time. I had had time to get a good hold of myself.

"Well, Amelie?" I said.

"Oh, madame," she replied. "I shall stay."

"And so shall I," I answered . . .

It was a little after one o'clock when the cannonading suddenly became much heavier, and I stepped out into the orchard, from which there is a wide view of the plain. I gave one look; then I heard myself say, "Amelie"—as if she could help,—and I retreated. Amelie rushed by me. I heard her say, *"Mon Dieu."* I waited, but she did not come back. After a bit I pulled myself together, went out again, and followed down to the hedge where she was standing, looking off to the plain.

The battle had advanced right over the crest of the hill. The sun was shining on silent Mareuil and Chauconin, but Monthyon and Penchard were enveloped in smoke. From the eastern and western extremities of the plain we could see the artillery fire, but owing to the smoke hanging over the crest of the hill on the horizon, it was impossible to get an idea of the positions of the army. So often, when

I first took this place on the hill, I had looked off at the plain and thought, "What a battlefield!" But when I thought that, I had visions very different from what I was seeing. I had imagined long lines of marching soldiers, detachments of flying cavalry, like the war pictures at Versailles and Fontainebleau. Now I was actually seeing a battle, and it was nothing like that. There was only noise, belching smoke, and long drifts of white clouds concealing the hills.

In the field below me the wheat was being cut. I remembered vividly afterward that a white horse was drawing the reaper, and the women and children were stacking and gleaning. Now and then the horse would stop, and a woman, with her red handkerchief on her head, would stand, shading her eyes a moment, and look off. Then the white horse would turn and go plodding on. The grain had to be got in if the Germans were coming. Talk about the duality of the mind—it is sextuple. I would not dare tell you all that went through mine that long afternoon.

It was just about six o'clock when the first bomb that we could really see came over the hill. The sun was setting. For two hours we saw them rise, descend, explode. Then a little smoke would rise from one hamlet, then from another; then a tiny flame—hardly more than a spark—would be visible; and by dark the whole plain was on fire, lighting up Mareuil in the foreground, silent and untouched. There were long lines of grain-stacks and mills stretching along the plain. One by one they took fire, until by ten o'clock, they stood like a procession of huge torches across my beloved panorama.

From *A Hilltop on the Marne,* by Mildred Aldrich; Houghton Mifflin; Boston, 1915.

## *Its Purpose is Death*
### —Richard Harding Davis

The change came to Brussels at ten in the morning. The boulevards fell suddenly empty. There was not a house that was not closely shuttered. Along the route by which we now knew the Germans were advancing, it was as though the plague stalked. That no one should fire from a window, that to the conquerors no one should offer insult, Burgomaster Max sent out as special constables men he trusted. Their badge of authority was a walking-stick and a piece of paper fluttering from a buttonhole. These, the police, and the servants and caretakers of the houses that lined the boulevards alone were visible. At eleven o'clock, unobserved but by this official audience, down the Boulevard Waterloo came the advance-guard of the German army. It consisted of three men, a captain and two privates on bicycles. Their rifles were slung across their shoulders, they rode unwarily, with as little concern as the members of a touring-club out for a holiday. Behind them, so close upon each other that to cross from one sidewalk to the other was not possible, came the Uhlans, infantry, and the guns. For two hours I watched them, and then, bored with the monotony of it, returned to the hotel.

After an hour, from beneath my window, I still could hear them; another hour and another went by. They still were passing. Boredom gave way to wonder. The thing fascinated you, against your will, dragged you back to the sidewalk and held you there open-eyed. No longer was it regiments of men marching, but something uncanny, inhuman, a force of nature like a landslide, a tidal wave, or lava sweeping down a mountain. It was not of this earth, but mysterious, ghostlike. It carried all the mystery and menace of a fog rolling toward you across the seat. The gray uniforms aided this impression. In it each man moved under a cloak of invisibility. It is the gray of the hour just before daybreak, the gray of unpolished steel, of mist among green trees. It was impossible to tell if in that noble square there was a regiment or a brigade. You saw only a fog that melted in to the stones, blended with the ancient house fronts, that shifted and drifted, but left you nothing at which to point.

All through the night, I could hear the steady roar of the passing army. And when early in the morning I went to the window the chain was still unbroken. For three days and three nights the column of gray, with hundreds of thousands of bayonets and hundreds of thousands of lances, with gray transport wagons, gray ammunition carts, gray ambulances, gray cannon, like a river, of steel, cut Brussels in two.

It is the most efficient organization of modern times; and its purpose only is death.

From *With the Allies,* by Richard Harding Davis; Charles Scribner's Sons; New York, 1918.

## *Stench of the battlefield*
### —Frances Wilson Huard

That night we slept in a shed hospitably offered by a lone peasant woman, and the next morning crossed the river and set our faces homeward.

Branching northwards into the open country we chose all the by-roads and short cuts where our carts would pass, in order to avoid the long streams of ambulances and ammunition vans, as well as in the hope of finding better thoroughfares. A drizzling rain had set in the night before, making the roads slippery and uncomfortable. Highways which heretofore had been seldom trodden were full of ruts and bumps, and from Langy to Villiers there was hardly a corner but what showed signs of the invaders' progress. Over these green and fertile fields whose crops had proudly waved their heads above the lovely Marne, were strewn straw and empty bottles in unimaginable quantities. Thousands of blackened or charred spots dotting the countryside, told of campfires and hasty bivouacs, and as we silently plodded on towards Charny, the growing evidences of recent battle met our saddened gaze.

Here a shell had burst on the road, in the midst of a bicycle squadron, scattering men and machines to the four winds of Heaven. A little mound, a rough-hewn cross, marked the spot where some sixty soldiers lay in their peaceful sleep, while the *melee* of tangled wire and iron which had once been machines, as well as blood-stained garments, bits of shell, and human flesh, made a gruesome and indescribable picture.

Souvenirs? The idea never entered my head. And my kodak, which I had been so prompt to use to commemorate various events, seemed a vulgar, inquisitive instrument, and was left unheeded in the bottom of the cart. Each step brought us face to face with the horrors of warfare. Toward Villeroy a number of battered Parisian taxicabs gave us the first hint of General Gallieni's clever maneuver which saved the capital—and then the wind brought towards us a nauseating odor, which paralyzed our appetites, and sent us doggedly onwards: the stench of the battlefield.

The girls in the cart drew closer together, shivering, though the air was warm and muggy. No one murmured as we passed the first bloated carcasses of dead horses and came upon that far more horrid sight—human bodies—swelled to twice their natural size, lying as death had met them—some in piles, some further apart—all unrecognizable, but once proud mothers' petted darlings. I think they were our enemies. I did not stop to investigate; the flies bothered us so terribly, and long low mounds with red *kepis* piled on them told of the graves of France's defenders. Far ahead I could discover groups of men with shovels, hastily burying those who remained. To the right a lazy column of dense smoke rose reluctantly in the heavy air. I fancied it came from a funeral pyre; we certainly smelled tar and petrol. The ground beneath rocked with the thundering of the distant cannon, and as one peal burst louder a flock of jet black crows mounted heavenward, mournfully cawing in the semi-twilight.

Again the wind shifted in our direction, bringing with it that same loathsome smell.

From *My Home in the Field of Honour*, by Frances Wilson Huard; Grosset & Dunlap; New York, 1916.

## *The Swathe of Stillness*
### —Henry Beston

After Dieulouard a strange stillness pervaded the air; not a stillness of death and decay, but the stillness of life that listens. The sun continued to shine on the brown moorland hills across the gray-green river, the world was quite the same, yet one sensed that something had changed. A village lay ahead of us, disfigured by random shells and half deserted. Beyond the still, shell-splattered houses, a great wood rose, about a mile and a half away, on a ridge that stood boldly against the sky. Running from the edge of the trees down across an open slope to the river was a brownish line that stood in a little contrast to the yellower grass. There slowly rose from this line a great puff of grayish-black smoke which melted away in the clear, autumnal air.

"See," said our lieutenant calmly, with no more emotion than he would have shown at a bonfire. "Those are the German trenches. We have just fired a shell into them."

Two minutes more took us into the dead, deserted city of Pont-a-Mousson. The road was now everywhere screened carefully with lengths of light-brown burlap, and there was not a single house that did not bear witness to the power of a shell. The sense of "the front" began to possess me, never to go, the sense of being in the vicinity of a tremendous power. A ruined village, or a deserted town actually on the front does not bring to mind any impression of decay, for the intellect tends rather to consider the means by which the destruction has been accomplished. One sees villages of the swathes so completely blown to pieces that they are literally nothing but earthy mounds of rubbish, and seeing them thus, in a plain still fiercely disputed night and day between one's own side and the invisible enemy, the mind feels itself in the presence of force, titanic, secret, and hostile . . .

A room in a bourgeois flat on the third floor of a deserted apartment house had been assigned to me. It was nine o'clock, and I was getting ready to roll up in my blankets and go to sleep. The street below was black as pitch save when a trench light, floating serenely down from the sky, illuminated with its green-white glow the curving road and the line of dark, abandoned, half-ruinous villas. There was not a sound to be heard outside of an occasional rifle shot in the trenches, sounding for all the world like the click of giant croquet balls. I went round to the rear of the house and looked out of the kitchen windows to the lines. A little action, some quarrel of sentries, was going on behind the trees, just where the wooded ridge sloped to the river. Trench light after trench light rose, showing the disused railroad tracks running across the un-harvested fields. Gleaming palely through the French window at which I was standing, the radiance revealed the deserted kitchen, the rusty stove, the dusty pans, and the tarnished water-tap above the stone sink. The hard, wooden crash of grenades broke upon my ears . . .

I am a light sleeper, and the arrival of the first shell awakened me. Kicking off my blankets, I sat up in bed just in time to catch the swift ebb of a heavy concussion. A piece of glass, dislodged from a broken pane by the tremor, fell in a treble tinkle to the floor. For a minute or two there was a full, heavy silence, and then several objects rolled down the roof and fell over the gutters into the street. It sounded as if some one had emptied a hodful of coal onto the house-roof from the height of the clouds. Another silence followed. Suddenly it was broken by a swift, complete sound, a heavy boom-roar, and on the heels of this noise came a throbbing, whistling sigh that, at first faint as the sound of ocean on a distant beach, increased with incredible speed to a whistling swish, ending in a HISH of tremendous volume, and a roaring, grinding burst. The sound of a great shell is never a pure bang; one hears, rather, the end of the arriving HISH, the explosion, and the tearing disintegration of the thick wall of iron in one grinding hammer-blow of terrific violence.

I got up and went to the kitchen window. More lumps, fragments of shell that had been shot into the air by the explosion, rained down upon the roof. A house on one of the silent streets between the city and the lines was on fire, great volumes of smoke were rolling off into the starlit night, and voices were heard all about murmuring in the shadows. I hurried on my clothes and went down to the cellar.

From *A Volunteer Poilu*, by Henry Beston; Houghton Mifflin; Boston, 1916.

## *Little Household Gods Shiver and Blink*
—Edith Wharton

From the thronged high-road we passed into the emptiness of the deserted Poperinghe, and out again on the way to Ypres. Beyond the flats and wind-mills to our left were the invisible German lines, and the staff-officer who was with us leaned forward to caution our chauffeur: "No tooting between here and Ypres." There was still a good deal of movement on the road, though it was less crowded with troops that near Poperinghe; but as we passed through the low line of houses ahead, the silence and emptiness widened about us. That low line was Ypres; every monument that marked it, that gave it an individual outline, is gone. It is a town without a profile.

The motor slipped through a suburb of small brick houses and stopped under cover of some slightly taller buildings. Another military motor waited there, the chauffeur relic-hunting in the gutted houses.

We got out and walked toward the centre of the Cloth Market. Not a human being was in the streets. Endless lines of houses looked down on us from vacant windows. Our footsteps echoed like the tramp of a crowd, our lowered voices seemed to shout. In one street we came upon three English soldiers who were carrying a piano out of a house and lifting it onto a hand-cart. They stopped to stare at us, and we stared back. It seemed an age since we had seen a living being. One of the soldiers scrambled into the cart and tapped out a tune on the cracked key-board, and we all laughed with relief at the foolish noise. Then we walked on and were alone again.

We had seen other ruined towns, but none like this. Ypres has been bombarded to death, and the outer walls of its houses are still standing, so that it presents the distant semblance of a living city, while near by it is seen to be a disembowelled corpse. Every window-pane is smashed, nearly every building unroofed, and some house-fronts are sliced clean off, with the different stories exposed, as if for the stage-setting of a farce. In these exposed interiors the poor little house-hold gods shiver and blink like owls surprised in a hollow tree. A hundred signs of intimate and humble tastes, of humdrum pursuits, of family association, cling to the unmasked walls. Whiskered pho-tographs fade on morning-glory wallpapers, plaster saints pine under glass bells, antimacassars droop from plush sofas, yellowing diplomas display their seals on office walls. It was all so still and familiar that it seemed as if the people for whom these things had a meaning might at any moment come back and take up their daily business. And then—crash! the guns began, slamming out volley after volley all along the English lines, and the poor frail web of things that had made up the lives of a vanished city hung dangling before us in that deathly blast.

We were turning to go when we heard a whirr overhead, followed by a volley of machine guns. High up in the blue, over the centre of the dead city, flew a German aero-plane; and all about it hundreds of white shrapnel bursts out in the summer sky like the miraculous snow-fall of Italian legend. Up and up they flew, on the trail of the Taube, and on flew the Taube, faster still, till quarry and pack were lost in mist, and the barking of the *mitrailleuse* died out.

So we left Ypres to the death-silence in which we had found her.

From *Fighting France*, by Edith Wharton; Charles Scribner's Sons; New York, 1919.

## *The Gothas*
### —Mildred Aldrich

On Wednesday night I went to bed early. I wakened suddenly with the impression that I heard someone running along the terrace under my window. I sat up and listened, half believing that I had been dreaming, when I saw a ray of light in the staircase—my door was open.

I called out, *"Qui est la?"*

Amelie's trembling voice replied, *"Cest moi, madame,"* and I had the sudden wide vision of possibilities, which I am told is like that of a drowning man, for I realized she was not coming to me in the middle of the night for nothing, when she appeared in the doorway, all dressed, even to her hood, and with a lighted candle in her hand.

"Oh, Madame?" she exclaimed, "you were sleeping? You heard nothing?" and at that moment I heard the cannon. *"Oh, mon Dieu, Madame,* what is happening out at the front? It is something terrible, and you slept!"

I listened.

"That is not at the front, Amelie," I said. It is much nearer, in the direction of Paris. It's the guns of the forts." At that moment a bomb exploded, and I knew at once. "It's the Gothas, Amelie. Give me something to put on. What time is it?"

"Nearly midnight."

It took me less than ten minutes to dress—it was bitterly cold—and I wrapped myself in my big military cloak, put a cap over my tumbled hair, and a big fur round my neck, grabbed my field glasses, and went out into the orchard, which looks directly across the fort at Chelles in the direction of Paris.

It was a beautiful night, cold and still, white with moonlight, and the sky spangled with stars. For three hours we stood there listening to that bombardment, seeing nothing—ignorant of what was going on. The banging of the guns, the whirring of the *moteurs,* the exploding shells seemed over us and around us—yet we could see nothing. It only took us a little while to distinguish between the booming of the guns at Chelles and Vauclure, endeavouring to prevent the Gothas from passing, by putting up barrage firing, and the more distant bombs dropped by the flyers that had arrived near or over the city.

It was all the more impressive because it was so mysterious. At times it seemed as if one of three things must have been happening—either that we were destroying the fleet in the air, or they were destroying us, or that Paris was being wiped out. It did not, during those hours that I stood there, seem possible that such a cannonading could be kept up without one of these results. It was our first experience, and I assure you that it was weird. The beauty of the night, the invisibility of the machines, our absolute ignorance of what was going on, the humming of the motors overhead, the infernal persistent firing of the cannon and the terrific explosion of the bombs, followed, now and then, by a dull glow in the west, was all so mysterious.

It was four o'clock when we finally went into the house, leaving silence under the stars and the moonlit night. Amelie stirred up the embers, threw on a little wood, put the screen around me, made me a hot drink and I sat there to wait for daybreak. It seemed strange to go out of doors in the morning, and see nothing changed, after such a night.

From *The Peak of the Load*, by Mildred Aldrich; Small, Maynard and Co.; Boston, 1918.

## *It Is No Pleasure to Tell What I Saw*
—Richard Harding Davis

At a distance of six miles, as you approach from Paris along the valley of the Marne, Rheims has more the appearance of a fortress than a church. But when you stand in the square beneath and look up, it is entirely ecclesiastic, of noble and magnificent proportions, in design inspired, much too sublime for the kings it has crowned. It has been called "the most beautiful structure produced in the Middle Ages." On the west facade, rising tier upon tier, are five hundred and sixty statues and carvings. The statues are of angels, martyrs, patriarchs, apostles, the vices and virtues, the Virgin and Child. In the centre of these is the famous rose window; on either side giant towers.

At my feet down the steps leading to the three portals were pools of blood. There was a priest in the square, a young man with white hair and with a face as strong as one of those of the saints carved in stone, and as gentle. He explained the pools of blood. After the Germans retreated, the priests had carried the German wounded up the steps into the nave of the cathedral and for them had spread straw upon the stone flaggings.

The curé guided me to the side door, unlocked it, and led the way into the cathedral. From north and south the windows shed a radiance of deep blue, like the blue of the sky by moonlight on the coldest night of winter, and from the west the great rose window glowed with the warmth and beauty of a thousand rubies. Beneath it, bathed in crimson light, where for generations French men and women have knelt in prayer, where Joan of Arc helped place the crown on Charles VII, was piled three feet of dirty straw, and on the straw were gray-coated Germans, covered with the mud of the fields, caked with blood, white and haggard from the loss of it, from the lack of sleep, rest and food. The entire west end of the cathedral looked like a stable, and in the blue and purple rays from the gorgeous windows the wounded were as unreal as ghosts.

Two of them, done with pack-drill, goose-step, half rations and forced marches, lay under the straw the priests had heaped upon them. The toes of their boots pointed grotesquely upward. The gray hands were clasped rigidly as though in prayer.

Half hidden in the straw, the others were as silent and almost as still. Since they had been dropped upon the stone floor they had not moved, but lay in twisted, unnatural attitudes. Only their eyes showed that they lived. These were turned beseechingly upon the French Red Cross doctors, kneeling waist-high in the straw and unreeling long white bandages. The wounded watched them drawing slowly nearer, until they came, fighting off death, clinging to life as shipwrecked sailors cling to a raft and watch the boats pulling toward them.

A young German officer, his smart cavalry cloak torn and slashed, and filthy with dried mud and blood and with his eyes in bandages, groped toward a pail of water, feeling his way with his foot, his arms outstretched, clutching the air. To guide him a priest took his arm, and the officer turned and stumbled against him. Thinking the priest was one of his own men, he swore at him, and then, to learn if he wore shoulder-straps, ran his fingers over the priest's shoulders, and finding a silk cassock, said quickly in French, "Pardon me, my father; I am blind."

As the young curé guided me through the wrecked cathedral his indignation and his fear of being unjust waged a fine battle. "Every summer," he said, "thousands of your fellow countrymen visit the cathedral. They come again and again. They love these beautiful windows. They will not permit them to be destroyed. Will you tell them what you saw?"

It is no pleasure to tell what I saw. Shells had torn out some of the windows, the entire sash, glass, and stone frame—all was gone; only a jagged hole was left. On the floor lay broken carvings, pieces of stone from flying buttresses outside that had been hurled through the embrasures, tangled masses of leaden window-sashes, like twisted coils of barbed wire, and great brass candelabra. The steel ropes that had supported them had been shot away, and they had plunged to the flagging below, carrying with them their scarlet silk tassels heavy with the dust of centuries. And everywhere was broken glass. Not one of the famous blue windows was intact. None had been totally destroyed, but each had been shattered, and through the apertures the sun blazed blatantly.

We walked upon glass more precious than precious stones. It was beyond price. No one can replace it. Seven hundred years ago the secret of the glass died. Diamonds can be bought anywhere, pearls can be matched, but not the stained glass of Rheims. And under our feet, with straw and caked blood, it lay crushed into tiny fragments. When you held a piece of it between your eye and the sun it glowed with a light that never was on land or sea.

I have seen a lot of war—and real war is a high-born officer with his eyes shot out, peasant soldiers with their toes sticking stiffly through the straw, and the windows of Rheims, that for centuries with their beauty glorified the Lord, swept into a dust heap.

From *With the Allies*, by Richard Harding Davis; Charles Scribner's Sons; New York, 1918.

## *The War Capital of Serbia*
### —John Reed

Nish. We took a tumble-down cab—whose bottom-board immediately fell out—attached to two dying horses and driven by a bandit in a high fur cap, and jolted up a wide street paved with mud and wide-set sharp cobbles. Round about the city the green hills rose, beautiful with new leaves and with every flowering fruit-tree, and over the wide-flung Turkish roofs, and the few mean plaster buildings in the European style, loomed the bulbous Greek domes of the cathedral. Here and there was the slender spire of a minaret, crisscrossed with telephone-wires. The street opened into a vast square, a sea of mud and cobbles bounded by wretched huts, across which marched steel poles carrying hundreds of wires and huge modern arc-lights. At one side an ox lay on his back, feet clewed up to a wooden beam, while peasants shod him with solid iron plates, as they had done it for half a thousand years.

Austrian prisoners in uniform wandered freely everywhere, without a guard. Some drove wagons, others dug ditches, and hundreds loitered up and down in idleness. We learned that by paying fifty *dinars* to the government, you could have one for a servant. All the legations and consulates were manned with them. And the prisoners were glad to be servants, for there was no decent place for them to live, and scanty food. Now and then an Austrian officer passed along, in full uniform and with his sword.

"Escape?" said one government official we interrogated. "No, they do not try. The roads are metres deep in mud, the villages are depopulated and full of disease, there is no food . . . It is difficult enough to travel by train in Serbia—on foot it would be impossible. And there are the guards along the frontier."

We passed a big hospital where pale prisoners leaned from windows upon dirty blankets, dragged themselves in and out of the doors, and lay propped up on piles of drying mud along the road. These were only survivors; for out of the sixty thousand Austrians captured in the war, twelve thousand were already dead of typhus.

Beyond the square was the street again, between rough one-story houses, and we were in the market-place. A dull roar rose from the haggling of hundreds of peasants in ten different national costumes— homespun linen embroidered with flowers, high fur hats, fezzes, turbans, and infinite varieties and modifications of Turkish trousers. Pigs squealed, hens squawked; underfoot were heaped baskets of eggs and herbs and vegetables and red peppers; majestic old men in sheep-skins shuffled along with lambs in their arms. Here was the centre of the town. There were two or three restaurants and foul-smelling cafes, the dingy Hotel Orient, the inevitable American shoe-store, and amid cheap little shops, sudden windows ablaze with expensive jewelry and extravagant women's hats.

Along the sidewalks elbowed a multitude of strangely assorted people: gypsies, poverty-stricken peasants, gendarmes with great swords, in red and blue uniforms, tax-collectors dressed like generals, also with swords, smart army officers hung with medals, soldiers in filthy tatters, their feet bound with rags—soldiers limping, staggering on crutches, without arms, without legs, discharged from the over-crowded hospitals still blue and shaking from the typhus—and everywhere the Austrian prisoners. Government officials hurried by with portfolios under their arms. Fat Jewish contractors hobnobbed with political hangers-on over maculate cafe tables. Women government clerks, wives and mistresses of the officers, society ladies, shouldered the peasant women in their humped-up gay skirts and high-colored socks. The government from Belgrade had taken refuge in Nish, and a mountain village of twenty thousand inhabitants had become a city of one hundred and twenty thousand—not counting those who died.

For the typhus had swept the town, where people were living six and ten in a room, until everywhere the black flags flapped in long, sinister vistas, and the windows of the cafes were plastered with black paper death-notices.

We crossed the muddy Nishava River on the bridge which leads to the heavy, arabesqued gate of the ancient Turkish citadel, which was Roman before the Turks, and where Constantine the Great was born. On the grass along the foot of the great wall sprawled hundreds of soldiers, sleeping, scratching themselves, stripping and searching their bodies for lice, tossing and twisting in fever. Everywhere about Nish, wherever there was a spot of worn grass, the miserable people clustered, picking vermin from each other.

Such was Nish, as we first saw it. Two weeks later we returned, after the rains had altogether ceased, and the hot sun had dried the streets. It was a few days after the feast of St. George, which marks the coming of the spring in Serbia. On that day all Serbia rises at dawn and goes out into the woods and fields, gathering flowers and dancing and singing and feasting all day. And even here, in this filthy, overcrowded town, with the tragic sadness of war and pestilence over every house, the streets were a gay sight. The men peasants had changed their dirty heavy woolens and sheepskins for the summer suit of embroidered dazzling linen. All the women wore new dresses and new silk kerchiefs, decorated with knots of ribbon, with leaves and flowers—even the ox-yokes and the oxen's heads were bound with purple lilac branches. Through the streets raced mad young gypsy girls in Turkish trousers of extravagant and gorgeous colors, their bodices gleaming with gold braid, gold coins hung in their ears. And I remember five great strapping women with mattocks over their shoulders, who marched singing down the middle of the road to take their dead men's places in the work of the fields.

From *The War in Eastern Europe*, by John Reed; Charles Scribner's Sons; New York, 1916.

## *That Sepia Waste*
### —Winston Churchill

One night we entered the danger zone. There had been an entertainment in the little salon which, packed with passengers, had gradually achieved the temperature and humidity of a Turkish bath. For the ports had been closed as tight as gaskets could make them, the electric fans, as usual, obstinately "refused to march." After the amateur speechmaking and concert pieces an Italian violinist, who had thrown over a lucrative contract to become a soldier, played exquisitely; and one of the French sisters we had seen walking the deck with the mincing steps of the cloister sang, somewhat precariously and pathetically, the *Ave Maria*. Its pathos was of the past, and after she had finished, as we fled into the open air, we were conscious of having turned our backs irrevocably yet determinedly upon an era whose life and convictions the music of the composer so beautifully expressed.

On deck a fine rain was blowing through a gap in our burlap shroud, a phosphorescent fringe of foam hissed along the sides of the ship, giving the illusory appearance of our deadlights open and ablaze, exaggerating the sinister blackness of the night. We were, apparently, a beacon in that sepia waste where modern underseas monsters were lurking.

There were on board other elements which in the normal times gone by would have seemed disquieting enough. The evening after we had left New York, while we were still off the coast of Long Island, I saw on the poop a crowd of steerage passengers listening intently to harangues by speakers addressing them from the top of a pile of life rafts. Armenians, I was told, on their way to fight the Turks, all recruited in America by one frenzied woman who had seen her child cut in two by a German officer. Twilight was gathering as I joined the group, the sea was silvered by the light of an August moon floating serenely between swaying stays. The orator's passionate words and gestures evoked wild responses from his hearers, whom the drag of an ancient hatred had snatched from the peaceful asylum of the west. This smiling, happy folk, which I had seen in our manufacturing towns and cities, were now transformed, atavistic—all save one, a student, who stared wistfully through his spectacles across the water. Later, when twilight deepened, when the moon had changed from silver to gold, the orators gave place to a singer. He had been a bootblack in America. Now he had become a bard. His plaintive minor chant evoked, one knew not how, the flavour of that age-long history of oppression and wrong these were now determined to avenge. Their conventional costumes were proof that we had harboured them— almost, indeed, assimilated them. And suddenly they had reverted. They were going to slaughter the Turks.

On a bright Saturday afternoon we steamed into the wide mouth of the Gironde, a name stirring vague memories of romance and terror. The French passengers gazed wistfully at the low-lying strip of sand and forest, but our uniformed pilgrims—the American lawyers, doctors, newspaper correspondents, movie photographers, and millionaires—crowded the rail and hailed it as the promised land of self-realization.

A richly colored watering-place slid into view, as in a moving-picture show. There was, indeed, all the reality and unreality of the cinematograph about our arrival; presently the reel would end abruptly, and we should find ourselves pushing our way out of the emptying theatre into a rainy street. The impression of unreality in the face of visual evidence persisted into the night when, after an afternoon of anchor, we glided up the river, our decks and and ports ablaze across the land. Silhouettes of tall poplars loomed against the blackness; occasionally a lamp revealed the milky-blue facade of a house. This was France!

War-torn France—at last vividly brought home to us when a glare appeared on the sky, growing brighter and brighter until, at a turn of the river, abruptly we came abreast of vomiting furnaces, thousands of electric lights strung like beads over the crest of a hill, and below these, dim rows of houses, all of a sameness, stretching along monotonous streets. A munitions town in the night! One could have tossed a biscuit on the stone wharfs where workmen, crouching over their tasks, straightened up at the sight of us and cheered. And one cried out hoarsely, "*Vous venez nous sauver, vous Americains*"—"You come to save us" . . .

The skies were of a darkness seldom known in America. The countryside was no longer smiling. After some two hours of progress we came, in that devastated district near the front, to a sepia expanse where many monsters were clumsily cavorting like dinosaurs in the primeval slime. At some distance from the road others stood apparently tethered in line, awaiting their turn for exercise. These were the far-famed tanks. Their commander, or chief mahout—as I was inclined to call him— was a cheerful young giant of colonial origin, who has often driven them serenely across No Man's Land and into the German trenches. He had been expecting us, and led me along a duck board over the morass, to where one of these leviathans was awaiting us.

You crawl through a greasy hole in the bottom, and the inside is as full of machinery as the turret of the *Pennsylvania*, and you grope your way to the seat in front beside that of the captain and conductor, looking out through a slot in the armour over a waste of water and mud. From here you are supposed to operate a machine gun. Behind you two mechanics have started the engines with a deafening roar, above which are heard the hoarse commands of the captain as he grinds in the gears. Then you realize that the thing is actually moving, that the bosses on the belt have managed to find a grip on the slime—and presently you come to the brink of what appears, to your exaggerated sense of perception, a bottomless chasm, with distant steep banks on the farther side that look unattainable and insurmountable. It is an old German trench which the rains have widened. You brace yourself, you grip desperately a pair of brass handles in front of you, while leviathan hesitates, seems to sit up on his haunches, and then gently buries his nose in the pasty clay and paws his way upward into the field beyond. It was like sitting in a huge rocking chair. That we might have had a bump, and a bone-breaking one, I was informed after I had left the scene of the adventure. It all depends on the skill of the driver. The monsters are not as tractable as they seem . . .

The English officer directed our chauffeur to Bapaume, across that wilderness which the Germans had so wantonly made in their retreat to the Hindenburg line. Nothing could have been more dismal than our slow progress in the steady rain, through the deserted streets of this town. Home after home had been blasted—their intimate yet harrowing interiors were revealed. The shops and cafes, which had been thoroughly looted, had their walls blown out, but in many cases the signs of the vanished and homeless proprietors still hung above the door. The church, the great cathedral on its terrace, the bishop's house, all dynamited, all cold and wet and filthy.

It was dismal, but scarcely more dismal than that which followed; for at Bapaume we were on the edge of the battle-field of the Somme. And I chanced to remember that the name had first been indelibly impressed on my consciousness at a comfortable breakfast-table at home, where I sat looking out on a bright New England garden. In the headlines and columns of my morning newspaper I had read again and again, during the summer of 1916, of Thiepval and La Boisselle, of Fricourt and Mametz and the Bois des Trones. Then they had had a sinister but remote significance; now I was to see them, or what was left of them.

As an appropriate and characteristic setting for the tragedy which had happened here, the indigo afternoon could not have been better chosen. Description fails to do justice to the abomination of the desolation of that vast battle-field in the rain, and the imagination refuses to reconstruct the scene of peace—the chateaux and happy villages, the forests and pastures, that flourished here so brief a time ago. In my fancy the long, low swells of land, like those of some dreary sea, were for the moment like subsiding waves of the cataclysm that had rolled here and extinguished all life. Beside the road only the blood-red soil betrayed the sites of powdered villages; and through it, in every direction, trenches had been cut. Between the trenches the earth was torn and tortured, as though some suddenly fossilizing process, in its moment of supreme agony, had fixed it thus.

On the hummocks were graves, graves marked by wooden crosses, others by broken rifles thrust in the ground. Shattered gun-carriages lay in the ditches, modern cannon that had cost priceless hours of skilled labour, and once we were confronted by one of those monsters, wounded to death, I had seen that morning. The sight of this huge, helpless thing oddly recalled the emotions I had felt, as a child, when contemplating dead elephants in a battle picture of the army of a Persian king.

From *A Traveller in War-Time*, by Winston Churchill; Macmillan; New York, 1918.

# Chapter Four:

# Lie

The status, influence, and respect that serious creative writers enjoyed in 1914–18 did not come without a cost. They were establishment figures, the pals of press barons, prime ministers, and kings, well paid and much honored, and thus with a stake in preserving the status quo, not only politically and socially, but in terms of victory and what it would take to insure it. When they were asked to contribute to the war effort with their writing, they knew what was expected of them—at the minimum, a certain flexibility in regards to the truth; at the maximum, a willingness to lie.

"Prevaricate" might be the most generous verb to apply here, or, borrowing a term from our own day, "slant." Rudyard Kipling, himself one of the most enthusiastic slanters, would publish after the war—and the death of his son in combat—this bitter couplet from "Epitaphs of War."

"If any question why we died
Tell them, because our fathers lied."

The pressure on writers to do this was enormous, and their response—speaking now in their defense—was probably sincere and not cynical. They saw the war as a fight for civilization and they genuinely hated the enemy. They felt guilty at not taking part in the battles themselves. They had their status, their careers, their income to worry about. Many of them were given official duties and titles, to which their vanity was not immune. Some had sons serving in the trenches; all had friends and relatives there. They had genuine respect for the fighting men. Taken on tours of the battlefields, they were shown what the military staff wanted them to see and kept tight on the leash.

Lie? They wouldn't have seen it that way. "Propagandize" is the worst they would have admitted to, a word that did not then carry the negative connotation it has today. Words contributing to victory were to them no bad thing.

The war was going badly now, becoming the endless nightmare writers only slowly realized was upon them. The year 1916 saw the bloodlettings at Verdun and on the Somme, catastrophes which not only killed hundreds of thousands of young men, but affected the Western imagination in ways that were and are incalculable.

Yet there were writers willing to portray these battles as total victories, never mind the death toll or the continued stalemate. Take the infamous First Day of the Somme, July 1, 1916, and the British writers' response.

"The most bloody defeat in the history of Britain," wrote C. E. Montague, who served in the trenches.

> "And our Press came out bland and copious and graphic, with nothing to show that we had not had quite a good day—a victory really. Men who lived through the massacre read the stuff open-mouthed."

Even today's historians have to reach to explain how truly terrible July 1 was.

"The casualties suffered by the British on the opening day of the Battle of the Somme," Martin Middlebrook points out,

> "[s]tands comparison not only with other battles, but with complete wars. The British Army's loss on that one

day easily exceeds the battle casualties in the Crimean War, the Boer War, and the Korean War combined."

John Keegan puts the July 1 casualties, on the British side alone, at over sixty thousand killed, wounded, and missing, or, to bring it home to Americans, about the same number of names that appear on the Vietnam Memorial in Washington; many of these casualties occurred in the battle's first ten minutes.

> "To the British army, it was and would remain their greatest military catastrophe of their national history. The Somme marked the end of an age of vital optimism in British life that has never been recovered."

It's well to remember that last line when reading some of the writers included in this chapter.

What angered the soldiers most—and can still anger you today—was the manly breeziness of style many writers felt the need for when writing of the war. Montague, whose wartime job included shepherding VIP writers on their official tours of the trenches, wrote how they invariably adopted

> "a certain jauntiness of tone that roused the fighting troops to fury against the writer. Through his dispatches there ran a brisk implication that regimental officers and men enjoyed nothing better than 'going over the top;' that a battle was just a rough, jovial picnic; that a fight never went on long enough for these men; that their only fear was lest the war should end on this side of the Rhine. This, the men reflected in helpless anger, was what people at home were offered as faithful accounts of what their friends in the field were thinking and suffering."

And writers could be guilty of something far worse than jauntiness. Many of them too easily believed tales of German atrocities . . . Huns poisoning the wells, Huns spreading influenza germs, Huns putting ground glass in Red Cross bandages . . . the better to whip up war fever and spur enlistments. Twenty-five years later, this would come back to haunt the world, when a new German army, a new German regime, committed atrocities that made World War I's seem like harmless misdemeanors. Because a credulous public had been sold crucified nuns and burning babies in the First War, they were fatally slow to buy Auschwitz and ovens in the Second.

As historian Rick Atkinson points out, the exaggerated reports of German atrocities in 1914–18, when subsequently discovered to be mostly fabrications, "left an enduring legacy of skepticism," with a poll finding that barely one-third of the British public in 1944 believed rumors of the concentration camps.

Some Great War writers, even figures of the establishment with much to lose, responded more honestly. Included here, along with the lies and the jauntiness, are more measured responses by Richard Harding Davis and H. G. Wells, the first writing about the difficulties correspondents faced in getting out the truth, the latter agonizing, via his Mr. Britling, over the writer's role in all the horror.

Still other writers, ones we'll examine in a later chapter, found the courage to protest the killing, not from the safety and hindsight of the 1920s, but while it was actually taking place. Another of the war's many ironies: the writers who expected honors and rewards for their wholehearted support of the war are now looked upon as little better than liars, while the ones who had nothing but obloquy heaped on them in 1916 now seem like prescient heroes who command our respect.

The propagandists were not without their critics even at the time. George Bernard Shaw, reading Kipling and his ilk, railed at "the incitements and taunts of elderly non-combatants, and the verses of poets jumping at the cheapest chance in their underpaid profession."

Perhaps the fairest thing that can be said of them, looking back, is that their writing, in its forced jauntiness and optimism, represents the last struggle of a doomed way of looking at the world as it confronts the horrors of a century that would demand a much darker response.

Arnold J. Toynbee would by the 1940s become perhaps the best-known historian in the Western world, thanks to his twelve-volume *A Study of History,* which got his face on the cover of *Time* magazine in 1947. In the years since, his reputation has declined, with historians finding his emphasis on religious and spiritual factors in the workings of history to be exaggerated.

He was twenty-five when the war broke out, and he went to work for the Intelligence Department of the British Foreign Service, later serving as a delegate to the Paris Peace Conference. His 1917 book, *The German Terror in Belgium; A Historical Record,* is prefaced with his assurance that "with the documents now published on both sides it is at last possible to present a clear narrative of what actually happened to the civil population in the countries overrun by the German Armies during the first three months of the European war."

But was it clear? Toynbee repeats every rumor and unsubstantiated report as fact, though he admits to exercising his "own judgement as to which of the inferences is truth." It's written in a hard-hitting documentary style, with specific names, dates, and places giving the feel of unbiased reportage.

After the war, many of these atrocities were discovered to be either fabricated for propaganda purposes, or the tragic, unavoidable result of the chaos that enveloped the battle zone. Still, war crimes against non-combatants, including women and children, *were* committed, particularly in Belgium, by German soldiers (whose fears were whipped up by their own writers at home) fearful of *franc-tireurs* like those the army had faced in France in 1870. A recent history puts the number of Belgian civilians killed at well over five thousand, and shows that the terrorizing of the populace was condoned and actively promoted by the German general staff, just as British writers originally claimed.

Many prominent German intellectuals, including the scientists Max Planck and Wilhelm Röntgen, defended their army, blaming Belgian civilians for the atrocities and insisting upon the army's right of reprisal.

Ernest Lissauer, a thirty-two-year-old German-Jewish poet and dramatist, is only remembered now for two moments of inspired vitriol. He coined the phrase *Gott strafe England,* May God punish England, which became the vow of the Germany army—and, in the Second World War, the origin of the word "strafing" as slang for machine-gunning from the air.

His poem set to music, *Hassgesang,* the notorious "Hymn of Hate," did even more to stir up German morale, and, when recited in England, stirred up morale there just as thoroughly. Arthur Conan Doyle, for one, found it absolutely beyond the pale.

> "This sort of thing is very painful and odious, and fills us with a mixture of pity and disgust, and we feel as if—instead of a man—we are really fighting with a furious screaming woman."

Lissauer's hymn made him famous in Germany. The Kaiser decorated him, and *Hassgesang* was printed and distributed to German soldiers on the western front.

If Lissauer's poem had any permanent value, it was its role in inspiring one of the great minor poems of World War I, written by the British satirist J. C. Squire.

"God heard the embattled nations sing and shout
'*Gott strafe England!*' and 'God Save the King!'
Gott save this, God that, and God the other thing
'Good God!' said God. 'I've got my work cut out.'"

The Kaiser, with his pompous military garb and knack for inflammatory comments, was an easy target for Allied writers, included the eighty-one-year-old novelist and critic W. D. Howells, who represented all that was good and bad in the American literary establishment at the turn of the twentieth century. Another old-timer asked to contribute to the war effort, a few months before his death, was Edmond Rostand, the author of *Cyrano de Bergerac,* who managed to turn the German destruction of Rheims cathedral to good propaganda purpose. However, Howells was famous for being a literary realist, Rostand for being a literary romantic, but the aging writers obviously saw eye-to-eye on the war, and the German's alleged policy of *Schrecklickeit*—Frightfulness.

The young "war poets" like Sassoon, Graves, and Owen, would become famous for their antiwar stance and their graphic descriptions of suffering in battle, but the most famous poet *during* the war continued to be the forty-nine-year-old Rudyard Kipling, the first English writer to win the Nobel Prize (1907); he was known for his wholehearted jingoism, if not his outright bloodthirstiness. Beloved before the war for his depiction of common English soldiers embroiled in one Imperialistic scrap after another, he didn't see any reason to soften his pro-military stance once Germans across the Channel became the enemy and not just some Zulu tribesmen on the fringes of Empire.

His enthusiasm for war would have tragic consequences. His seventeen-year-old son John wanted to enlist in the army, but was rejected because of his weak eyesight. Kipling pulled strings with his friends in the army to get him past the physical to a commission in the Irish Guards. John died in the Battle of Loos in 1915, and Kipling and his wife never got over it. Kipling's lament, "My Boy Jack," continues to be one of his most often read poems today.

I have Kipling's account of a battlefield tour (taken before his son's death), *France at War; on the Frontiers of Civilization,* on the desk beside me. The cover depicts, in a softly colored patina, the three furled flags of England, France, and Russia; on the flyleaf is a small sticker showing it was purchased from The Corner Book Store in Boston. Even more interesting, at least to me, is the page with the publishing information. "Doubleday and Page" it says, "1915," and "Garden City, New York."

This was the famous Country Life Press, only a block or two from the house I grew up in, and only a few blocks farther from the old site of Camp Mills where my friends and I played touch football near the monument to the Rainbow Division.

After the war, Kipling worked on behalf of the Imperial War Graves Commission in establishing the dignified and moving western front cemeteries. He selected the phrase "Their Name Liveth for Evermore" from Ecclesiastes, found on the Stone of Remembrance in many of these cemeteries, and suggested "Known Unto God" for the headstones of the unidentified. Further, he chose the phrase "The Glorious Dead" for the Cenotaph in Whitehall—a phrase that, when used now, has become mostly ironic.

No writer in World War I worked more industriously than John Buchan—or was more tightly embedded in his nation's military and political establishment. Already famous for his adventure novels (including *The Thirty-Nine Steps,* made into one of Hitchcock's early films), Buchan would be the writer the soldiers read in the trenches, with his novel *Greenmantle,* with its plot of wartime espionage and suspense, being their special favorite.

Buchan, who was thirty-nine and suffering ill health, still managed to make major contributions to the war effort. He served on Haig's staff in France, writing communiques and weekly battle summaries; worked for the Intelligence Corps escorting journalists on tours of the front; wrote, for the War Propaganda Bureau, the multi-volume *History of the War,* which became a huge bestseller; was put in charge of foreign propaganda for the Department of Information; and, to cap it all, became the man responsible for briefing King George V on the progress of the war.

"I have had many queer jobs in my life," he said of the last, "but this is the queerest."

*The Battle of the Somme*—with vivid photos and detailed maps—was published only a few months after the battle, though it has the remote tone of a history written many years later. Buchan's summary of the first day's fighting—along with Mrs. Humphrey Ward's description that follows—should be compared with what the historians had to say about it in the chapter introduction.

Critic Peter Buitenhuis sums up Buchan's *Somme* thusly:

> "The account contains all the ringing clichés and exaggerations of the genre, and by representing that almost unmitigated hell in such glowing colors, Buchan falsifies the whole military situation on the Western Front. By his omission and exaggerated claims he makes not only the common soldier but also the commanding generals look superb."

Buchan's brother and many of his friends were killed in the war. He felt slighted at its conclusion at not receiving more honors for his contributions, though this was rectified in 1935, when the King appointed him the first Baron Tweedsmuir and Governor General of Canada.

Thanks to his "thrillers" and their star, superspy Richard Hannay, Buchan is still read today, and is regarded as one of the founders of the modern suspense story and a formative influence on writers like Ian Fleming and John Le Carré. The John Buchan Society publishes a journal to keep his work alive; this includes operating a John Buchan Museum in Peebles, Scotland.

## *Babies on Bayonets*
—Arnold J. Toynbee

The devastation done by the Germans in their advance was light compared with the outrages they committed when the Belgian sortie of August 25th drove them back from Malines towards the Aerschot-Louvain line.

In Malines itself, they destroyed 1,500 houses from first to last, and revenged themselves atrociously on the civil population. A Belgian soldier saw them bayonet an old woman in the back, and cut off a young woman's breasts. Another saw them bayonet a woman and her son. They shot a police inspector in the stomach as he came out of his door, and blew off the head of an old woman at a window. A child of two came out into the street as eight drunken soldiers were marching by. A man in the second file stepped aside and drove his bayonet with both hands into the child's stomach. He lifted the child into the air on his bayonet and carried it away, he and his comrades still singing. The child screamed when the soldier stuck it with his bayonet, but not afterwards. This incident was reported by two witnesses. Another woman was found dead with twelve bayonet wounds between her shoulders and her waist. Another—between 16 and 20 years old—who had been killed by a bayonet, "was kneeling, and her hands were clasped, and the bayonet had pierced both hands. I also saw a boy of about 16," continues the witness, "who had been killed by a bayonet thrust through his mouth. In the same house there was an old woman lying dead."

The next place from which the Germans were driven was Hofstade, and here, too, they revenged themselves before they went. They left the corpses of women lying in the streets. There was an old woman mutilated with the bayonet. There was a young pregnant woman who had been ripped open. In the lodge of a chateau the porter's body was found lying on a heap of straw. He had been bayonetted in the stomach—evidently, while in bed, for the empty bed was soaked with blood. The blacksmith of Hofstade—also bayonetted—was lying on the doorstep. Adjoining the blacksmith's house there was cafe, and here a middle-aged woman lay dead, and a boy of about 16. The boy was found kneeling in an attitude of supplication. Both his hands had been cut off. "One was on the ground, the other hanging by a bit of skin." His face was smeared with blood. He was seen in this condition by twenty-five separate witnesses.

"I went with an artilleryman," states another Belgian soldier, "to find his parents who lived in Hofstade. All the houses were burning except the one where this man's parents lived. On forcing the door we saw lying on the floor of the room on which it opened the dead bodies of a man, a woman, a girl, and a boy, who, the artilleryman told us, were his father and mother and brother and sister. Each of them had both feet cut off just above the ankle, and both hands just above the wrist. The poor boy rushed straight off, took one of the horses from his gun, and rode in the direction of the German lines. We never saw him again."

At Sempst, as the Germans evacuated the village, they dragged the inhabitants out by firing into the cellars. The hostages were taken to the bridge. "One young man was carrying in his arms his little brother, 10 or 11 years old, who had been run over before the war and could not walk. The soldiers told the man to hold up his arms. He said he could not, as he must hold his brother, who could not walk. Then a German soldier hit him on the head with a revolver, and he let the child fall."

At Weerde, 34 houses were burnt. As the Germans retreated they bayonetted two little girls standing in the road and tossed them into the flames of a burning house—their mother was standing by. At Capelle-au-Bois, the Belgian troops found two girls hanging naked from a tree with their breasts cut off, and two women bayonetted in house, caught as they were making preparations to flee. A woman told them how German soldiers had violated her daughter successively in an adjoining room.

The Belgian troops found the body of a woman on the road, stripped to the waist with her breasts cut off. There was another woman with her head cut off and her body mutilated. There was a child with its stomach slashed open with a bayonet, and another—two or three years old—nailed to a door by its hands and feet.

From *The German Terror in France*, by Arnold J. Toynbee; George H. Doran Co.; New York, 1917.

## *Hymn of Hate*

—Ernest Lissauer

French and Russian, they matter not
A blow for a blow, and a shot for a shot
We love them not, we hate them not,
We hold the Weichsel and Vosges gate.
We have but one and only hate,
We love as one, we hate as one,
We have one foe and one alone.
He is known to you all, he is known to you all,
He crouches behind the dark gray flood
Full of envy, of rage, of craft, of gall,
Cut off by waves that are thicker than blood.
Come, let us stand at the Judgement Place,
An oath to swear to, face to face.
An oath of bronze no wind can shake,
An oath for our sons and their sons to take.
Come, hear the word, repeat the word,
Throughout the Fatherland make it heard.
We will never forego our hate,
We have but a single hate,
We love as one, we hate as one,
We have one foe and one alone—
                    ENGLAND!


Take you the folk of earth in pay,
With bars of gold your ramparts lay
Bedeck the ocean with bow on bow,
Ye reckon well, but not well enough now,
French and Russian, they matter not,
A blow for a blow, a shot for a shot,
We fight the battle with bronze and steel,
And the time that is coming Peace will seal.

You we will hate with a lasting hate,
We will never forego our hate,
Hate by water and hate by land,
Hate of the head and hate of the hand,
Hate of the hammer and hate of the crown,
Hate of seventy million choking down.
We love as one, we hate as one,
We have one foe and one alone—
                    ENGLAND!

From *Current History; the European War*, The New York Times Co., New York, 1915; translation Barbara Henderson.

## *Mother is the Name of the Gun*
### —Arthur Conan Doyle

It was to an artillery observation post that we were bound, and once again my description must be bounded by discretion. Suffice it, that in an hour I found myself, together with a razor-keen young artillery observer and an excellent old sportsman of a Russian prince, jammed into a very small space, and staring through a slit at the German lines. In front of us lay a vast plain, scarred and slashed, with bare places at intervals, such as you see where gravel pits break a green common. Not a sign of life or movement, save some wheeling crows. And yet down there, within a mile or so, is the population of a city. Far away a single train is puffing at the back of the German lines. We are here on a definite errand. Away to the right, nearly three miles off, is a small red house, dim to the eye but clear in the glasses, which is suspected as a German post. It is to go up this afternoon.

The gun is some distance away, but I hear the telephone directions. "Mother will soon do her in," remarks the gunner boy cheerfully. "Mother" is the name of the gun. "Give her five six three four," he cries through the 'phone. "Mother" utters a horrible bellow from somewhere on our right. An enormous spout of smoke rises ten seconds later from near the house.

"Raise her seven five," says our boy encouragingly. "Mother" roars more angrily than ever. "How will that do?" she seems to say.

I wonder how the folk in the house are feeling as the shells creep ever nearer. "Gun laid, sir," says the telephone. "Fire!" I am looking through my glass. A flash of fire on the house, a huge pillar of dust and smoke—then it settles and an unbroken field is there. The German post has gone up. "It's a dear little gun," says the officer boy.

We are all led off to be introduced to "Mother," who sits, squat and black, amid twenty of her grimy children who wait upon and feed her. She is an important person is "Mother," and her importance grows. It gets clearer with every month that it is she, and only she, who can lead us to the Rhine. She can and she will if the factories of Britain can beat those of the Hun. See to it, you working men and women of Britain. Work now if you rest for ever after, for the fate of Europe and of all that is dear to us is in your hands. For "Mother" is a dainty eater, and needs good food and plenty . . .

That night we dined with yet another type of the French soldier, General A., who commands the corps of which my friend has one division. Each of these French generals has a striking individuality of his own which I wish I could fix on paper. Their only common point is that each seems to be a rare good soldier. The corps general is Athos with a touch of d'Artagnan. He is well over six feet high, bluff, jovial, with a huge, upcurling moustache, and a voice that would rally a regiment. It is a grand figure which should have been done by Van Dyck with lace collar, hand on sword, and arm akimbo. Jovial and laughing was he, but a stern and hard soldier was lurking behind the smiles.

His name may appear in history, and so may Humbert's, who rules all the army of which the other corps is a unit. Humbert is a Lord Robert's figure, small, wiry, quick-stepping, all steel and elastic, with a short, sharp upturned moustache, which one could imagine as crackling with electricity in moments of excitement like cat's fur. What he does or says is quick, abrupt and to the point. He fires his remarks like pistol shots at this man or that.

Once to my horror he fixed me with his hard little eyes, and demanded, *"Sherlock Holmes, est ce qu'il est un soldat dans l'armee Anglaise?"*

The whole table waited in an awful hush.

*"Mais, mon general,"* I stammered. *Il est trop vieux pour service."*

There was general laughter, and I felt that I had scrambled out of an awkward place.

And talking of awkward places, I had forgotten about that spot upon the road whence the Boche observer could see our motor-cars. He had actually laid a gun upon it, the rascal, and waited all the long day for our return. No sooner did we appear upon the slope than a shrapnel shell burst above us, but somewhat behind me, as well as to the left. Had it been straight the second car would have got it, and there might have been a vacancy in one of the chief editorial chairs in London. The General shouted to the driver to speed up, and we were soon safe from the German gunners.

One gets perfectly immune to noises in these scenes, for the guns which surround you make louder crashes than any shell which bursts about you. It is only when you actually see the cloud over you that your thoughts come back to yourself, and that you realise that in this wonderful drama you may be a useless super, but none the less you are on the stage and not in the stalls.

From *A Visit to Three Fronts*, by Arthur Conan Doyle; George M. Doran Co.; New York, 1916.

# *The Master Spirit of Hell*
## — W. D. Howells

### The Little Children

"Suffer little children to come unto me,"
Christ said, and answering with infernal glee,
"Take them!" the arch-fiend scoffed, and from the tottering walls

Of their wrecked homes, and from the cattle's stalls,
And the dogs' kennels, and the cold
Of the waste fields, and from the hapless hold
Of their dead mothers' arms, famished and bare
And maimed by shot and shell,
The master-spirit of hell
Caught them up, and through the shuddering air
Of the hope-forsaken world
The little ones he hurled,
Mocking that Pity in his pitiless might—
The anti-Christ of Schrecklickeit.

From *The Book of the Homeless*, edited by Edith Wharton; Charles Scribner's Sons, New York, 1916.

## *Vandal Guns of Dull Intent*
—Edmond Rostand

### The Cathedral

"Deathless" is graven deeper on thy brow;
Ghouls have no power to end thy endless sway.
The Greek of old, the Frenchman of today,
Before thy riven shrine are bending now.

A wounded fortress straightaway lieth prone,
Not so the Temple dies; its roof may fall,
The sky its covering vault, an azure pall,
Doth droop to crown its wealth of lacework stone.

Praise to you, Vandal guns of dull intent!
We lacked till now our Beauty's monument.
Twice hallowed o'er by insult's brutal hand,

As Pallas owns on Athens' golden hill,
We have it now, thanks to your far-flung brand!
Your shame—our gain, misguided German skill!

From *Current History; the European War*, The New York Times Co.,
New York, 1915; translation Frances C. Fay.

## *These Terrific Symbols*
—Rudyard Kipling

The ridge with the scattered pines might have hidden children at play. Certainly a horse would have been quite visible, but there was no hint of guns, except a semaphore which announced it was forbidden to pass that way, as the battery was fighting. The Boches must have looked for that battery, too. The ground was pitted with shell holes of all calibres—some of them as fresh as mole-casts in the misty damp morning; others where the poppies had grown from seed to flower all through the summer.

"And where are the guns?" I demanded at last.

They were almost under one's hand, their ammunition in cellars and dug-outs beside them. As far as one can make out, the 75 gun has no pet name. The bayonet is Rosalie, the virgin of Bayonne, but the 75, the watchful nurse of the trenches and the little sister of the Line, seems to be always *soixante-quinze*. Even those who love her best do not insist she is beautiful. Her merits are French—logic, directness, simplicity, and the supreme gift of "occasionality." She is equal to everything on the spur of the moment. One sees and studies the few appliances that make her do what she does, and one feels that any one could have invented her.

"As a matter of fact," says a commandant, "anybody—or rather, everybody did. The general idea is after such-and-such a system, the patent of which has expired, and we improved it; the breech action, with slight modification, is somebody else's; the sighting is perhaps a little special; and so is the traversing, but, at bottom, it is only an assembly of variations and arrangements."

That, of course, is all that Shakespeare ever got out of the alphabet. The French Artillery make their own guns as he made his plays. It is just as simple as that.

The gun-servers stood back with the bored contempt of the professional for the layman who intrudes on his mysteries. Other civilians had come that way before—had seen, and grinned, and complimented and gone their way, leaving the gunners high up on the bleak hillside to grill or mildew or freeze for weeks and months.

Then she spoke. Her voice was higher pitched, it seemed, than ours—with a more shrewish tang to the speeding shell. Her recoil was as swift and as graceful as the shrug of a French-woman's shoulders; the empty case leaped forth and clanged against the trail; the tops of two or three pines fifty yards away nodded knowingly to each other, though there was no wind.

"They'll be bothered down below to know the meaning of our single shot. We don't give them one dose at a time as rule," somebody laughed.

We waited in the fragrant silence. Nothing came back from the mist that clogged the lower grounds, though no shell of this war was ever launched with more earnest prayers that it might do hurt . . .

A shell must fall somewhere, and by the law of averages occasionally lights straight as a homing pigeon on the one spot it can wreck most. Then earth opens for yards around, and men must be dug out—some merely breathless, who shake their ears, swear, and carry on, and others whose souls have gone loose among terrors. These have to be dealt with as their psychology demands, and the French officer is a good psychologist. One of them said: "Our national psychology has changed. I do not recognize it myself."

"What made the change?"

"The Boche. If he had been quiet for another twenty years the world must have been his—rotten, but all his. Now he is saving the world."

"How?"

"Because he has shown us what Evil is. We—you and I, England and the rest—had begun to doubt the existence of Evil. The Boche is saving us."

Then we had another look at the animal in its trench—a little nearer this time than before, and quieter on account of the mist. Pick up the chain anywhere you please, you shall find the same observation post, table, map, observer, and telephonist; the same always-hidden, always-ready guns; the same vexed foreshore of trenches, smoking and shaking from Switzerland to the sea. The handling of war varies with the nature of the country, but the tools are unaltered. One looks upon them at last with the same weariness of wonder as the eye receives from endless repetitions of Egyptian hieroglyphics. A long, low profile, with a lump to one side, means the field-gun and its attendant ammunition case; a circle and slot stand for an observation-post; the trench is a bent line, studded with vertical plumes of explosion; the great guns of position, coming and going on their motors, repeat themselves as scarabs; and man himself is a small blue smudge, no larger than a foresight, crawling and creeping or watching and running among all these terrific symbols . . .

"This is the end of the line," said the Staff Officer, kindest and most patient of chaperons. It buttressed itself on a fortress among the hills. Beyond that, the silence was more awful than the mixed noise of business to the westward. In mileage on the map the line must be between four and five hundred miles; in actual trench-work many times that distance. It is too much to see at full length; the mind does not readily break away from the obsession of its entirety or the grip of its detail. One visualizes the thing afterwards as a white-hot gash, worming all across France between intolerable sounds and lights, under ceaseless blasts of whirled dirt. Nor is it any relief to lose one-self among wildernesses of piling, stoning, timbering, concreting, and wire-work, or incalculable quantities of soil thrown up raw to the light and cloaked by the changing seasons—as the unburied dead are cloaked.

Yet there are no words to give the essential simplicity of it. It is the rampart put up by Man against the Beast, precisely as in the Stone Age. If it goes, all that keeps us from the Beast goes with it.

Where the rifle and bayonet serve, men use those tools along the front. Where the knife gives better results, they go in behind the hand-grenades with the naked twelve-inch knife. Each race is supposed to fight in its own way, but this war has passed beyond all known ways. They say that the Belgians in the north settle accounts with a certain dry passion which has varied very little since their agony began. Some sections of the English line have produced a soft-voiced, rather reserved type, which does its work with its mouth shut. The French carry an edge to their fighting, a precision, and a dreadful knowledge coupled with an insensibility to shock, unlike anything one has imagined of mankind.

From *France at War*, by Rudyard Kipling; Doubleday, Page & Co., Garden City, 1915.

## *Few Wished Themselves Elsewhere*
### —John Buchan

The first day of July dawned hot and cloudless, though a thin fog, the relic of the damp of the past week, clung to the hollows. At half-past five the hill just west of Albert offered a singular view. It was almost in the centre of the section allotted to the Allied attack, and from it the eye could range on the left up and beyond the Ancre to the high ground around Beaumont Hamel and Serre; in front of the great lift of tableland behind which lay Bapaume; and to the right past the woods of Fricourt to the valley of the Somme. Every gun along the front was speaking, and speaking without pause. Great spurts of dust on the slopes showed where a heavy shell had burst, and black and white gouts of smoke dotted the middle distance like the little fires in a French autumn field. Lace-like shrapnel wreaths hung in the sky, melting into the morning haze. The noise was strangely uniform, a steady rumbling, as if the solid earth were muttering in a nightmare, and it was hard to distinguish the deep tones of the heavies, the vicious whip-like crack of the field guns and the bark of the trench mortars.

About 7:15 the bombardment rose to that hurricane pitch of fury which betokened its close. It was as if titanic machine guns were at work all around the horizon. Then appeared a marvellous sight, the solid spouting of the enemy slopes—as if they were lines of reefs on which a strong tide was breaking. In such a hell it seemed that no human thing could live. Through the thin summer vapour and the thicker smoke which clung to the foreground there were visions of a countryside actually moving—moving bodily in debris into the air. And now there was a fresh sound—a series of abrupt and rapid bursts which came gustily from the first lines. These were the new trench mortars—wonderful little engines of death.

The staff officers glanced at their watches, and at half-past seven precisely there came a lull. It lasted for a second or two, and then the guns continued their tale. But the range had been lengthened every-where, and from a bombardment the fire had become a *barrage*. For, on a twenty-five mile front, the Allied infantry had gone over the parapets.

The point of view of the hill-top was not that of the men in the front trenches. The crossing of the parapets is the supreme moment in modern war. The troops are outside defences, moving across the open to investigate the unknown. It is the culmination of months of train-ing for officers and men, and the least sensitive feels the drama of the crisis. Most of the British troops engaged had twenty months before been employed in the peaceable civilian trades. In their ranks were every class and condition—miners from north central England, factory hands from the industrial centers, clerks and shop-boys, ploughmen and shepherds, Saxon and Celt, college graduates and dock labour-ers, men who in the wild places of the earth had often faced danger, and men whose chief adventure had been a Sunday bicycle ride. Nerves may be attuned to the normal risks of trench warfare and yet shrink from the desperate hazard of a charge into the enemy's line.

But to one who visited the front before the attack the most vivid impression was that of quiet cheerfulness. There were no shirkers and few who wished themselves elsewhere. One man's imagination might be more active than another's, but the will to fight, and to fight desperately, was universal. With the happy gift of the British soldier they had turned the ghastly business of war into something homely and familiar. Accordingly they took everything as part of the day's work, and awaited the supreme moment without heroics and without tremor, confident in themselves, confident in their guns, and confident in the triumph of their cause. There was no savage lust of battle, but that far more formidable thing—a resolution which needed no rhetoric to support it. Norfolk's words were true of every man of them:

"As gentle and as jocund as to jest
Go I to fight. Truth hath a quiet breast."

In that stubborn action against impossible odds the gallantry was so universal and absolute that it is idle to select special cases. In each mile there were men who performed the incredible. Nothing finer was done in the war. The splendid troops, drawn from those volunteers who had banded themselves together for another cause, now shed their blood like water for the liberty of the world.

That grim struggle from Thiepval northward was responsible for by far the greater number of Allied losses of the day But, though costly, it was not fruitless, for it occupied the bulk of the German defence. It was the price that had to be paid for the advance of the rest of the front. For, while in the north the living wave broke vainly and gained little, in the south "by creeks and inlets making" the tide was flowing strongly shoreward. Our major purpose was attained . . .

No great thing is achieved without a price, and on the Somme fell the very flower of our race, the straightest of limb, the keenest of brain, the most eager of spirit. The young men who died almost before they had gazed on the world, the makers and the doers who left their tasks unfinished, were greater in their deaths than in their lives. Out of their loss they won for mankind an enduring gain.

From *The Battle of the Somme*, by John Buchan; Grosset & Dunlap, New York, 1917.

## *Nearer Than Any Other Woman*
—Mrs. Humphrey Ward

A young artillery officer was asked to show us the way. We reached a ruined village from which all normal inhabitants had been long since cleared away. The shattered church was there, and I noticed a large crucifix quite intact still hanging on its chancel wall. A little farther and the boyish artillery-officer, our leader, turned and beckoned to the General. Presently we were creeping through seas of mud down into the gun emplacement, so carefully concealed that no aeroplane overhead could guess it.

There it was—how many of its fellows I had seen in the Midland and northern workshops!—its muzzle just showing in the dark, and nine or ten high-explosive shells lying on the bench in front of the breech. One is put in. We stand back a little, and the sergeant tells me to put my fingers in my ears and look straight at the gun. Then comes the shock—not so violent as I expected—and the cartridge case drops out. The shell has sped on its way to the German trenches—with what result to human flesh and blood? But I remember thinking very little of that.

Now indeed we were in the battle! It was discussed whether we should be taken zigzag through the fields to the entrance of the com-munication-trench. But the firing was getting hotter, and the Captain was evidently relieved when we elected to turn back. Shall I always regret that lost opportunity? That was the nearest that any woman could personally have come to it! But I doubt whether anything more—anything, at least, that was possible—could have deepened the whole effect. We had been already nearer than any woman—even a nurse—had been, in this war, to the actual fighting on the English line, and the cup of impressions was full . . . .

The first of July dawned, a beautiful summer morning, and the British and French infantry sprang over their parapets and rushed to the attack on both sides of the Somme. Twelve hours after the fighting began, Sir Douglas Haig telegraphed: "Heavy fighting has continued all day between the rivers Somme and Ancre. On the right of our attack we have captured the German labyrinth of trenches on a front of seven miles to a depth of 1,000 yards, and have stormed and occupied the strongly fortified villages of Montauban and Mametz. In the centre, we have gained many strong points. Up to date, 2,000 German prisoners have passed through our collecting stations. The large number of the enemy dead on the battle-fields indicate that the German losses have been very severe."

So much for the first day's news. The attack was well begun . . .

The result on the Somme has set the heart of England aflame; even while we ponder those long, long casualty lists which represent the bitter price that British fathers and mothers, British wives and daughters have paid, and must still pay, for the only victory which will set up once again the reign of law and humanity in Europe.

From *England's Effort,* by Mrs. Humphrey Ward; Charles Scribner's Sons; New York, 1918.

## *The World Has a Right to Know*
### —Richard Harding Davis

When I returned to New York every second man I knew greeted me sympathetically with: "So you had to come home, hey? They wouldn't let you see a thing." And if I had time I told him all I saw was the German, French, Belgian, and English armies in the field, Belgium in ruins and flames, the Germans sacking Louvain, in the Dover Straits dreadnoughts, cruisers, torpedo destroyers, submarines, hydroplanes; in Paris bombs falling from air-ships and a city put to bed at 9 o'clock; battle-fields covered with dead men; fifteen miles of artillery firing across the Aisne at fifteen miles of artillery; the bombardment of Rheims with shells lifting the roofs as easily as you would lift the cover of a chafing-dish and digging holes in the streets, and the cathedral on fire; I saw hundreds of thousands of soldiers from India, Senegal, Morocco, Ireland, Australia, Algiers, Bavaria, Prussia, Scotland, saw them at the front in action, saw them marching over the whole northern half of Europe, saw them wounded and helpless, saw thousands of women and children sleeping under hedges and haystacks with on every side of them their homes blazing in flames or crashing in ruins.

That was part of what I saw. What during the same two months did the man at home see? If he were lucky he saw the Braves win the World Series, or the Vernon Castles dance the fox-trot . . .

The army calls for your father, husband, son—calls for your money. It enters upon a war that destroys your peace of mind, wrecks your business, kills the men of your family, the man you were going to marry, the son you brought into the world. And to you the army says: "This is our war. We will fight it in our own way, and of it you can only learn what we choose to tell you. We will not let you know whether your country is winning the fight or is in danger, whether we have blundered and the soldiers are starving, whether they gave their lives gloriously or through our lack of preparation or inefficiency are dying of neglected wounds." And if you answer that you will send with the army correspondents to write reports home and tell you, not the plans for the future and the secrets of the army, but what are already accomplished facts, the army makes reply: "No, these men cannot be trusted. They are spies."

Not for one moment does the army honestly think those men are spies. But it is the excuse nearest at hand.

This is a world war, and my contention is that the world has a right to know, not what is going to happen next, but at least what has happened. If men have died nobly, if women and children have cruelly and needlessly suffered, if for no military necessity and without reason cities have been wrecked, the world should know that.

Those who are carrying on this war behind a curtain, who have enforced this conspiracy of silence, tell you that in their good time the truth will be known.

It will not.

Some men are trained to fight, others are trained to write. The latter can tell you of what they have seen so that you, safe at home at the breakfast table, also can see it. Any newspaper correspondent would rather send his paper news than a descriptive story. But news lasts only until you have told it to the next man, and if in this war the correspondent is not to be permitted to send the news I submit he should at least be permitted to tell what has happened in the past. The war is a world enterprise, and in it every man, woman and child is an interested stockholder. They have a right to know what is going forward. The directors' meetings should not be held in secret.

From *With the Allies*, by Richard Harding Davis; Charles Scribner's Sons; New York, 1918.

## *Old Men Don't Go*
### —H. G. Wells

Mr. Britling's conception of his own share in the great national uprising was a very modest one. He was a writer, a footnote to reality; he had no trick of command over men, his role was observation rather than organisation, and he saw himself only as an insignificant individual dropping from his individuality into his place in a great machine, taking a rifle in a trench, guarding a bridge, filing a cartridge until the great task was done. Sunday night was full of imaginations of order, of the countryside standing up to its task, of roads cleared and resources marshalled, of the petty interests of private life altogether set aside. And mingling with that it was still possible for Mr. Britling, he was still young enough, to produce such dreams of personal service, of sudden emergencies swiftly and bravely met, of conspicuous daring and exceptional rewards, such dreams as hover in the brains of every imaginative recruits . . .

It was acutely shameful to him that all these fine lads should be going off to death and wounds while the men of forty and over lay snug at home. How stupid it was to fix things like that! Here were the fathers, who had done their work, shot their bolts, returned some value for the costs of their education, unable to get training, unable to be of service, shamefully safe, doing April fool work as special constables; while their young innocents, untried, all their gathering possibilities of service unbroached, went down into the deadly trenches . . . The war would leave the world a world of cripples and old men and children . . .

He felt himself as a cowardly brute, fat, wheezy, out of training. He writhed with impotent humiliation.

How stupidly the world is managed.

He began to fret and rage. He could not lie in peace in his bed; he got up and prowled about his room, blundering against chairs and tables in the darkness . . . We were too stupid to do the most obvious things; we were sending all these boys into hardship and pitiless danger; we were sending them ill-equipped, insufficiently supported, we were sending our children through the fires of Moloch, because essentially we English were a world of indolent, pampered, sham good-humored, old and middle-aged men. (So he distributed the intolerable load of self-accusation.) Why was he doing nothing to change things, to make them better? What was the good of an assumed modesty, an effort at tolerance for and confidence in these boozy old lawyers, those ranting platform men, those stiff-witted officers and hide-bound officials? They were butchering the youth of England.

Old men sat out of danger contriving death for the lads in the trenches. That was the reality of the thing. "My son!" he cried sharply in the darkness. His sense of our national deficiencies became tor-mentingly, fantastically acute. It was as if all his cherished delusions had fallen from the scheme of things . . . What was the good of making believe that up there they were planning some great counterstroke that would end in victory? It was as plain as daylight that they had neither the power of imagination nor the collective intelligence ever to conceive of a counterstroke. The old men would sit at their tables, replete and sleepy, and shake their cunning old heads. The press would chatter and make odd ambiguous sounds like a shipload of monkeys in a storm. The political harridans would get the wrong men appointed, would attack every possible leader with scandal and abuse and falsehood . . .

The spirit and honour and drama had gone out of this war.

Our only hope now was exhaustion. Our only strategy was to barter blood for blood—trusting that our tank would prove the deeper . . .

While into this tank stepped Hugh, young and smiling . . .

The war became a nightmare vision.

From *Mr. Britling Sees It Through*, by H. G. Wells; Macmillan; New York, 1917.

# Chapter Five:
# Pity

Probably no war before and certainly no war after has brought civilian novelists, poets, and dramatists into such close proximity to wounded soldiers as did World War I. The Civil War saw Whitman nursing dying Union soldiers in Washington, but it would be hard to think of another nineteenth-century poet demonstrating this kind of hands-on compassion; in World War II, ambulance services and hospitals were militarized, and no amateurs would be allowed as close to the fighting as they were in the Great War. As the terrible year of 1916 gave way to the even more horrible year of 1917, writers would turn from writing diatribes, analyses, and exhortations, to focus on individual soldiers caught up in the tragedy, needing all the sympathy and pity a nurse—or a novelist—could bring them.

More and more it's not the "Hun" that's the enemy, but the war itself, so, in a way that wouldn't have been possible in 1914, writers begin moving away from abstractions and "great issues"—the wounded are individualized and made vivid, if only in brief vignettes; out of the millions who served in the war, these are the ones we see up close and remember, thanks to the writers sitting beside them, tending their wounds—and going back to their huts at night to write about them.

Changes in writing style and tone that began to emerge as writers witnessed the war in person now intensify; after a writer tended a soldier whose gangrenous leg had just been cut off, there was no going back to a florid nineteenth-century writing style or a cheery way of looking at things.

The more ironic, harder sensibility is very much of the twentieth century. A writer like Mrs. Humphrey Ward writes of 1917 from the vantage point of 1878, but Enid Bagnold and May Sinclair, with their striking mix of pity for the wounded and fretful self-absorption (they focus again and again, not only on what the soldiers feel, but on what they feel themselves) read like writers of the 1920s or, for that matter, of 2016. Even Henry James, whom we saw earlier torturing his way to a baroquely phrased understanding of what the war meant, now finds enough pity to get past his own circumlocutions to his simple and tender point: the wounded boys he nurses in the London hospital are "the very flowers of the human race."

Another change: more and more the writers worth remembering and reading today are female. Many of them served as nurses—the traditional role for women in war, though hardly a passive one, not with what was demanded of them in the surgical wards of station hospitals. And even women waiting at home like the Jenny of Rebecca West's novel *The Return of the Soldier*—their role was a lot more wrenching than merely "waiting" would imply.

The literary historian Samuel Hynes points out how significant a change this represented—women at home being able to picture how horrible the war truly was.

> "Jenny, the narrator, can picture these things because Rebecca West could, because any English civilian could by 1916. From the war's beginning its terrible particulars were brought home continually to England and into the lives and minds of the people there. The First World War was the first English war to be reported and photographed in the daily newspapers, and the first to be filmed and shown to the public in cinemas. Jenny doesn't know the whole story of the

war, but she knows the worst of it—the horror stories
that we all have in our heads, and visualize as the reality of the Western Front. Such knowledge would not
have been available to a sheltered woman like Jenny
during any previous English war; this was the first war
that women *could* imagine, and so it was the first that
a woman could write into a novel."

(Jane Austen, writing exactly 100 years before West, famously
could *not* imagine the Napoleonic Wars she and her characters lived
through, and so could not or would not write about them.)

Pity was the response that moved many women to write—a great,
all-embracing pity that can still move us today. It's a word they use
often, wondering whether they feel too much of it or not anywhere
near enough. Vera Brittain, whose *Testament of Youth* became one of
the war's best-known memoirs, worried that nursing in front-line hospitals would eventually turn her compassion into ice; she prayed to be
spared "the bright immunity from pity which the highly trained nurse
seems so often to possess."

Brittain, as writer and nurse, never lost this pity—or the anger
that ran just beneath.

"I wish those people who write so glibly about this
being a holy war could see a case of mustard gas in its
early stages—could see the poor things burnt and blis-
tered all over with great mustard-colored suppurating
blisters, with blind eyes all sticky and stuck together,
and always fighting for breath, with voices a mere
whisper, saying that their throats are closing and they
know they will choke."

Male writers, of course, felt pity too. Wells's Mr. Britling nurses a
very different kind of victim—his own aunt, who has been wounded

in a German Zeppelin raid on the English coast; a particularly heinous crime, in Britling's view, because England hasn't been attacked on her own soil for so many centuries, let alone had bombs rained down from the air on its innocent civilians. He—and the other writers included here—would have to get used to this kind of barbarity very fast if they wished to stay relevant, to find a way to write about what, when it first happened, must have seemed like the modern age announcing its appearance in one high-explosive burst.

The pity writers brought to their writing was not evoked only by the wounded. Many describe the simple, long-suffering, "ordinary" men caught up in the fighting through no fault of their own, and in particular the wrenching disparity between what they experienced on the battlefield and what civilians at home thought the war was like.

May Sinclair joined the Munro Ambulance Corps when war broke out, and spent seventeen days in Belgium during the early retreats; not a young woman (she was fifty-one), her nerves quickly broke under the strain and she was sent back to England. Her book on the experience, *A Journal of Impressions in Belgium,* was one of the very first books written and published by a woman on the war. Rebecca West, soon to write her own war book, called it "This gallant, humiliated book," and its complicated mix of irony, pity, and self-doubt can only be termed "Modern."

"This country is formed for the very expression of peace," Sinclair writes, as her ambulance carries her toward the fighting,

> "It is all unspeakably beautiful and it comes to me with the natural, inevitable shock and ecstasy of beauty. I am going straight into the horror of war. For all I know it may be anywhere, here, behind this sentry; or there, beyond that line of willows. I don't know. I don't care. I cannot realize it. All that I can see or feel at the moment is this beauty. I look and look, so that

I may remember. All your past is soaking in the vivid
dye of these days . . . I would rather die than go back
to England."

Her novel, *The Tree of Heaven,* became a bestseller later in the war;
an influential critic, she is given credit for inventing the term "stream
of consciousness" in 1918 to describe the latest literary innovation.

Enid Bagnold, with her writing career already well launched in
England, volunteered as a nurse when the war broke out and was stationed at a hospital in Woolrich. Her *A Diary Without Dates* was so
frank and critical of the hospital administration that she was fired;
still wanting to serve, she went on to drive an ambulance in France,
and got from the experience her second wartime book, *The Happy
Foreigner.* She was twenty-five.

She achieved popular success after the war with her novel about
horse racing, *National Velvet,* the film version of which made Eliza-
beth Taylor a star. Her play *The Chalk Garden* is still performed; when
it appeared on Broadway in 1956, Arthur Miller wrote, "It is the most
steadily interesting, deeply felt, and civilized piece of work I have seen
in a very long time."

*Diary Without Dates,* published in 1917, shows a modern
sensibility fully at work. She writes on the title page, "I apologize to
those I may hurt. Can I soothe them by pleading that one may only
write what is true for oneself?"

Hugh Walpole was thirty when the war broke out and was already
a highly successful English novelist. Like so many writers, he volunteered for Red Cross ambulance work, but unlike most, who were sent
to France, he ended up on the eastern front in Russia, which gave him
a unique perspective and the material for two wartime novels, *The
Dark Forest* and *The Secret City.* He won the Russian "Cross of Saint
George" for rescuing a wounded soldier under fire.

While in Russia, he helped establish the Anglo-Russian Propaganda Bureau in Petrograd and witnessed the first stages of the Revolution; returning to England, he wrote more propaganda for John Buchan's wartime bureau.

His close friend Henry James was terrible impressed by Walpole's bravery, writing that he was showing "the last magnificence of pluck, the finest strain of resolution."

Rebecca West first made her literary reputation by publishing an attack on the old school of English writers, particularly Mrs. Humphrey Ward; this brought her to the attention of, among others, H. G. Wells. She and Wells became lovers just before the war broke out (West was twenty-one), never mind that West had referred to him in print as "the Old Maid among novelists." They had a son together, and West was supported by Wells throughout the war years. Wells wrote of being struck by her "curious mix of maturity and infantilism; I had never met anything quite like her before, and I doubt if there was anything like her before."

Her novel, *The Return of the Soldier,* published in 1918, examines the relationship between three women and a soldier suffering shell shock. Samuel Hynes (the soldier/writer who was one of the most astute students of the war's literature) called it "an extraordinary book, a perfect small work of art, a war novel that makes its perfection out of its limitations; a novel of an enclosed world invaded by public events, a private novel containing history."

West herself didn't have to go to war—it came to her, when in 1918 German Gotha aircraft bombed the village on the Thames where she was staying with her son; one incendiary bomb dropped only a few yards away. Wells may have had this in mind when he wrote the scene excerpted at this chapter's end.

H. M. Tomlinson is mostly forgotten now, but in 1914 he was an essayist and travel writer who was often compared to Thoreau and/

or Conrad; his classic account of a trip up the Amazon on a tramp
steamer, *The Sea and the Jungle,* is still in print.

He was an official correspondent with the British troops in France
(he was forty-five), but managed to rise above the restrictions and cen-
sorship to produce some of the most sensitive civilian writing about
the war, showing a real fellow feeling for soldiers and what they had
to deal with.

Tomlinson blames the well-born, the clever, the haughty, and the
greedy for making the war out of "the perplexity of their scheming"—
and then, panicking when it breaks out, calling upon the masses to
save them.

> "Then out from their obscurity, where they
> dwelt because of their own worth, arise the Nobodies;
> because theirs is the historic job of restoring again the
> upset balance of affairs. They make no fuss about it.
> Theirs is always the hard and dirty work. They have
> always done it. If they don't do it, it will not be done.
> They fall with a will and without complaint upon the
> wreckage willfully made of generations of such labor
> as theirs, to get the world right again, to make it hab-
> itable again, though not for themselves; for them, they
> must spend the rest of their lives recreating order out
> of chaos."

In the 1920s, Tomlinson became one of the first critics to write
intelligently and movingly of the literature produced by the war.

G. M. Trevelyan, born into the aristocracy, was forty by the time the
war broke out. He was one of Britain's most highly regarded literary
historians, especially for his *Garibaldi Trilogy* on the famous Italian
patriot. His brother Charles Trevelyan resigned from Asquith's government to protest the war, and was vilified, but George, exempted from

the army because of his eyesight, led the first Red Cross ambulance unit to Italy and spent three years close to the front lines.

He was caught up in the disastrous retreat at Caporetto, but, as the excerpt makes clear, was a long way from blaming Italian coward-ice for the disaster, as other commentators were (and are) quick to do.

My copy of *Scenes from Italy's War* has an elegant bookplate pasted in front—John Hampton Barnes is the owner's name—and the pages, a hundred years old now, have edges that seem freshly cut. Like many books included here, it includes a few token photographs, including one stirring shot of a tattered Italian flag flying defiantly over Monte Santo on the Isonzo River that saw so much fighting. Pasted on the title page is a little one-by-three insert of "Errata," making sure the reader knows to correct "October" for "November" on page 222, line 5, "six and nine" for "eight and twelve" on page 183, line 4, and—italics being important—"*Bersaglieri ciclisti*" for "Bersaglieri ciclisti" on page 84, line 8.

Some World War I literature is forgotten because, having written one book on the war that received little attention, the author went on to write another on the same experience that became famous, thereby condemning the earlier book to extinction.

John Dos Passos's novel *Three Soldiers* is firmly within what would become, in the 1920s and 30s, the "official" literary canon of the war, but, as a young volunteer (he was twenty-two), he wrote a totally for-gotten novel while the war was still being fought: *One Man's Initiation: 1917*, a title he later changed to *First Encounter*; it is drawn from his experience in the Norton-Harjes Ambulance Corps on the front lines with the French.

Dos Passos had the book republished in 1942, when another war was in progress, writing, in his preface:

> "I think the brutalities of war and oppression come as
> less of a shock to people who grew up in the Thirties

than they did to Americans of my generation, raised as we were during the quiet afterglow of the nineteenth century, among comfortably situated people who were confident that industrial progress meant an improved civilization, more of the good things of life, more freedom, a more human and peaceful society. To us, the European war of 1914–18 seemed a horrible monstrosity, something outside of the normal order of things, like an epidemic of yellow fever in some place where yellow fever had never been heard of before. Now these things are more familiar."

In writing *One Man's Initiation,* Dos Passos admits to having been heavily influenced by the recently published novel *Under Fire (Le Feu)* by Henri Barbusse, which appeared in 1916 and became an immediate sensation (my copy is the twelfth printing from 1918) with its graphic, searing account of life on the western front as seen by a disillusioned *Poilu.* After Barbusse's book, civilian writers—except for the hacks—would find it hard to cling to any last romantic illusions about the war.

## *All That This War Has Annihilated*
### —May Sinclair

I don't want to describe that ward, or the effect of those rows upon rows of beds, those rows upon rows of bound and bandaged bodies, the intensity of their physical anguish suggested by sheer force of multiplication, by the diminishing perspective of the beds, by the clear light and nakedness of the great hall that sets these repeated units of torture in a world apart, a world of insufferable space and agonizing time, ruled by some inhuman mathematics and given over to pure transcendent pain. A sufficiently large ward full of wounded really does leave an impression very like that. But the one true thing about this impression is its transcendence. It is utterly removed from and unlike anything that you have experienced before. From the moment that the doors have closed behind you, you are in another world, and under its strange impact you are given new senses and a new soul. If there is horror here you are not aware of it as horror. Before these multiplied forms of anguish what you feel—if there is anything of *you* left to feel—is not pity, because it is so near to adoration.

If you are tired of the burden and malady of self, go into one of these great wards and you will find instant release. You and the sum of your little consciousness are not things that matter any more. The lowest and least of these wounded is of supreme importance and significance. You, who were once afraid of them and of their wounds, may think that you would suffer for them now, gladly; but you are not allowed to suffer; you are marvellously and mercilessly let off. In this sudden deliverance from yourself you have received the ultimate absolution, and their torment is your peace . . .

I am to look after Mr._____. He has the pick of the Belgian Red Cross women to nurse him, and they are angelically kind and very skillful, but he is not very happy with them. He says: "These dear people are so good to me, but I can't make out what they say. I can't tell them what I want." He is pathetically glad to have any English people with him.

I sat with him all morning. The French boy has gone and he is alone in his room now. The morning went like half an hour, while it was going, but when it was over I felt as if I had been nursing for weeks on end. There were so many little things to be done, and so much that you mustn't do, and the anxiety was appalling. I don't suppose there is a worse case in the Hospital. He is perhaps a shade better to-day, but none of the medical staff think that he can live.

Madame E_____ and Dr. Bird have shown me what to do, and what not to do. I must keep him all the time in the same position. I must give him sips of iced broth, and little pieces of ice to suck every now and then. I must not let him try to raise himself in bed. I must not try to lift him myself. If we do lift him we must keep his body tilted at the same angle. I must not give him any hot drinks and not too much cold drink.

And then he is six foot high, so tall that his feet come through the blankets at the bottom of the bed; and he keeps sinking down it all the time and wanting to raise himself up again. He must be kept very quiet. I must not let him talk more than is necessary to tell me what he wants, or he will die of exhaustion. And what he wants is to talk every minute that he is awake.

He drops off to sleep, breathing in jerks and with a terrible rapidity. And I think it will be all right as long as he sleeps. But his sleep only lasts for a few minutes. I hear the rhythm of his breathing alter; it slackens and goes slow; then it jerks again, and I know that he is awake.

And then he begins. He says things that tear at your heart. He has looks and gestures that break it—the adorable, willful smile of a child that knows that it is being watched when you find his hand groping too often for the glass of iced water that stands beside his bed; a still more adorable and utterly gentle submission when you take the glass from him; when you tell him not to say anything more just yet but to go to sleep again. You feel as if you were guilty of act after act of nameless and abominable cruelty.

He sticks to it that he has seen me before, that he has heard of me, that his people know me. And he wants to know what I do and where I live and where it was that he saw me. Once, when I thought he had gone to sleep, I heard him begin again: "Where did you say you lived?"

I tell him. And I tell him to go to sleep again.

He closes his eyes obediently and opens them the next instant.

"I say, may I come and call on you when we get back to England?"

You can only say: "Yes. Of course," and tell him to go to sleep.

His voice is so strong and clear that I could almost believe that he will get back and that some day I shall look up and see him standing at my garden gate.

Mercifully, when I tell him to go to sleep again, he does go to sleep. And his voice is a little clearer and stronger every time he wakes.

And so the morning goes on. The only thing he wants you to do for him is to sponge his hands and face with iced water and give him little bits of ice to suck. Over and over again I do these things. And over and over again he asks me, "Do you mind?"

He wears a little grey woolen cord round his neck. Something has gone from it. Whatever he has lost, they have left him his little woolen cord, as if some immense importance attached to it.

He has fallen into a long doze. And at the end of the morning I left him sleeping.

Some of the Corps have brought in trophies from the battlefield—a fine grey cloak with a scarlet collar, a spiked helmet, a cuff with three buttons cut from the coat of a dead German.

These things make me sick. I see the body under the cloak, the head under the helmet, and the dead hand under the cuff.

We shall never know all that the War has annihilated.

From *A Journal of Impressions in Belgium*, by May Sinclair; Macmillan; New York, 1915.

## *A Bit of Metal Turned Them for Home*
### —Enid Bagnold

When one shoots at a wooden figure it makes a hole. When one shoots at a man it makes a hole, and the doctor must make seven others.

I heard a blackbird sing in the middle of the night last night— two bars, and then another. I thought at first it might be a burglar whistling to his mate in the black and rustling garden.

But it was a blackbird in a nightmare.

Those distant guns again to-night . . .

Now a lull and now a bombardment; again a lull, and then batter, batter, and the windows tremble. Is the lull when *they* go over the top?

I can only think of death to-night. I tried to think just now, "What is it, after all! Death comes anyway; this only hastens it." But that won't do; no philosophy helps the pain of death. It is pity, pity, pity, that I feel, and sometimes a sort of shame that I am here to write at all . . .

Waker had a birthday yesterday and got ten post cards and a telegram. But that is as nothing to another anniversary.

"A year to-morrow I got my wound—two o'clock to-morrow morning."

"Shall you be awake, Waker?"

"Yes."

How will he celebrate it? I would give a lot to know what will pass in his mind. For I don't yet understand this importance they attach to such an anniversary. One and all, they know the exact hour and minute on which their bit of metal turned them for home.

Sometimes a man will whisper, "Nurse . . ." as I go by the bed; and when I stop I hear, "In ten minutes it will be a twelvemonth!" and he fixes his eyes on me.

What does he want me to respond? I don't know whether I should be glad or sorry that he got it. I can't imagine what he thinks of as the minute ticks. For I can see by his words that the scene is blurred and no longer brings back any picture. "Did you crawl back or walk?"

"I . . . walked." He is hardly sure.

I know that for Waker that moment at two o'clock in the morning changed his whole career. From that moment his arm was paralysed, the nerves severed; from that moment football was off, and with it his particular ambition. And football, governing a kingdom, or painting a picture—a man's ambition is his ambition, and when it is wiped out his life is changed.

But he knows all that, he has had time to think of all that. What, then, does this particular minute bring him?

They think I know; for when they tell me in that earnest voice that the minute is approaching they take for granted that I too will share some sacrament with them.

Waker is not everything a man should be: he isn't clever. But he is so very brave.

From *A Diary Without Dates*, by Enid Bagnold; William Heinemann; London, 1918.

## *The Very Flower of the Human Race*
### —Henry James

It would be the essence of these remarks, could I give them within my space all the particular applications naturally awaiting them, that they pretend to refer here to the British soldier only—generalisation about his officers would take us so considerably further and so much enlarge our view. The high average of the beauty and modesty of these, in the stricken state, causes them to affect me, I frankly confess, as probably the very flower of the human race. One's apprehension "Tommy"—and I scarce know whether more to dislike the liberty this mode of reference takes with him, or to incline to retain it for the tenderness really latent in it—is in itself a theme for fine notation, but it has brought me thus only to the door of the boundless hospital ward in which, these many months, I have seen the successive and the so strangely quiet tides of his presence ebb and flow, and it stays me there before the incalculable vista. The perspective stretches away, in its mild order, after the fashion of a tunnel boring into the very character of the people, and so going on forever—never arriving or coming out, that is, at anything in the nature of a station, a junction or a terminus. So it draws off through the infinite of the common personal life, but planted and bordered, all along its passage, with the thick-growing flower of the individual illustration, this sometimes vivid enough and sometimes pathetically pale. The great

fact, to my now so informed vision, is that it undiscourageably continues and that an unceasing repetition of its testifying particulars seems
never either to exhaust its sense or to satisfy that of the beholder. Its
sense indeed, if I may so far simplify, is pretty well always the same, that
of the jolly fatalism above-mentioned, a state of moral hospitality to the
practices of fortune, however outrageous, that may at times fairly be felt
as providing amusement, providing a new and thereby a refreshing turn
of the personal situation, for the most interested party. It is true that one
may be sometimes moved to wonder which *is* the most interested party,
the stricken subject in his numbered bed or the friendly, the unsated
inquirer who has tried to forearm himself against such a measure of the
"criticism of life" as might well be expected to break upon him from
the couch in question, and who yet, a thousand occasions for it having
been, all round him, inevitably neglected, finds this ingenious provision
quite left on his hands. He may well ask himself what he is to do with
people who so consistently and so comfortably content themselves with
*being*—for the most part incuriously and instinctively admirable—that
nothing whatever is left of them for reflection as distinguished from
their own practice; but the only answer that comes is the reproduction
of the note. He may, in the interest of appreciation, try the experiment
of lending them some scrap of a complaint or a curse in order that they
shall meet him on congruous ground, the ground of encouragement to
his own participating impulse. They are imaged, under that possibility,
after the manner of those unfortunates, the very poor, the victims of a
fire or shipwreck, to whom you have to lend something to wear before
they can come to thank you for helping them. The inmates of the long
wards, however, have no use for any imputed or derivative sentiments
or reasons; they feel in their own way, they feel a great deal, they don't
at all conceal from you that to have seen what they have seen is to have
seen things horrible and monstrous—but there is no estimate of them
for which they seek to be indebted to you, and nothing they less invite
from you than to show them that such visions must have poisoned their
world. Their world isn't in the least poisoned; they have assimilated their

experience by a process scarce at all to be distinguished from their having healthily gotten rid of it.

The case thus becomes for you that they consist wholly of their applied virtue, which is accompanied with no waste of consciousness whatsoever. The virtue may strike you as having been, and as still being, greater in some examples than others, but it has throughout the same sign of differing at almost no point from a supreme amiability. How can creatures so amiable, you allow yourself vaguely to wonder, have welcomed even for five minutes the stress of carnage? and how can the stress of carnage, the murderous impulse at its highest pitch, have left so little distortion of the moral nature? It has left none at all that one has at the end of many months been able to discover; so that perhaps the most steadying and refreshing effect of intercourse with these hospital friends is through the almost complete rest from the facing of generalisations to which it treats you.

From *The Book of the Homeless*, edited by Edith Wharton; Charles Scribner's Sons; New York, 1916.

## *With the Wounded I was at Home*
### —Hugh Walpole

There comes now a difficult matter. During the later months when I was to reflect on the whole affair I saw quite clearly that the hour between our leaving the wooden house and arriving in the trenches bridged quite clearly for me the division between imagination and reality: that is, I was never after this to speak of war as I would have spoken of it an hour before. I was never again to regard the paraphernalia of it with the curiosity of a stranger—I had become part of it. This hour then may be regarded as in some ways the most important of all my experiences. It is certainly the occasion to which if I were using my invention I should make the most. Here then is my difficulty.

I have nothing to say about it. There's nothing at all to be made of it.

I may say at once there was no atom of drama in it. At one moment I was standing with Maria Ivanovna under the sunrise, at another I was standing behind a trench in the heart of the forest with a battery to my left and a battery to my right, a cuckoo somewhere not very far away, and a dead man with his feet sticking out from beneath a tree at my side. There had, of course, been that drive in the wagons, bumping over the uneven road while the sun rose gallantly in the heavens and the clanging of the iron door grew, with every roll of our wheels, louder and louder. But it was rather as though I had been lifted in a sheet from one life—a life of speculation, of viewing war from a superior and safe distance, of viewing indeed all catastrophe and reality from the same distance—into the other. I had been caught up, had hung for a moment in mid-air, had been "planted" in this new experience. For all of us there must have been at this moment something of this passing from an old life into a new one, and yet I dare swear that not for any one of us was there any drama, any thrill, any excitement. We stood, a rather lonely little group, in the forest clearing whilst the soldiers in the trench flung us a careless glance, then turned back to their business of the day with an indifference that showed how ordinary and drab a thing custom had made it . . .

A dream, I know, yesterday's experiences seemed to me as I settled down to the business that had filled so much of my earlier period at the war. Here, with the wounded, I was at home—the bare little room, the table with the bottles and bandages and scissors, the basins and dishes, the air even thicker and thicker with that smell of dried blood, unwashed bodies, and iodine that is like no other smell in the world. The room would be crowded, the sanitars supporting legs and arms and heads, nurses dashing to the table for bandages or iodine or scissors, three or four stretchers occupying the floor of the room with the soldiers who were too severely wounded to sit or stand, these soldiers often utterly quiet, dying perhaps, or watching with eyes that realised only dreams and shadows, the little window square, the strip of sky, the changing colours of the day; then the sitting soldiers, on ordinary of a marvellous and most simple patience, watching the bandaging of their arms and hands and legs, whispering sometimes *"Boje moi! Boje moi!"* dragging themselves up from their desperate struggle for endurance to answer the sanitars who asked their name, their regiments, the nature of their wounds. Sometimes they would talk, telling how the thing had happened to them:

"And there, your Honour, before I could move, she had come— such a noise—eh, eh, a terrible thing—I called out '*Zemliac.* Here it is!' I said, and he . . ."

But as a rule they were very quiet, starting perhaps at the sting of iodine, asking for a bandage to be tighter or not so tight, suddenly slipping in a faint to the ground, and then apologising afterwards. And in their eyes always that look as though, very shortly, they would hear some story so marvellous that it would compensate for all their present pain and distress.

And these wounded knew something that we did not. In the first moments of their agony when we met them their souls had not recovered from the shock of their encounter. It was, with many of them, more than the mere physical pain. They were still held by some discovery at whose very doors they had been. The discovery itself had not been made by them, but they had been so near to it that many of them would never be the same man again. "No, your Honour," one soldier said to me. "It isn't my arm . . . That is nothing, *Slava Bogu* . . . but life isn't so real now. It is half gone." He would explain no more.

In the early morning, when the light was so cold and inhuman, when the candles stuck in bottles on the window-sills shivered and quavered in the little breeze, when the big basin on the floor seemed to swell ever larger and larger, with its burden of bloody rags and soiled bandages and filthy fragments of dirty clothes, when the air was weighted down with the smell of blood and human flesh, when the sighs and groans and cries kept up a perpetual undercurrent that one did not notice and yet faltered before, when again and again bodies, torn almost in half, legs hanging almost by a thread, rose before one, passed and rose again in endless procession, then, in those early hours, some fantastic world was about one. The poplar trees beyond the window, the little beech-wood on the hill, the pond across the road, a round grey sheet of ruffled water, these things in the half-light seemed to wait for our defeat. One instant on our part and it seemed that all the pain and torture would rise in a flood and overwhelm one . . . in those early morning hours the enemy crept very close indeed. We could almost hear his hot breath behind the bars of our fastened doors.

There was a peculiar little headache that I have felt nowhere else, before or since, that attacked on those early mornings. It was not a headache that afflicted one with definite physical pain. It was like a cold hand pressed upon the brow, a hand that touched the eyes, the nose, the mouth, then remained, a chill weight upon the head; the blood seemed to stop in its course, one's heart beat feebly and things were dim before one's eyes. One was stupid and chose one's words slowly, looking at people closely to see whether one really knew them, even unsure about oneself, one's history, neither sad nor joyful, neither excited nor dull, only with the cold hand upon one's brow, catching the beating of one's heart.

While there was work to do nothing mattered, but now in the silence the whole world seemed as empty and foul as a drained and stinking tub.

From *The Dark Forest*, by Hugh Walpole; George M. Doran Co., New York, 1916.

## *The Boche Bread is Bad*
### —Henry Beston

That night we were given orders to be ready to evacuate the chateau in case the Boches advanced from Verdun. The drivers slept in the ambulances, rising at intervals through the night to warm their engines. The buzz of the motors sounded through the pines of the chateau park, drowning out the rumbling of the bombardment and then the monotonous roaring of the flood. Now and then a trench light, rising like a spectral star over the lines on the Hauts de Meuse, would shine reflected in the river. At intervals attendants carried down the swampy paths to the chapel the bodies of soldiers who had died during the night. The cannon flashing was terrific. Just before dawn, half a dozen batteries of seventy-fives came in a swift trot down the shelled road; the men leaned over on their steaming horses, the harnesses rattled and jingled, and the cavalcade swept on, outlined a splendid instant against the motor flashes and the streaks of day.

On my morning trip a soldier with bandaged arm was put beside me on the front seat. He was about forty years old; a wiry black beard gave a certain fullness to his thin face, and his hands were pudgy and short of finger. When he removed his helmet, I saw that he was bald. A bad cold caused him to speak in a curious whispering tone, giving to everything he said the character of a grotesque confidence.

"What do you do en civil?" he asked.

I told him.

"I am a pastry cook," he went on. "My speciality is Saint-Denis apple tarts. Have you ever had one? They are very good when made with fresh cream."

"How did you get wounded?"

"Eclat d'obus," he replied, as if that were the whole story. After a pause he added, "Douamont—yesterday."

I thought of the shells I had seen bursting over that fort.

"Do you put salt in chocolate?" he asked professionally.

"Not as a rule," I replied.

"It improves it," he pursued, as if he were revealing a confidential dogma. "The Boche bread is bad, very bad, much worse than a year ago. Full of crumbles and lumps. Degoutant!"

The ambulance rolled up to the evacuation station, and my pastry cook alighted.

"When the war is over, come to my shop," he whispered benevolently, "and you shall have some tartes aux pommes a la mode de Saint-Denis with my wife and me."

"With fresh cream?" I asked.

"Of course," he replied seriously.

I accepted gratefully, and the good old soul gave me his address.

Two weeks later, when the back of the attack had been broken and the organization of the defense had developed into a trusted routine, I went again to Verdun. The snow was falling heavily, covering the piles of debris and sifting into the black skeletons of the burned houses. Untrodden in the narrow streets lay the white snow. Above the Meuse, above the ugly burned areas in the old town on the slope, rose the shell-spattered walls of the citadel and the cathedral towers of the still, tragic town. The drumming of the bombardment had died away. The river was again in flood. In a deserted wine-shop on a side street well protected from shells by a wall of sandbags was a post of territorials.

To the tragedy of Verdun, these men were the chorus; there was something Sophoclean in this group of older men alone in the silence and ruin of the beleaguered city. A stove filled with wood from the wrecked houses gave out a comfortable heat, and in an alley-way, under cover, stood a two-wheeled hose cart, and an old-fashioned seesaw fire pump. There were old clerks and bookkeepers among the soldier firemen—retired gendarmes who had volunteered, a country schoolmaster, and a shrewd peasant from Lyonnais. Watch was kept from the heights of the citadel, and the outbreak of fire in any part of the city was telephoned to the shop. On that day only a few explosive shells had fallen.

"Do you want to see something odd, mon vieux?" said one of the pompiers to me; and he led me through a labyrinth of cellars to a cold, deserted house. The snow had blown through the shell-splintered window-panes. In the dining-room stood a table, the cloth was laid and the silver spread; but a green feathery fungus had grown in a dish of food and broken straws of dust floated on the wine in the glasses. The territorial took my arm, his eyes showing the pleasure of my responding curiosity, and whispered,—

"There were officers quartered here who were called very suddenly. I saw the servant of one of them yesterday; they have all been killed."

Outside there was not a flash from the batteries on the moor. The snow continued to fall, and darkness, coming on the swift wings of the storm, fell like a mantle over the desolation of the city.

From *A Volunteer Poilu*, by Henry Beston; Houghton Mifflin; Boston, 1916.

## *I Was Wishing for the Return of a Soldier*
### —Rebecca West

The house lies on the crest of Harroweald, and from its windows the eye drops to miles of emerald pastureland lying wet and brilliant under a westward line of sleek hills blue with distance and distant woods, while nearer it ranges the suave decorum of the lawn and the Lebanon cedar whose branches are like darkness made palpable, and the minatory gauntness of the topmost pines in the wood that break downwards, its bare boughs a close texture of browns and purple, from the pond on the hill's edge.

That day in its beauty was an affront to me, because like most Englishwomen of my time I was wishing for the return of a soldier. Disregarding the national interest and everything except the prehensile gesture of our hearts toward him, I wanted to snatch my cousin Christopher from the wars and seal him in this green pleasantness his wife and I now looked upon. Of late I had had bad dreams about him. By night I saw Chris running across the brown rottenness of No Man's Land, starting back here because he trod upon a hand, not even looking there because of the awfulness of an unburied head, and not till my dream was packed full of horror did I see him pitch forward on his knees as he reached safety—if it was that. For on the war-films I have seen men slip down as softly from the trench parapet, and none but the grimmer philosophers would say that they had reached safety by their fall. And when I escaped into wakefulness it was only to lie stiff and think of stories I had heard in the boyish voice, that rings indomitable yet has most of its gay notes flattened, of the modern subaltern.

"We were all of us in a barn one night, and a shell came along. My pal sang out, '*Help me, old man I've got no legs!*' and I had to answer, '*I can't, old man, I've got no hands!*'"

Well, such are the dreams of Englishwomen today; I could not complain. But I wished for the return of our soldier.

(From *The Return of the Soldier*, by Rebecca West; The Century Co.; New York, 1918.)

## *On Leave*

### —H. M. Tomlinson

Coming out of Victoria Station into the stir of London again, on leave from Flanders, must give as near the sensation of being thrust suddenly into life from the beyond and the dead as mortal man may expect to know. It is a surprising and providential wakening into a world which long ago went dark. That world is strangely loud, bright and alive. Plainly it did not stop when, somehow, it vanished once upon a time. There its vivid circulation moves, and the buses are so usual, the people so brisk and intent on their own concerns, the signs so startlingly familiar, that the man who is home again begins to doubt that he has been absent, that he has been dead. But his uniform must surely mean something, and its stains something more!

And there can be no doubt about it, as you stand there a trifle dizzy in London once more. You really have come back from another world; and you have the curious idea that you may be invisible in this old world in a sense you know you are unseen. These people will never know what you know. There they gossip in the hall, and leisurely survey the bookstall, and they would never guess it, but you have just returned from hell. What could they say if you told them? They would be embarrassed, polite, forbearing, kindly, and smiling, and they would mention the matter afterwards as a queer adventure with a poor devil who was evidently a little overwrought; shell shock, of course. Beastly thing, shell shock. Seems to affect the nerves.

They would not understand. They will never understand. What is the use of standing in veritable daylight, and telling the living, who have never been dead, of the other place?

The man who comes back from the line has lost more than years. He has lost his original self. People failed to recognize Rip Van Winkle because they did not know his beard. Our friends do recognize us when they greet us on our return from the front, but they do not know us because we are not the men they remember. They are the same as ever; but when they address us, they talk to a mind which is not there, though the eyes betray nothing of the difference. They talk to those who have come back to life to see them again, but who cannot tell them what has happened, and dare not try . . .

The youngster who is home on leave, though he may not have reasoned it out, knows that what he wants to say, often prompted by indignation, cannot be said. He feels intuitively that this is beyond his power to express. Besides, if he were to begin, where would he end? He cannot trust himself. What would happen if he uncovered, in a sunny and innocent breakfast-room, the horror he knows? If he spoke out? His people would not understand him. They would think he was mad. They would be sorry, dammit. Sorry for him! Why, he is not sorry for himself. He can stand it now he knows what it is like. He can stand it—if they can. And he realizes they can stand it, and are merely anxious about his welfare, the welfare which does not trouble him in the least, for he has looked into the depth of evil, and for him the earth has changed; and he rather despises it. He has seen all he wants to see of it. Let it go, dammit. If they don't mind the change, and don't kick, why should he? What a hell of a world to be born into; and once it did look so jolly good, too! He is shy, cheery, but inexorably silent on what he knows. Some old fool said to him once, "It must be pretty bad out there?" Pretty bad? What a lark!

It is difficult for him to endure hearing the home folk speak with the confidence of special revelation of the war they have not seen, when he, who has been in it, has contradictory minds about it. They are so assured that they think there can be no other view and they bear out their mathematical arguments with maps and figures. It might be a chess tournament. He feels at last his anger beginning to smoulder. He feels a bleak and impalpable alienation from those who are all the world to him. He understands at last that they also are in the mirror, projected from his world that was, and that now he cannot come near them. Yet though he knows, they do not. The greatest evil of war—that is what staggers you when you come home, feeling you know the worst of it—is the unconscious indifference to war's obscene blasphemy against life of the men and women who have the assurance that they will never be called on to experience it. Out there, comrades in a common and unlightened affliction shake a fist humorously at the disregarding stars, and mock them. Let the Fates do their worst. The sooner it is over, the better; and, while waiting, they will take it out of Old Jerry. He is the only one out of whom they can take it. They are to throw away their world and die, so they must take it out on somebody.

But what is the matter with London? The men on leave, when they meet each other, always ask that question without hope, in the seclusion of their confidence and special knowledge. They feel perversely they would sooner be amid the hated filth and smells of the battle-ground than at home. Out there, though possibly mischance may suddenly extinguish the day for them, they will be with those who understand, with comrades who rarely discuss the war except obliquely and with quiet and bitter jesting. Seeing the world has gone wrong, how much better and easier it is to take the likelihood of extinction with men who have the same mental disgust as your own, and can endure it till they die, but who, while they live in the same torment with you, have the unspoken but certain conviction that Europe is a decadent old beast eating her young with insatiable appetite, than to sit in sunny breakfast-rooms with the newspaper maps and positive arguments of the unsaved!

From *Old Junk*, by H. M. Tomlinson; Alfred A. Knopf; New York, 1923.

## *Andiamo a Casa*
### —G. M. Trevelyan

Let us take the case of an imaginary "Giuseppe," and try to reconstruct in his person a type of the *povero fante*. Giuseppe comes from a farm in the Appenines, where, in the summer of 1915, he left a wife and five small children. His simple and intensely human thoughts and affections are all centred upon them, and upon his farm and a village made up of persons like himself. Outside that circle he has no experience, no knowledge, nor much interest in life beyond a good-natured but uninstructed curiosity in whatever may be going on under his eyes. Of politics he knows nothing. No one has attempted to instruct him in them, except the priest, who told him not to vote because the State was wicked, and the Socialist, who exhorted him to seize the land. He is silently suspicious, both of priest and of Socialist, as he is of every one pretending to authority. But their combined exhortations can have done little to fortify his sense of patriotism or of civic duty, which must in his case be instinctive, since they have never been inculcated. He has, indeed, heard of Garibaldi and knows that the Austrians are *brutte bestie*. Giuseppe can read, which is more than can be said of a quarter of his regiment, chiefly coming from the south. But he sets little store by the newspapers—they do not talk about things that interest him; besides, he regards them as being part of the system of authority, and, therefore, their statements are to be regarded with the respectful skepticism that he accords to all things official.

Between battles there is little drill, training, or discipline. The life of the soldier seems to Giuseppe dull and purposeless. His officers, who expose themselves well in battle, are patriotic, and know all the reasons for the war, but they live by themselves. Sometimes the Colonel reads the regiment a manifesto about the Italian eagle perching on the highest summit of the Alps, but some of Giuseppe's companions say under their breaths, "*Porca Madonna! Vogliamo andare a casa.*" The trenches are very wet and cold when they are not very hot, and they are always terribly dull; several times he has been left in them two months on end by some Staff muddle. And even when he is *in riposo* life is wet, dirty and dull. But "*Pazienza,*" Giuseppe says; that is his greatest peasant virtue, on which the ungrateful State is built.

There are several Socialists in the regiment who conduct most of the discussions. Some of them are patriots, but Aristodemo talks them all down. Giuseppe does not understand all that Aristodemo says; it is vague, distant talk coming from the world outside the village. But it seems to have some relation to things that are real to him; the chief of these are his wife's letters, saying that prices are so high that she can no longer feed the children on the separation allowance. She also writes that the priest says the Pope has declared there will be peace in a month, but that the chemist says they must go on fighting for another three months and then they will win. Giuseppe has just come off San Gabriele, and knows they will not win in three months. Half the regiment was killed there. He doubts if they will ever win at all. Russia has given in; he understands that much about world politics; also that the Inglesi are very stubborn.

Aristodemo says the Russians are sensible fellows. *Porca miseria!* he says, what are we doing shivering and starving and dying here to win these barren mountains where no one lives at all except a few barbarians who cannot even talk Italian? What are we fighting for? The Inglesi pay our masters to go on with the war, says Aristodemo, but none of it comes our way, except fivepence a day in the front line and threepence behind! Giuseppe has had two leaves of ten days each since he joined in 1915, and each time he went back his wife was more depressed and thinner, and every one in the village had turned against the war except the chemist—but he is always against the aging priest anyhow.

Oh yes, says Aristodemo, the Russians have got liberty, and so they have all gone home to their farms, and taken the land in the bargain! They have had a revolution, and so should we. All the "great guns," he says, keep their sons and nephews *imboscati;* they sit in the *retrovie,* eating beefsteak, and give us poor soldiers in the trenches dry chestnuts. Giuseppe laughs at that, and sings a song about it, a forbidden song. One verse says—

"*A Cividale e Udine ci sono imboscati;*
*Hanno le scarpe lucide e capelli profumati.*"
("At Cividale and Udine the *embuches* live.
They have shining boots and perfumed hair.")

Giuseppe has been two and a half years away from home, and here is a third winter coming on. When he gets away from Aristodemo he wishes he could talk about things to the young sub-lieutenant as he did one day last year, when the sub-lieutenant made it all so clear to him, and talked about Italia. But now the sub-lieutenant has gone. His arm was blown right off him on that accursed mountain, and he just said, "Viva l'Italia!" and then his skin grew like wax. But Giuseppe carried him away so that the *brutte bestie* never got him.

On the top of all this came the news of Caporetto, and Cardona's orders to retreat. So they trudged off, sad at first that it had all come to nothing, and sad to leave behind so many dead comrades on those barren hills. But as they went on they began to feel they were going home. The roads in the plain were so crowded that they soon began to pass the artillery and cars standing blocked in rows. It was raining like ruin. No one gave orders or made them keep rank. They just splashed on, getting more and more like a mob, in the mood of children coming back from school. "Andiamo a casa," they said. Evidently Cardona had given it up, and the war was over. As there is going to be peace now, said Aristodemo, let us throw away our rifles, and then no fool of an officer can turn us back to fight when it is of no use. Well, says Giuseppe, the rifles are very heavy, and we have not eaten for two days.

To me the thing that needs explaining is not why the Retreat occurred, but why it did not occur long before.

From *Scenes from Italy's War*, by G. M. Trevelyan; Houghton Mifflin, Boston, 1919.

## *What Manner of Man*
### —John Dos Passos

The woods all about him were a vast rubble-heap; the jagged, splintered boles of leafless trees rose in every direction from heaps of brass shell-cases, of tin cans, of bits of uniform and equipment. The wind came in puffs laden with an odor as of dead rats in an attic. And this was what all the centuries of civilization had struggled for. For this had generations worn away their lives in mines and factories and forges, in fields and workshops, toiling, screwing higher and higher the tension of their minds and muscles, polishing brighter and brighter the mirror of their intelligence. For this!

The German prisoner and another man had appeared in the road again, carrying a stretcher between them, walking with the slow, meticulous steps of great fatigue. A series of shells came in, like three cracks of a whip along the road. Martin followed the stretcher-bearers into the dugout.

The prisoner wiped the sweat from his grime-streaked forehead, and started up the step of the dugout again, a closed stretcher on his shoulder. Something made Martin look after him as he strolled down the rutted road. He wished he knew German so that he might call after the man and ask him what manner of man he was.

Again, like snapping of a whip, three shells flashed yellow as they exploded in the brilliant sunlight of the road. The slender figure of the prisoner bent suddenly double, like a pocket-knife closing, and lay still. Martin ran out, stumbling in the hard ruts. In a soft child's voice the prisoner was babbling endlessly, contentedly. Martin kneeled beside him and tried to lift him, clasping him round the chest under the arms. He was very hard to lift, for his legs dragged limply in their soaked trousers, where the blood was beginning to saturate the muddy cloth. Sweat dripped from Martin's face on the man's face, and he felt the arm-muscles and the ribs pressed against his body as he clutched the wounded man tightly to him in the effort of carrying him toward the dugout. The effort gave Martin a strange contentment. It was as if his body were taking part in the agony of the man's body. At last they were washed out, all the hatreds, all the lies, in blood and sweat. Nothing was left but the quiet friendliness of beings alike in every part, eternally alike.

Two men with a stretcher came from the dugout, and Martin laid the man's body, fast growing limper, less animated, down very carefully.

As he stood by the car, wiping the blood off his hands with an oily rag, he could still feel the man's ribs and the muscles of the man's arm against his side. It made him strangely happy.

From *One Man's Initiation: 1917*, by John Dos Passos; George H. Doran; New York, 1922.

## *Smashed in Some Complicated Manner*
### —H. G. Wells

Abruptly and shockingly, this malignity of warfare, which had been so far only a festering cluster of reports and stories and rumours and suspicions, stretched out its arms to Essex and struck a barb of grotesque cruelty into the very heart of Mr. Britling. Late one afternoon came a telegram from Filmington-on-Sea, where Aunt Wilshire had been recovering her temper in a boarding-house after a round of visits in Yorkshire and the moorlands. And she had been "very seriously" injured by an overnight Zeppelin air raid. It was a raid that had not been even mentioned in the morning's papers. She had asked to see him.

It was, ran the compressed telegraphic phrase, "advisable to come at once."

Hugh found her in the hospital very much hurt indeed. She had been smashed in some complicated manner that left the upper part of her body intact, and lying slantingly upon pillows. Over the horror of bandaged broken limbs and tormented flesh below sheets and a counterpane were drawn. Morphia had been injected, he understood, to save her from pain, but presently it might be necessary for her to suffer. She lay up in her bed with an effect of being enthroned, very white and still; her strong profile with its big nose and her straggling hair and a certain dignity gave her the appearance of some very important, very old man, of an aged pope for instance, rather than of an old woman.

He was not sure at first that she knew of his presence.

"Here I am, Aunt Wilshire," he said. "Your nephew Hugh."

"Mean and preposterous," she said very distinctly.

But she was not thinking of Mr. Britling. She was talking of something else.

She was saying: "It should not have been known I was here. There are spies everywhere. Everywhere. There is a spy now—or a lump very like a spy. They pretend it is a hot-water bottle. Pretext . . . Oh yes! I admit—absurd. But I have been pursued by spies. Endless spies. Endless, endless spies. Their devices are almost incredible . . . He has never forgiven me . . . All this on account of a carpet. A palace carpet. Over which I had no control. I spoke my mind. He knew I knew of it. I never concealed it. So I was hunted. For years he had mediated revenge. Now he has it. But at what cost! And they call him Emperor.

Emperor! . . . His arm is withered; his son—imbecile. He will die—without dignity . . ."

The story was like a page from some fantastic romance of Jules Verne's; the peace of the little old town, the people going to bed, the quiet streets, the quiet starry sky, and then for ten minutes an uproar of breaking glass, and then a fire here, a fire there, a child's voice pitched high by pain and terror, scared people going to and fro with lanterns, and the sky empty again, the Zeppelin raiders gone.

Five minutes before, Aunt Wilshire had been sitting in the boarding-house playing Patience. Five minutes later she was a thing of elemental terror and agony, bleeding wounds and shattered bones, plunging about in the darkness amidst a heap of wreckage. And already the German airmen were buzzing away to sea like boys who have thrown a stone through a window.

Her voice weakened, but it was evident she wanted to say something more.

"I'm here," said Mr. Britling. "Your nephew Hughie."

She listened.

"Can you understand me?"

She became suddenly an earnest, tender human being. "My dear!" she said and seemed to search for something in her mind and failed to find it.

"You have always understood me," she tried.

"You have always been a good boy to me, Hughie," she said, rather vacantly, and added after some moments of still reflection, "*au fond.*"

After that she was silent for some minutes, and took no notice of his whispers.

Then she recollected what had been in her mind. She put out a hand that sought for Mr. Britling's sleeve.

"Hughie!"

"I'm here, Auntie," said Mr. Britling. "I'm here."

"Don't let him get at *your* Hughie . . . Too good for it, dear. Oh! much—much too good . . . People let these wars and excitements run

away with them . . . They put too much into them . . . They aren't—
they aren't worth it. Don't let him get at your Hughie."

"No."

"You understand me, Hughie?"

"Perfectly, Auntie."

"Then don't forget it. Ever."

She had said what she wanted to say. She had made her testament.
He was amazed to find this grotesque old creature had suddenly
become beautiful, in that silvery vein of beauty one sometimes finds
in very old men. She was exalted as great artists will sometimes exalt
the portraits of the aged. He was moved to kiss her forehead.

At about seven o'clock that evening she died.

From *Mr. Britling Sees It Through*, by H. G. Wells; Macmillan; New
York, 1917.

# Chapter Six:

# Protest

Courage, martial courage, bravery in battle, was recognized and honored during the Great War. Medals, promotion, celebrity—all these were possible for those who killed or rescued under spectacular circumstances. The famous aces, fighter pilots like Georges Guynemer in France, Albert Ball in England, Eddie Rickenbacker in the United States, Hermann Goering in Germany, all became national heroes, as did soldiers like Captain Noel Chavasse, England's double Victoria Cross winner, and Sergeant Alvin York, the Tennessee hill farmer turned soldier who took thirty-two German machine gun nests single-handedly. (Though later, looking back on his wartime experience, he would admit, "I can't see we did any good.")

Other forms of courage were taken for granted and honored only in platitudes. Women who feared at any moment the knock on the door with the dreaded war office telegram; mothers and fathers dealing with the same kind of anxiety; civilians, across a huge swath of Europe, whose homes and livelihoods were destroyed. They were expected to "soldier on" without the support of their husbands or sons and, in the worst cases, to mourn them quickly, then get on with the job of winning the war.

Some of the greatest exemplars of courage during the war, those showing moral courage, were actively despised, and in some circumstances rigorously prosecuted: the very few writers who dared protest the war in print. They were rewarded with obloquy, loss of income, exile, or jail—the war-fighting establishment did not content itself with tsk-tsk shakes of the head. Yet—such are the ironies of literature and history—these are the very writers whose work can seem the most alive today, while the knee-jerk jingoism of their peers reads mostly as a curiosity. Antiwar writing from any war is always sadly relevant to contemporary conditions, and many of the specific arguments against World War I, so controversial in their day, have long since been accepted by historians as the truth.

As has been seen, almost all the famous fiction writers, playwrights, and poets wholeheartedly supported the war while it was being fought. The protestors (with the notable exception of Romain Rolland), were *not* imaginative writers; they were essayists, philosophers, professors, and social workers, more directly focused on political and social issues than were novelists, and with much less to lose by going against the popular mood.

Protest writing was a feature of the war right from the start, but it picked up in intensity as the war dragged on. In 1917, war weariness had settled over Europe—and not just over writers. One of the great myths of the war is that the average soldier just "took it," serving stolidly on through the carnage without complaint or protest. The fact is, by 1917 many soldiers had had enough, and voted with their feet. After twenty-nine thousand *poilus* were butchered in the failed French offensive along the Chemin des Dames, soldiers in fifty-four divisions, half the French army, refused to take part in any more offensives. Italian soldiers deserted *en masse* before and after the disaster at Caporetto. After the October Revolution in Russia, the army immediately began to melt away, with four million of them offering themselves up to captivity rather than fighting on, and many others simply laying down their arms and heading home. Not every World War I soldier thought he was enlisted in a great cause.

Since America dithered for three years before entering the war, there was more time and more opportunities for antiwar writing to be safely published there than in other Allied countries. One of dozens of hastily compiled books trying to cash in on the war, *The Great War In Europe; Most Terrible Conflict in History*, published in New York in 1915, could include an introduction by Bishop Samuel Fallows, "famous Civil War chaplain," that included this passionate antiwar peroration.

> "I arraign war in the name of the ghastly armies of the mangled dead; of the countless devastated and desolate homes; of the millions of broken-hearted, wailing widows fighting a grim and losing battle for bread; of helpless orphans knowing no father's providence and care; of aged parents without the strong hand of loving sons on which to lean. I arraign it in the name of our common Humanity; in the name of the christianity of the Prince of Peace."

Two years later this kind of writing could get you punished. The Espionage Act was passed in 1917 and the repressive Sedition Act the following year. Antiwar writers were persecuted with rigor, ostracized in some cases, censored and prosecuted in others. Jane Addams, the beloved founder of Hull House in Chicago, went from a saint to a pariah overnight, thanks to her leadership of the American Union Against Militarism, or, as the *New York Times* labeled it, "this little group of malcontents."

Another AUAM writer, Scott Nearing, was prosecuted under the newly passed Espionage Act (which, as whistleblower Edward Snowden discovered, is still very much in force 100 years later), charged with "obstruction to the recruiting and enlistment service of the United States."

I have on my desk one of the original short pamphlets Nearing was prosecuted for: *The Menace of Militarism; An Analysis, A Criticism, a Protest and a Demand*, published by the Rand School of

Social Science in New York City in 1917. It looks scruffy, amateurish, like a penny-dreadful western meant to be read on a train ride, then tossed into the trash, but having survived a century now, it still packs a powerful punch, not only because of its message ("War is built of fear and cemented with hate"), but because of the unmistakable urgency and passion with which it was printed and produced. On the back is the famous Boardman Robinson cartoon from *The Masses* called "The Deserter": Christ lined up against a wall as a firing squad composed of soldiers from all the combatant nations take aim at his heart.

Even such a beloved figure as Helen Keller received abuse for her pacifist views. At an antiwar rally in 1916 she urged workers to "Strike against the war, for without you no battles can be fought! Strike against manufacturing shrapnel and gas bombs and all other tools of murder!"

Were the protest writers much read? Did they have any influence? Most of their impact came *after* the war ended and the mood dramatically changed. Ignored and censored while the war was in progress, their writing became relevant in the 1920s, when the soldier writers began publishing their memoirs testifying to how truly awful the trenches had been, and a mood of disillusionment replaced war fever.

Now, a hundred years later, what comes across most strongly in the writing is the sheer moral and physical courage it took to publish it in the first place. Romain Rolland paid tribute to the dissenters while the war was still at its height.

> "The combatants, pitted against each other, agree in hating those who refuse to hate. Europe is like a besieged town. Fever is raging. Whoever will not rave like the rest is suspected. Whoever insists, in the midst of war, on defending peace among men knows that he risks his own peace, his reputation, his friends, for his belief. But of what value is a belief for which no risks are run?"

World War I was the turning point in Bertrand Russell's life. Forty-two when the war started, his reputation was that of a technical philosopher focused on rarefied abstractions, with his groundbreaking work on mathematical theory, *Principia Mathematica*, having been published in 1913. The horrors of the war changed the thrust of his writing; ever afterwards social issues would be his primary concern.

"When the War came I felt as if I heard the voice of God," this famous atheist would later write.

> "I knew that it was my business to protest, however futile protest might be. My whole nature was involved. As a lover of truth, the national propaganda of all the belligerent nations sickened me. As a lover of civilization, the return to barbarism appalled me. As a man of thwarted parental feeling, the massacre of the young wrung my heart. I hardly supposed that much good would come of opposing the War, but I felt that for the honour of human nature those who were not swept off their feet should show they stood firm."

Russell became one of the most prominent pacifists, and—though he was a member of the British aristocracy, the brother of an earl—the establishment struck back hard. He was stripped of his lectureship at Cambridge, denied a passport so he couldn't teach in America, mobbed when he tried to make antiwar speeches, and then, when he wrote a pamphlet for the No Conscription Fellowship, he was thrown into Brixton Prison for five months.

Russell would campaign for peace for the rest of his long life. At age eighty-nine, he was sent back to Brixton Prison, this time for his participation in a Campaign for Nuclear Disarmament demonstration in London.

The selection is from his "An Appeal to the Intellectuals of Europe," written in 1916 and included in his book, *Justice in War-Time,* published the same year.

No writer of the Great War was braver, suffered more and is now more forgotten than the forty-two-year-old German physiologist and professor, Dr. G. F. Nicolai. At the outbreak of the war, distraught over Germany's invasion of Belgium, he wrote a "Manifesto to the Europeans" demanding that the army withdraw, and circulated it among his fellow intellectuals for signatures; only three signed, one of them being Albert Einstein.

The government threw him into Graudenz Prison for this; when he was released, he immediately went to work on a five-hundred-page examination of war in general and the Great War in particular: *The Biology of War,* with its thesis that war ought to be regarded as we regard smallpox or the plague, something that can and ought to be eradicated by taking the proper preventive measures. He piled particular scorn on the favorite German argument that without war nations become degenerate and effeminate.

Back he went into prison; his property was confiscated, his family left penniless. ("Those who have seen him recently," writes his translator in the introduction, "declare that his imprisonment and suffering have greatly aged him, and he now looks quite a broken man.") He eventually made a daring escape to neutral Denmark in a commandeered German biplane. After the war, when he tried to resume his teaching duties at Berlin University, he was shouted down by angry mobs of veterans who considered him a traitor. After a few more years of this persecution, he was forced into exile in South America.

Jane Addams, reformist, feminist, and pacifist, was honored for her work in the Chicago slums and the book she wrote about it, *Twenty Years at Hull House.* Fifty-four when the war broke out, influenced (as many World War I dissidents were) by the writings of Tolstoy, she came to believe that women had a special mission to preserve peace. As president of the Women's International League for Peace and Freedom, she served as a delegate to the International Congress of Women at the Hague in 1915, where 1,200 delegates called upon combatant nations to begin "a process of continuous mediation until peace could be restored."

While in Europe on her peace mission, she had the opportunity to meet with soldiers, nurses, pacifists, and young people dealing with the issues she cared about so passionately. She co-authored a book on her experiences, *Women at the Hague.* My copy, stamped *Withdrawn,* comes from "The Somerset County Library," and shows it last being checked out in November 1965.

Addams's work for peace damaged her reputation once the United States joined the war, but in 1931 she became the first American woman to receive the Nobel Peace Prize.

W. E. B. Du Bois, forty-six, was at the height of his reputation as a militant spokesman for black Americans when war broke out in Europe. He published an essay in the *Atlantic Monthly* that was highly critical of the combatant countries' hidden imperialist agendas, but when the United States became involved in 1917, and thousands of African Americans immediately enlisted, Du Bois, like many heretofore antiwar liberals, quickly changed his opinion, writing an essay called "Close Ranks."

> "For long years to come men will point to the year 1917 as the great Day of Decision. We of the colored race have no ordinary interest in the outcome. That which the German power represents today spells death to the aspirations of negroes and all the darker races. Let us, while the war lasts, forget our special grievances, and close ranks brother to brother with our white fellow citizens."

Some in the black community criticized him for his flip-flop, citing his "crass moral cowardice," but the Military Intelligence Branch of the U. S. army, recognizing his influence, offered him a captaincy in return for his support. He did not end up serving, though the reason—he either failed the physical and/or there was a backlash among white officers—has never been made entirely clear.

After the war, his views on anti-imperialism reverted to those expressed in his original 1915 *Atlantic* essay.

Randolph Bourne, born in 1886 with a debilitating physical deformity, was considered one of the most brilliant young intellectuals in the United States, a spokesman for the spiritually sensitive, socially progressive generation just coming of age as the fighting in Europe began. He wrote for the liberal *New Republic* on literature, culture, and education, but when he tried to publish his antiwar essays there, he found his work was no longer welcome. He became a contributor to the more radical *The Masses* and *Seven Arts* until, with war fever reaching its height, these journals were suppressed and he had no outlets for his writing whatsoever. He died in the Spanish Flu epidemic a month after the war ended.

Bourne's writing and personality made a huge impression on all who came into contact with him, including the critic James Oppenheim.

> "No nerve of the young world was missing in Randolph
> Bourne; he was as sensitive to art as to philosophy, as
> politically-minded as he was psychologic, as brave in
> fighting for the conscientious objector as he was in
> opposing current American culture. He was a flaming
> rebel against our crippled life, as if he had taken the
> cue from the long struggle with his own body. And
> just as that weak child's body finally slew him before

he had fully triumphed, so the Great War succeeded in silencing him."

John Dos Passos apostrophized him in his novel *1919*.

> "If any man has a ghost
> Bourne has a ghost,
> a tiny twisted unscared ghost in a black cloak
> hopping along the grimy old brick and brownstone
> streets still left in downtown New York,
> crying out in a shrill soundless giggle:
> *War is the health of the state.*"

Emily G. Balch, at fifty, was a professor of economics and sociology at Wellesley College, very much involved in the kind of social issues that inspired her friend and colleague Jane Addams. She joined her at the International Congress of Women in Holland in 1915, and co-authored the account of their experiences in a Europe at war, *Women at the Hague*. As a founder of the Women's International League for Peace, she came under immediate suspicion with the climate of fear and repression taking hold in the United States, and was dismissed from her professorship by Wellesley in 1918.

Twenty-eight years later, she was awarded the Nobel Peace Prize.

Scott Nearing was thirty-four when America entered the war, and already had caused his share of controversy as a radical economist. He was dismissed from the University of Pennsylvania in 1915 for his dissident writings, and thanks to his antiwar views he was quickly fired from his next teaching job at a state university in Ohio. He moved to New York and became one of the founders of the pacifist People's Council of America for Democracy and Peace. During the war, his views moved ever leftward, and he became one of the guiding lights of the American Socialist Party.

Nearing's career had an unlikely epilogue. He moved to a farm in rural Vermont in 1947, then co-authored with his wife Helen the bestselling *Living the Good Life: How to Live Simply and Sanely in a Troubled World,* which became the bible of the modern homesteading/commune movement for the 1960s' counterculture.

He lived longer than any of the writers included in this volume, dying at age 100 in 1983.

Reinhold Niebuhr was twenty-five when America entered the war, serving as a pastor of a German-American congregation in Detroit; a young man, he already had a reputation as a theologian with passionate, courageous insights into a wide range of ethical, political, and cultural issues—a reputation that caused the *Atlantic Monthly* to commission a 1916 article on his antiwar views, which came at things from a different angle than most antiwar writers.

He retreated from this pacifism in later years, when he became known as the leading theologian of American Protestantism, and a founder of Americans for Democratic Action.

E. D. Morel made his prewar reputation as a radical journalist by helping to expose the horrors of Belgium's brutal exploitation of the Congo. Fifty-nine when the war broke out, he helped found one of the largest English pacifist organizations, the Union of Democratic Control, which numbered 650,000 members by 1917. He was physically assaulted when trying to deliver antiwar speeches, then accused of breaking the Defense of the Realm Act by sending a UDC pamphlet to Romain Rolland in Switzerland; he was sentenced to six months in prison.

Bertrand Russell was aghast at how prison changed him.

> "His hair is completely white (there was hardly a tinge of it before); he collapsed completely, physically and mentally, largely as a result of insufficient food."

After the war, he became a respected leader of the Labor Party. George Orwell, writing in 1946, remembered him as a "heroic but rather forgotten man."

## *This War is Trivial*
### —Bertrand Russell

Leibniz, writing to a French correspondent at a time when France and Hanover were at war, speaks of "this war, in which philosophy takes no interest." We have travelled far since those days. In modern times, philosophers, professors and intellectuals generally undertake willingly to provide their respective governments with those ingenious distortions and those subtle untruths by which it is made to appear that all good is on one side and all wickedness on the other. Side by side, in the pages of *Scientia,* are to be read articles by learned men, all betraying shamelessly their national bias, all as incapable of justice as any cheap newspaper, all as full of special pleading and garbled history. And all accept, as a matter of course, the inevitability of each other's bias; disagreeing with each other's conclusions, yet they agree perfectly with each other's spirit. All agree that the whole of a writer's duty is to make out a case for his own country.

To this attitude there have been notable exceptions among literary men—for example, Romain Rolland and Bernard Shaw—and even among politicians, although political extinction is now everywhere the penalty for a sense of justice. Among men of learning, there are no doubt many who have preserved justice in their thoughts and their private utterances. But these men, whether from fear or from unwillingness to seem unpatriotic, have almost kept silence.

I cannot but think that the men of learning, by allowing partiality to color their thoughts and words, have missed the opportunity of performing a service to mankind for which their training should have specially fitted them. The truth, whatever it may be, is the same in England, France, and Germany, in Russia and in Austria. It will not adapt itself to national needs; it is in its essence neutral. It stands outside the clash of passions and hatreds, revealing, to those who seek it, the tragic irony of strife with its attendant world of illusions. Men of learning, who should be accustomed to the pursuit of truth in their daily work, might have attempted, at this time, to make themselves the mouthpiece of truth, to see what was false on their own side, what was valid on the side of their enemies. They might have used their reputation and their freedom from political entanglements to mitigate the abhorrence with which the nations have come to regard each other, to help towards mutual understanding, to make the peace, when it comes, not a mere cessation due to weariness, but a fraternal reconciliation, springing from a realisation that the strife has been a folly of blindness. They have chosen to do nothing of all this. Allegiance to country has swept away allegiance to truth. Thought has become the slave of instinct, not its master. The guardians of the temple of Truth have betrayed it to idolators, and have been the first to promote the idolatrous worship . . .

This war is trivial, for all its vastness. No great principle is at stake, no great human purpose is involved on either side. The supposed ideal ends for which it is being fought are merely part of the myth. This war is not being fought for any rational end; it is being fought because, at first, the nations wished to fight, and now they are angry and determined to win victory. Everything else is idle talk, artificial rationalising of instinctive actions and passions. When two dogs fight in the street, no one supposes that anything but instinct prompts them, or that they are inspired by high and noble ends. If their fighting were accompanied by intellectual activity, the one would say he was fighting to promote the right kind of smell (*Kultur*), and the other to uphold the inherent canine right of running on the pavement (democracy). Yet this would not prevent the bystanders from seeing that their action was foolish, and that they ought to be parted as soon as possible. And what is true of dogs in the street is equally true of nations in the present war . . .

Men of learning should be the guardians of one of the sacred fires that illumine the darkness into which the human spirit is born: upon them depends the ideal of just thought, of disinterested pursuit of truth, which, if it had existed more widely, would have sufficed alone to prevent the present horror. To serve this ideal, to keep alive a purpose remote from strife, is more worthy of the intellectual leader of Europe than to help Governments in stimulating hatred or slaughtering more of the young men upon whom the future of the world depends. It is time to forget our supposed separate duty toward Germany, Austria, Russia, France, or England, and remember that higher duty to mankind in which we can still be at one.

From *Justice in War-Time*, by Bertrand Russell; Open Court Publishing; Chicago, 1916.

## *The Last Great Carouse*
### —G. F. Nicolai

War is the solvent, for without war no one would be interested in patriotism or chauvinism. The man who loved his country would have an additional form of happiness, but if a man did not love it, no one would disturb him. The merchant and manufacturer of their own accord try to increase their trade and sales, and thus add to the national welfare. The scientists and artist do their best by reason of some power within them, and thus add to national civilization. They do not require a special stimulus.

When money is to be appropriated for a school, theater, harbor, or canal, certain questions are considered, such as whether the costs will be proportionate to the increased comfort, wealth, civic improvement, or any other advantage that may ensue. In accordance with this the decision is made; no patriotism is required. In short, patriotism does not play the slightest practical role in any of the activities of peace.

But whenever the question is one of an army increase, of new cannons, or new battle-ships, we have to appeal to patriotism, because such armaments are *per se* unproductive, and demand deprivations on our part. Therefore even during peace patriotism has to be stirred up by the threat of possible war. As a rule the glowing spark is just barely kept alive. Were it to flare up too brightly, it might disturb the activities of the diplomats, and governments are almost as proud of them as they are of the deeds of warlike valor.

When war has once begun, such considerations are superfluous, for war generally puts many deprivations upon a population both in respect to mental and material necessities of life. Consequently, patriotism must be augmented, for only the highest patriotic tension can bring about long-continued and voluntary self-denial in a people. Then, too, the uncertainty and fear with which the possible horrors of war are viewed brings about a closer association of all those who are weak.

Both these feelings are played upon and artificially stimulated. A closer study of the press shows that the wire-pullers have an empiric understanding of the instincts of the crowd. Probably few people, except perhaps the late P. T. Barnum, would envy them this understanding. The whole performance essentially amounts to this. Either there is exaggeration of things favorable to one's own country or of those favorable to the opponent. In one case the desire is to stimulate the mass feeling by the feeling of activity; in the other to increase the need for cohesion . . .

War is wrong, harmful and needless. Then why do we wage war, we twentieth-century mortals? And why do we even love war?

War stirs us to the very depths of our being, and is perhaps the last great carouse of which even a degenerate nation can dream. Such simple things as truth and beauty, freedom and progress, evoke merely a tired smile, like that of an old man recalling his youthful follies. Something stronger and more tangible in the way of a stimulant is now needed to arouse the enthusiasm. Such a stimulant for a nation is war. It is a reminder of its youthful days, with their wonderful lightheartedness, their pardonable selfishness, and their boundless capacity for self-sacrifice.

Even the Americans, who are, after all, quite a recent con-glomeration of miscellaneous peoples, are becoming patriots and imperialists . . .

Let us assume that the righteous Germans had none but chivalrous motives for taking the field. Now he hears that the enemy sometimes kill and sometimes do violence to defenseless women, old men and children, and sometimes send them on in front in order to protect themselves against German bullets. Next he hears that ves-sels engaged in the dangerous work of mine-sweeping are manned by defenseless German prisoners; or, as stated in a grand general staff report of May, 1915, that the French, when digging trenches, made German prisoners stand in a row, thus forming a living wall to protect them against German attacks. Next he hears that the Turcos are cutting off Germans' heads, and carrying them about in their knapsacks as souvenirs; that the Russians are cutting off German children's hands; that Belgian girls are gouging out soldiers' eyes; that the English want to starve German women and children to death; that the Serbians are assassins, and the Montenegrins sheep-stealers, the Italians a pack of scoundrels, and the Japanese half-monkeys. In short, he is so overwhelmed by all these mean and baseless statements which he hears that, however kindly may be his nature, he must inevitably be convinced that all mankind except the inhabitants of the German Empire, the Austro-Hungarian monarchy, the Sultanate of Turkey, and the territories of the Turko-Tatar Bulgarian people is rotten to the core.

Whoever thinks thus cannot continue to have any respect for human dignity, and the foundations of his own morality are consequently sapped.

From *The Biology of War*, by Dr. G. F. Nicolai, translated by Constance and Julian Grande; The Century Co.; New York, 1918.

## *Courage There is No Room For*
### —Jane Addams

It gradually became clear to us that whether it is easily recognized or not, there has grown up a generation in Europe, as there has doubtless grown up a generation in America, who have revolted against war. It is a god they know not of, whom they are not willing to serve; because all of their sensibilities and their training upon which their highest ideals depend, revolt against it.

We met a young man in Switzerland who had been in the trenches for three months and had been wounded there. He did not know that he had developed tuberculosis but he thought he was being cured, and he was speaking his mind before he went back to the trenches. He was, I suppose, what one would call a fine young man, but not an exceptional one. He had been in business with his father and had travelled in South Africa, in France, England, and Holland. He had come to know men as *Mensch,* that *gute Menschen* were to be found in every land. And now here he was, at twenty-eight, facing death because he was quite sure when he went back to the trenches that death awaited him. He said that never during that three months and a half had he once shot his gun in a way that could possibly hit another man and nothing in the world could make him kill another man. He could be ordered into the trenches and "to go through the motions," but the final act was in his own hands and with his own conscience. And he said: "My brother is an officer." He gave the name and rank of his brother, for he was quite too near the issues of life and death for any shifting and concealing. "He never shoots in a way that will kill. And I know dozens and dozens of young men who do not."

We talked with nurses in hospitals, with convalescent soldiers, with mothers of those who had been at home on furlough and had gone back into the trenches, and we learned that there are surprising numbers of young men who will not do any fatal shooting because they think that no one has the right to command them to take human life. From one hospital we heard of five soldiers who had been cured and were ready to be sent back to the trenches, when they committed suicide, not because they were afraid to die but they would not be put into a position where they would have to kill others.

I recall a spirited young man who said: "We are told that we are fighting for civilization but I tell you that war destroys civilization. The highest product of the university, the scholar, the philosopher, the poet, when he is in the trenches, when he spends his days and nights in squalor and brutality and horror, is as low and brutal as the rudest peasant. They say, those newspaper writers, that it is wonderful to see the courage of the men in the trenches, singing, joking, playing cards, while the shells fall around them. Courage there is no room for, just as there is no room for cowardice. One cannot rush to meet the enemy, one cannot even see him. The shells fall here or they fall there. If you are brave, you cannot defy them; if you are a coward, you cannot flee from them; it is all chance."

It is such a state of mind which is responsible for the high percentage of insanity among the soldiers. In the trains for the wounded there is often a closed van in which are kept the men who have lost their minds.

From *Women at the Hague*, by Jane Addams, Emily G. Balch, Alice Hamilton; Macmillan; New York, 1916.

## *This Unspeakably Inhuman Outrage*
### —W. E. B. Du Bois

Most men assume that Africa lies far afield from the center to our burning social problems, and especially from our present problem of World War. Yet in a very real sense Africa is a prime cause of this terrible overturning of civilization, and these words seek to show how in the Dark Continent are hidden the roots, not simply of war to-day, but of the menace of wars to-morrow . . .

The present world war is the result of jealousies engendered by the recent rise of armed national associations of labor and capital, whose aim is the exploitation of the wealth of the world mainly outside the

European circle of nations. These associations, grown jealous and suspicious at the division of spoils of trade-empire, are fighting to enlarge
their respective shares; they look for expansion, not in Europe, but
in Asia, and particularly in Africa. "We want no inch of French territory," said Germany to England, but Germany was unable to give
similar assurances as to France in Africa.

The resultant jealousies and bitter hatreds tend continually to
fester along color lines. We must keep Negroes in their places, or
Negroes will take our jobs. All over the world there leaps to articulate
speech and ready action that singular assumption that if white men
do not throttle colored men, then China, India, and Africa will do to
Europe what Europe has done to them . . .

Hitherto the peace movement has confined itself chiefly to figures
about the cost of war and platitudes on humanity. What do nations care
about the cost of war, if by spending a few hundred millions in steel and
gunpowder they can gain a thousand millions in diamonds and cocoa?
How can love of humanity appeal as a motive to nations whose love
of luxury is built on the inhuman exploitation of human beings, and
who, especially in recent years, have been taught to regard these human
beings as inhuman? I appealed to the last meeting of peace societies in
St. Louis, saying "Should you not discuss racial prejudice as a prime
cause of war?" The secretary was sorry but was unwilling to introduce
controversial matters!

If we want real peace and lasting culture, we must extend the
democratic ideals to the yellow, brown, and black peoples. To say this
is to evoke on the faces of modern men a look of blank hopelessness.
Impossible! we are told, and for so many reasons—scientific, social,
and what not—that argument is useless. But let us not conclude too
quickly. Suppose we had to choose between this unspeakably inhuman outrage on decency and intelligence and religion which we call
the World War and the attempt to treat black men as human, sentient,
responsible beings? We have sold them as cattle. We are working them
as beasts of burden. We shall not drive war from this world until we

treat them as free and equal citizens in a world-democracy of all races and nations.

Colored people endure the contemptuous treatment meted out by whites to those not "strong" enough to be free. These nations and races, composing as they do a vast majority of humanity, are going to endure this treatment just as long as they must and not a moment longer. Then they are going to fight and the War of the Color Line will outdo in savage inhumanity any war this world has yet seen. For colored folk have much to remember and they will not forget.

From *The Atlantic Monthly*; Boston, May 1915.

## *A War Made Deliberately by Intellectuals*
—Randolph Bourne

To those of us who still retain an irreconcilable animus against war, it has been a bitter experience to see the unanimity with which the American intellectuals have thrown their support to the use of war-technique in the crisis in which America found itself. Socialists, college professors, publicists, new-republicans, practitioners of literature, have vied with each other in confirming with their intellectual faith the collapse of neutrality and the riveting of the war-mind on a hundred million more of the world's people. And the intellectuals are not content with confirming our belligerent gesture. They are now complacently asserting that it was they who effectively willed it, against the hesitation and dim perceptions of the American democratic masses. A war made deliberately by intellectuals! A calm moral verdict, arrived at after a penetrating study of inexorable facts! Sluggish masses, too remote from the world-conflict to be stirred, too lacking in intellect to perceive their danger! An alert intellectual class, saving the people in spite of themselves, biding their time with Fabian strategy until the nation could be moved into war without serious resistance! An intellectual class, gently guiding a nation through sheer force of ideas into what the other nations entered only through predatory craft or popular hysteria or militarist madness! A war free from any taint of self-seeking, a war that will secure the triumph of democracy and internationalize the world! This is the picture which the more self-conscious intellectuals have formed of themselves, and which they are slowly impressing upon a population which is being led no man knows whither by an indubitably intellectualized President. And they are right, in that the war certainly did not spring from either the ideals or the prejudices, from the national ambitions or hysterias, of the American people, however acquiescent the masses prove to be, and however clearly the intellectuals prove their putative intuition.

Those intellectuals who have felt themselves totally out of sympathy with this drag toward war will seek some explanation for this joyful leadership. They will want to understand this willingness of the American intellect to open the sluices and flood us with the sewage of war spirit . . .

The war sentiment, begun so gradually but so perseveringly by the preparedness advocates who came from the ranks of big business, caught hold of one after the other of the intellectual groups. With the aid of Theodore Roosevelt, the murmurs became a monotonous chant, and finally a chorus so mighty that to be out of it was at first to be disreputable and finally almost obscene. And slowly a strident chant was worked up against Germany which compared very creditably with the German fulminations against the greedy power of England. The nerve of war-feeling centered, of course, in the richer and older classes of the Atlantic seaboard, and was keenest where there were French or English business and particularly social connections. The sentiment then spread over the country as a class-phenomenon, touching everywhere those upper-class elements in each section who identified themselves with this Eastern ruling group. It must never be forgotten than in every community it was the least liberal and least democratic elements among whom the preparedness and later the war sentiment was found. The farmers were apathetic, the small business men and workingmen are still apathetic towards the war. The intellectuals, in other words, have identified themselves with the least democratic forces in American life. They have assumed the leadership for the war of those very classes whom the American democracy has been immemorially fighting. Only in a world where irony was dead could an intellectual class enter war at the head of such illiberal cohorts in the avowed cause of world-liberalism and world-democracy. No one is left to point out the undemocratic nature of this war-liberalism. In a time of faith, skepticism is the most intolerable of all insults . . . .

We go to war to save the world from subjugation! But the German intellectuals went to war to save their culture from barbarization! And the French went to war to save their beautiful France! And the English to save international honor! And Russia, most altruistic and self-sacrificing of all, to save a small State from destruction! Whence is our miraculous intuition of our moral spotlessness? Whence our confidence that history will not unravel huge economic and imperialist forces upon which our rationalizations float like bubbles? Are not our intellectuals fatuous when they tell us that our war of all wars is stainless and thrillingly achieving for good? . . .

Minor novelists and minor poets are still coming back from driving ambulances in France to write books that nag us into an appreciation of the "real meaning." No one can object to the generous emotions of service in a great cause or to the horror and pity at colossal devastation and agony. But too many of these prophets are men who have lived rather briskly among the cruelties and thinness of American civilization and have shown no obvious horror and pity at the exploitations and the arid quality of the life lived here around us. Their moral sense has been deeply stirred by what they saw in France and Belgium, but it was a moral sense relatively unpracticed by deep concern and reflection over the inadequacies of American democracy. Few of them had used their vision to create literature impelling us toward a more radiant American future. And that is why, in spite of their vivid stirrings, they seem so unconvincing. Their idealism is too new and bright to affect us, for it comes from men who never cared very particularly about great creative American ideals. So these writers come to us less like ardent youth, pouring its energy into the great causes, than like youthful mouthpieces of their strident and belligerent elders . . .

It is foolish to hope. Since the 30th of July, 1914, nothing has happened in the area of war-policy and war-technique except for the complete and unmitigated worst. We are tired of continued disillusionment, and of the betrayal of generous anticipations. One keeps healthy in wartime not by a series of religious and political consolations that something good is coming out of it all, but by a vigorous assertion of values in which war has no part.

From *Untimely Papers*, by Randolph Bourne; B. W. Huebsch; New York, 1919.

## *Women Who Dared*
### —Emily G. Balch

When I sailed on the *Noordam* in April 1915 with the forty-two other American delegates to the International Congress of Women at The Hague, it looked doubtful to me, as it did to many others, how valuable the meeting could be made. I felt, however, that even a shadow of chance to serve the cause of peace could not to-day be refused. Never have I been so thankful for any decision. As I look at it now, the undertaking repaid all that it cost us a hundred-fold.

In this world upheaval the links that bind the peoples have been strained and snapped on every side. Of all the international gatherings that help to draw the nations together, since the fatal days of July, 1914, practically none have been convened. Science, medicine, reform, labor, religion—not one of these causes has yet been able to gather its followers from across the dividing frontiers.

Our whole experience has been an interesting one. Sunny weather and a boat steadied by a heavy load of grain made it possible for the American delegates to study and deliberate together during the voyage. We were stopped one evening under the menace of a little machine gun trained full upon us by a boat alongside while two German stowaways were taken off and searched and carried away. If the proceeding had been staged for dramatic purpose, it could not have been more effective. One prisoner, with a rope about him to prevent his escaping or falling overboard, shouted *Hoch der Kaiser, Deutschland uber Alles,* before he stepped upon the swaying ladder over the ship's side; both prisoners in the boat below us, with hands held up above their heads, were searched in front of that ever-pointing little cannon, then the sailors carried blankets and cups of hot coffee to them in the hold. All this, lighted by the ship's lanterns, was just below us as we hung over the ship's side.

At last we were allowed to proceed, but not for long. Next morning not far from Dover we were stopped again and there we were held motionless for four mortal days, almost like prisoners of war. We chafed and fretted and telegraphed and brought to bear all the influence that we could command, but there we stuck, not allowed to land, not allowed to have any one come aboard. When telegrams were possible, they were severely censored, and no indication of our whereabouts was allowed.

As the days slipped by and the date of the Congress drew nearer and people spoke of possible weeks of delay, it grew harder and harder to bear. At last, we were released as mysteriously as we had been stopped, and by Tuesday afternoon were landing in Rotterdam . . .

The Congress was too large for any of the rooms at the Peace Palace and met in a great hall at the Dierentuin. In general the mornings were given over to business and the evenings to public addresses. The programme and rules of order agreed on from the first shut out all discussions of relative national responsibility for the present war or the conduct of it or of methods of conducting future wars. We met on the common ground beyond—the ground of preparation for permanent peace.

The two fundamental planks, adherence to which was a condition of membership, were: (*a*) That international disputes should be settled by pacific means; (*b*) that the Parliamentary franchise should be extended to women . . .

What stands out most strongly among all my impressions of those thrilling and strained days at The Hague is the sense of the wonder of the beautiful spirit of the brave, self-controlled women who dared ridicule and every sort of difficulty to express a passionate human sympathy, not inconsistent with patriotism, but transcending it.

There was something profoundly stirring and inexpressibly inspiriting in the attitude of these women, many of them so deeply stricken, so closely bound to the cause of their country as they understand it, yet so full of faith in the will for good of their technical enemies and so united in their common purpose to find the principles on which permanent relations of international friendship and cooperation can ultimately be established.

There was not one clash or even danger of a clash over national differences; on every hand was the same moving consciousness of the development of a new spirit which is growing in the midst of the war as the roots of wheat grow under the drifts and tempests of winter. In the distress of mind that the war breeds in every thinking and feeling person, there is a poignant relief in finding a channel through which to work for peace. The soldiers in the hospitals say to their nurses: "We don't know why we are fighting. Can't you women help us? We can't do anything." That is the very question we are trying to answer.

From *Women at the Hague*, by Emily G. Balch, Jane Addams, Alice Hamilton; Macmillan; New York, 1916.

# *The Bitterness of Gall*

—Scott Nearing

They lied to us!

Consciously, deliberately, with premeditation and malice aforethought, they lied to us! The shepherds of the flock, the bishops of men's souls, the learned ones, the trusted ones—with fear in their hearts and a craven falsehood on their lips, they betrayed us.

Not all of them!

There were some who believed sincerely that they were in the right; there were some who knew no better; there were some who should have known better and were duped, and there were some, oh!, so very, very few, who kept the faith—all through the bitter years—and who were reviled, attacked and jailed—but we had trusted them all and most of them betrayed us.

First of all—most conspicuous and most notorious there were the newspapers—the channels of information that reached the greatest number of American people—that shamelessly and almost without exception, threw their news-columns as well as their editorial pages on the side, first of preparedness and then of war. A meeting called to advocate war would be heralded beforehand in blazing type across the page, and would be reported in elaborate detail. A meeting of the same number of people, addressed by speakers of equal ability, called to consider peace, would be treated with indifference or ignored. Every device that could be relied upon to stimulate fear and to arouse hate was resorted to—the papers seeming to vie with each other in their efforts to lash American public opinion to a spate of war fury.

My life has brought me into contact with many newspaper men. I sat in the office of one managing editor recently, discussing this very matter. At first, by way of defense, he insisted that there was only one side to the question. Then, when I asked him whether he, as a newspaper man of long experience, was willing to state that there was only one side

to the greatest public issue that had confronted the world for a generation, he protested, shamefacedly, that the owner of the paper, a business
man of prominence, was for war, "and that settles the matter as far as
this paper is concerned," he said.

The great, outstanding, bitter fact is that the newspapers, instead
of informing us, lied to us—consistently.

The newspapers were not alone. Others lied to us whose conduct
is far less excusable than that of the press. There were the scientists,
teachers, research-men—who have given their lives to study; men
charged with the sacred duty of seeking out the truth and telling it to
the people. And they lied to us. The same thing that has happened in
Europe has happened also in the United States and the college halls
and class rooms, almost without exception, have been ringing with a
note of partisanship, antagonism, and hate that is not met even in the
recruiting station or the training camp.

Children come out of the schools with an unintelligent
acceptance of war as a matter of course. Many of them come out
feeling that war is a grand, fine, splendid thing. The kind of emphasis
now laid in the American schools upon war and military training is
bad for the children and bad for the nation, nor is it of any particular value in creating the basis for successful army or military life.
It is jingoistic and militaristic in the cheapest sense in which these
terms may be used.

Then there are the churches. Here and there a minister has raised
his voice for peace and brotherhood, but his has been merely one
voice, crying in the wilderness of militaristic propaganda.

When I think that these men of the cloth, sworn servants of God
and followers of Jesus of Nazareth, the men trusted as the spiritual
advisers of the people, have been among the most ardent propagandists of hatred and bitterness, I think that I may be pardoned if I
simply remind the reader that their Leader, after commanding purity,
meekness, justice and peace, said "Blessed are ye, when men shall
revile you, and persecute you and shall say all manner of evil against

you, falsely, for my sake. Rejoice and be exceedingly glad, for so prosecuted they the prophets that were before you," and to note that, in
this immense world crisis, most of the clergy have escaped reviling
and persecution.

The mighty ones—the masters in the land—the favored, trusted
leaders of American public opinion turned militaristic, and after
denouncing German jingoism, developed a jingoism of their own,
more vicious, because more unjustifiable than that of the Germans.
And the great mass of the common people of the land, who relied
upon those elect ones and trusted them, have turned away empty, or
else with the bitterness of gall and wormwood on their lips.

Shepherdless—for the moment leaderless—the common folk of
America are turning this way and that, in an effort to extricate themselves
from the network of falsehood that has enmeshed their minds and poisoned their souls. Perhaps, in seeking they may decide with the common
people of Russia that the only sure way to have a thing done right is to do
it for themselves.

From *The Menace of Militarism,* by Scott Nearing; The Rand School of
Social Science; New York, 1917.

## *Crime Against the Individual*
### —Reinhold Niebuhr

The incurable optimists who feel called upon to find a saving virtue
in every evil and in every loss a compensation have been comforting
the world since the outbreak of the great war with the assurance that the
nations of Europe would arise purified and ennobled from the ashes of
the war's destruction. It is not difficult to share this hope, but it gives
us little comfort if we have any sense of proportion and are able to see
what the individual is paying for a possible ultimate gain to the nations.
We cannot help but think of the thousands of graves on the countryside
of Europe that are mute testimonies to the tragedy of individual life as
revealed in this war, when we are asked to accept these optimistic assur-

ances. The heroes and victims will not arise from their graves, though Europe may rise from its destruction . . .

No cause was too petty to be advanced by blood; no price in human values too high to be paid for its advancement. History is not lacking in national ventures that can be morally justified, but on the whole it presents a dismal succession of petty jealousies, often more personal than national, of cheap ambition and unrighteous pride, all of which claimed the individual as victim. To this history of individual life this war is a tragic climax, because it convinces us that the forces of history have not favored the individual as much as we thought. Modern warfare is cruel, not only because of its extravagant waste of human life, but because of its barbaric indifference to personal values . . .

What a pitiful thing it is that the Pomeranian peasant or the miner of Wales is asked to sacrifice his life in a struggle that is to determine whether future generations of Hamburg or Liverpool merchants shall wax rich from overseas commerce and the exploitation of undeveloped countries! That is the tragedy of modern nationalism—it offers modern man, with all his idealism and sensitive moral instincts, no better cause to hallow his sacrifices than the selfish and material one of securing his nation's prosperity . . .

By peculiar irony, history applies other standards to the actions of men than those of the tribunals of contemporary opinion. It sees many men as fools who were heroes in their own time. For its loyalty is not an end in itself. It looks to the ends that this virtue may serve. That is the reason posterity often honors men for their non-conformity, while contemporary opinion respects them for their conformity; that is why there are as many rebels as patriots on the honor rolls of history . . .

The willingness of men to die in struggles that effect no permanent good and leave no contribution to civilization makes the tragedy of individual life all the more pathetic. The crime of the nation against the individual is, not that it demands his sacrifices against his will, but that it claims a life of eternal significance for ends that have no eternal value.

From "The Nation's Crime Against the Individual," by Reinhold Niebuhr; *The Atlantic Monthly Magazine*; November 1916.

## *This Saturnalia of Massacre*
—E. D. Morel

### To the Belligerent Governments

Wider and wider the spread of your devastations.
Higher and higher the mountains of the dead—the dead
    because of you.
Ever more extensive the boundaries of the cemetery you
    fashion.
All the wars and all the plagues were as nought to the
    madness of your doings.
Like until the breath of a pestilence this madness sweeps
    through the plains and valleys of Europe, destroying
    in multitudes the children of men.
The weeping of women is unceasing; their tears mingle
    with the blood which flows continuously at your bidding.

What have the people done to you that you should treat
    them so?
Have they not sweated for you?
Have they not groveled to you and licked the hand that
    smote them?
Have they not stocked your Treasuries?
Have they not lacked that you might be filled?
Have not great masses of them submissively endured

poverty, squalor and want while you prated to them
of Liberty and Equality and Patriotism and Empire?

Continuously, cynically, deliberately, you have sacrificed
them to your secret maneuvers and your sordid quarrels.
You murder the body and you putrefy the mind.
For you are all guilty—every one.
One and all you prepared for this saturnalia of massacre.

From *Truth and the War*, by E. D. Morel; National Labour Press;
London, 1916.

# Chapter Seven:

# Mourn

Writers, along with the inarticulate and illiterate, would have mourning, deep mourning, thrust upon them during the war; talent with words brought no immunity when it came to loss. At least ten million soldiers died in the trenches; boys from the combatant nations born between 1892 and 1895, ages 19–22 when the fighting started, had their ranks reduced by over 35 percent. Their survivors would mourn them the rest of their lives. "Every day one meets saddened women, with haggard faces and lethargic movements, and one dare not ask about their husband or son," Beatrice Webb wrote in her diary in 1918. Writers, even the most illustrious, joined the ranks of the bereaved, having lost sons, brothers, nephews, colleagues, students, protégés, lovers, friends.

It's surprising then, reading the books they wrote while the war was still in progress, how few did their mourning in print. They wrote of tanks, trenches, cannon, strategy and tactics, political ramifications, moral issues, even the sick and wounded, but few wrote descriptions of the dead, especially *their* dead, and hardly any could bring themselves to describe their feelings of loss while the blow was still fresh. It seems, looking back on this now, as if they suffered a reversal of the usual order of things; they could write movingly of the larger tragedy, murder en masse, but the death of a single individual was too much for them to bear.

This reticence, in a confessional age like ours, can be hard to understand. Was the death of a friend or relation too painful for words, straining the limits of what even a Nobel Prize winner could do with language? Was it better, literarily speaking, to wait until later, when the war ended and perspective could be gained? Better to keep a stiff literary upper lip while everyone else suffered in silence? Had the long years of peace and security, writers' own privileged status, ill equipped them to write of sorrow?

When the dead appear, it's often as nameless bodies that move the writers to pity, but are too anonymous to mourn. Those going on VIP tours of the trenches did not often see corpses, and when they did, their reactions could be coldly impersonal. Edith Wharton, allowed farther into the front lines than ordinary visitors, spots "halfway between cliff and cliff, a gray uniform huddled in a dead heap," and feels, not sadness, not grief, but "relief to find it was after all a tangible enemy hidden over there across the meadow."

The ambulance drivers and war correspondents, writers like Henry Beston and Richard Harding Davis, saw more of death, and wrote about it with more specificity. Poets like Jean Cocteau, trying to make sense of the massacre, retreated (and, reading it now, it can seem like retreat) to the formalism of classic poetry. Writers like Katherine Mansfield, unable to deal with their losses publicly, wrote about them movingly in the privacy of their diaries, which were published only once the war was over.

In the end, their reactions were like those of everyone else whose loved ones died. Shock, horror, incomprehension, sadness, anger, fantasies of revenge. Wells's Mr. Britling experiences them all in one overwhelming wave when his son is killed, and whatever emotions he is spared are left for his young widowed friend Letty to express with a passion and intensity that can still burn when you read it today.

There is one aspect of the mourning writers did do in print that is striking, particularly among the British writers. The dead in their books that are actually named, mourned with specificity, are all upper-class officers, or, at the minimum, brilliant young graduates of Oxford and Cambridge. John Buchan, in his long bestselling book on the Somme, gives the specific name of only one of the dead hundred thousands, the son of the prime minister and his friend.

This kind of discrimination, while not particularly praiseworthy, is at least understandable. Writers, often enjoying a privileged position inside the elite, would know mostly officers, their prewar friends, or students; and with the war being particularly dangerous for junior officers, many of these would die. Enlisted men from Glasgow or York would not have novelist friends to mourn them, at least not until the 1920s, when the soldier-writers published their own memoirs and talked about the men they led.

You get the feeling, reading those elegies we do have, that writers were waiting for the war to end to do their serious mourning, until they had time—if they would ever have time—to make sense of it all. For now, the pain was too raw, the suffering too enormous. "The scarlet doom," Belgian poet Emile Verhaeren called this mood, while the war was yet in progress, "the scarlet doom hurled over a grave-strewn world." Few writers could lift it.

George Santayana's Spanish-Catholic background made him an outsider at prewar Harvard, and he left for Europe before the war started. He was fifty-two, and had a reputation as an urbane, skeptical philosopher and novelist, enhanced by his widely praised *The Last Puritan*. He's in Bartlett's for his quote, "Only the dead have seen the last of war," and, more famously, "Those who cannot remember the past are condemned to repeat it."

Bertrand Russell, in his autobiography, remembered Santayana's wartime attitude: "He had not enough respect for the human race to care whether it destroyed itself or not."

When Edith Wharton sent out invitations to the leading authors of the day to contribute to her fund-raising *The Book of the Homeless,* Jean

Cocteau, at twenty-three, was by far the youngest writer asked. By the time the war started, his reputation for a genius kind of self-absorption was already immense, though it wasn't until after the Armistice that his novels, poems, paintings, and films made him one of the leading lights of the French avant-garde. Today he's remembered mostly for his movie *La Belle et la Bete,* and his play *La Voix Humaine.*

A portrait of him is included in *The Book of the Homeless,* an "unpublished crayon sketch" by the Russian artist and Diaghilev set designer Leon Bakst. No less military figure could be imagined, with his finely chiseled yet delicate features, the open neck of his tunic, and his doe-like, curiously cold eyes, topped off by a Bohemian shock of wavy hair. A recruiting board would have taken one look at him and thrown up their hands; though, like so many other writers, he put in a shift, a short shift, as an ambulance driver in Belgium. (He was soon dismissed and sent home in disgrace, though biographies are vague on exactly why.) "How the Young Men died in Hellas" is very typical of his output at this stage of his career, with his intense interest in all things Greek.

There were few accounts written by a father about his son's death actually published while the war was being fought, which makes Harry Lauder's, taken from his *A Minstrel in France,* so moving. Lauder was in his fifties when the war started, at the height of his reputation as a beloved Scottish music hall comedian and singer, famous for his kilt, his crooked walking stick, his broad Scots dialect, and songs like "Roamin' in the Gloamin'."

If you go online, you can see an eight-minute film clip of Lauder and Charlie Chaplin hamming it up before the cameras in Hollywood during the war—Lauder more than holds his own with the Little Tramp.

Lauder's son John was a captain in the Argyll and Sutherland Highlanders, wounded twice, and twice sent back to France, only to die on the Somme in 1916.

Lauder all but collapsed under the pain of this, and it was only by devoting himself to entertaining the troops in France that he was able to find solace. (He was knighted for this after the war.) He performed close to the trenches and, when given the chance, took a measure of revenge.

> "I was swept by an almost irresistible desire to be fighting myself. If I could only play my part! If I could fire even a single shot—if I, with my own hands, could do that much against those who had killed my boy! And then, incredulously, I heard the words in my ear. It was the major."
>
> 'Would you like to try a shot, Harry?' he asked.
>
> They showed me my place. After all, it was the simplest of matters to fire even the biggest of guns. I had but to pull a lever. I was thrilled and excited as I had never been in all my life before.
>
> 'All ready? Fire!'
>
> It pleases me to think that the long snouted engine of war propelled that shell, under my guiding hand, with unwonted accuracy and effectiveness! Perhaps I was childish, to feel as I did; indeed, I have no doubt that was so. But I dinna care!"

It wasn't just soldiers who suffered in France during the war. Katherine Mansfield, the talented New Zealand short-story writer, had gone there, of all places, for her health; her description of her lonely, desperate battle against tuberculosis and crushing solitude makes for grim reading even today. She wasn't yet thirty, but already life was proving too much for her, and the last blow was the death of her beloved younger brother Leslie, who died while serving in the trenches as a British officer. It was his death that turned her fiction to reminiscences of their idyllic childhood together back in

New Zealand. Her diary wasn't published until after the war, but includes these poignant passages taken from 1915.

Paul Claudel was one of those characteristically French figures who combined literature with a career in the foreign service. Forty-six when war broke out, he was assigned to a diplomatic post in South America and helped ensure the delivery of vital foodstuffs to France; after the war, he briefly served as ambassador to the United States. His literary reputation was analogous to T. S. Eliot's in England—a politically conservative poet whose conversion to Catholicism is commemorated by a bronze plaque set in the floor of Notre Dame in Paris.

W. H. Auden would later take Claudel to task for his militaristic opinions in a famous stanza, though one suspects it was less for reasons of politics than it was for convenience of rhyme.

"Time that with this strange excuse
Pardoned Kipling and his views,
And will pardon Paul Claudel,
Pardons him for writing well."

## *And the Bullet Won*
### —Richard Harding Davis

The waste of human life in this war is so enormous, so far beyond our daily experience, that disasters less appalling are much easier to understand. The loss of three people in an automobile accident comes nearer home than the fact that at the battle of Sézanne thirty thousand men were killed. Few of us are trained to think of men in such numbers—certainly not of dead men in such numbers. We have seen thirty thousand men together only during the world's series or at the championship football matches. To get an idea of the waste of this war we must imagine all of the spectators at a football match between Yale and Harvard suddenly stricken dead. We must think of all the wives, children, friends affected by the loss of those thirty thousand, and we must multiply those thirty thousand by hundreds and imagine these hundreds of thousands lying dead in Belgium, in Alsace-Lorraine, and within ten miles of Paris. After the Germans were repulsed at Meaux and at Sézanne the dead of both armies were so many that they lay intermingled in layers three and four deep. They were buried in long pits and piled on top of each other like cigars in a box. Lines of fresh earth so long that you mistook them for trenches were in reality graves. Some bodies lay for days uncovered until they lost all human semblance. They were so many you ceased to regard them even as corpses. They had become just a part of the waste, a part of the shattered walls, uprooted trees, and fields ploughed by shells. What once had been your fellow men were only bundles of clothes, swollen and shapeless, like scarecrows stuffed with rags, polluting the air.

Each one had once been physically fit or he would not have been passed to the front; and those among them who are officers are finely bred, finely educated, or they would not be officers. But each matched his good health, his good breeding, and knowledge against a broken piece of shell or steel bullet, and the shell or bullet won.

From *With the Allies*, by Richard Harding Davis; Charles Scribner's Sons; New York, 1918.

## *He Loved His Youth*
### —John Buchan

In the Guards' advance, among many other gallant and distinguished officers, there fell one whose death was, in a peculiar sense, a loss to his country and the future. Lieutenant Raymond Asquith, of the Grenadier Guards, the eldest son of the British Prime Minister, died while leading his men through the fatal enfilading fire from the corner of Ginchy village. In this war the gods took toll of every rank and class. Few generals and statesmen in the Allied nations but had to mourn intimate bereavements. But the death of Raymond Asquith had a poignancy apart from his birth and position, and it may be permitted to one of his oldest friends to pay his tribute to a heroic memory.

A scholar of the ripe Elizabethan type, a brilliant wit, an accomplished poet, a sound lawyer—these things were borne lightly, for his greatness was not in his attainments but in himself. He had always a curious aloofness towards mere worldly success. He loved the things of the mind for their own sake—good books, good talk, the company of old friends—and the rewards of common ambition seemed to him too trivial for a man's care. He was of the spending type in life, giving freely of the riches of his nature, but asking nothing in return. His carelessness of personal gain, his inability to trim or truckle, and his aloofness from the facile acquaintances of the modern world made him incomprehensible to many, and his high fastidiousness gave him a certain air of coldness. Most noble in presence, and with every grace of voice and manner, he moved among men like a being of another race, scornfully detached from the common struggle; and only his friends knew the warmth and loyalty of his soul.

At the outbreak of war he joined a Territorial battalion, from which he was later transferred to the Grenadiers. More than most men he hated the loud bellicosities of politics, and he had never done homage to the deities of the crowd. His critical sense made him chary of enthusiasm, and it was no sudden sentimental fervour that swept him into the Army. He saw his duty, and, though it meant the shattering of every taste and interest, he did it joyfully, and did it to the full. For a little he had a post on the Staff, but applied to be sent back to his battalion, since he wished no privilege. In the Guards he was extraordinarily happy, finding the same kind of light-hearted and high-spirited companionship which had made Oxford for him a place of delectable memories. He was an admirable battalion officer, and thought seriously of taking up the Army as a profession after the war, for he had all the qualities which go to the making of a good soldier.

In our long roll of honour no nobler figure will find a place. He was a type of his country at its best—shy of rhetorical professions, austerely self-respecting, one who hid his devotion under a mask of indifference, and, when the hour came, revealed it only in deeds. Many gave their all for the cause, but few, if any, had so much to give. He loved his youth, and his youth has become eternal.

From *The Battle of the Somme*, by John Buchan; Grosset & Dunlap; New York, 1917.

# *Demons of the Whirlwind*
## —George Santayana

### The Undergraduate Killed In Battle

Sweet as the lawn beneath his sandalled tread
Or the scarce rippled stream beneath his oar,
For its still, channelled current constant more,
His life was, and the few blithe words he said.

One or two poets read he, and reread;
One or two friends in boyish ardour wore
Next to his heart, incurious of the lore
Dodonian woods might murmur o'er his head.

Ah, demons of the whirlwind, have a care
What, trumpeting your triumphs, ye undo!
The earth once won, begins your long despair
That never, never is his bliss for you.
He breathed betimes this clement island air
And in unwitting lordship saw the blue.

From *The Book of the Homeless*, edited by Edith Wharton; Charles Scribner's Sons; New York, 1916.

## *All Four Lie Buried on the Western Front*
—Gilbert Murray

Four New College scholars of exceptional intellect and character entered the university in 1905—Arthur Heath, Leslie Hunter, R. C. Woodhead, and Phillip Brown. And now all four lie buried on the Western Front. Each had his special character and ways and aims; but to one who knew them well, there comes from all of them a certain uniform impression, the impression of an extraordinary and yet unconscious high-mindedness. It is not merely that they were clever, hard-working, conscientious, honourable, lovers of poetry and beauty; the sort of men who could never be suspected of evading a duty, or, say, voting for their own interest rather than the common good. It was, I think, that the standards which had become the normal guides of life to them were as a matter of plain fact spiritual standards, and not of the world nor the flesh.

Such language may sound strained as applied to a group of men who were earning their living among us in perfectly ordinary ways, as teachers, writers, doctors, civil servants, some of them in the law or in business; but it implies nothing strained or specially high-strung in the quality of their daily lives. There is always a religion of some sort at the root of every man's living. Every man is either willing or not willing to sacrifice himself to something which he feels to be higher than himself, though if he is sensible, he will probably not talk much about it. And men of conscience and self-mastery are fully as human, as varied, and as interesting as any weaklings or picturesque scoundrels are.

Perhaps the first thing that struck one about Arthur Heath was his gentleness and modesty. "It was fine," says one of his superior officers, "to see a first-rate intellect such as his applied to a practical matter that was strange of him. And he was so modest about himself, and never dreams how we all admired him." The last words strike one as exactly true. Another quality was his affectionateness, or rather the large space that affection occupied in his mind. Affection, indeed, is too weak a term to describe the feeling that seems to glow behind the words of his letters home; for instance, the beautiful letter to his mother, written on July 11, about the prospect of death. He was a devoted son and brother, interested in every detail of home life, and not forgetting family birthdays. And the same quality pervaded much of his relations towards friends and acquaintances. He was the sort of man whom people confide in, and consult in their troubles.

Heath was a bold thinker; he held clear opinions of his own on all sorts of subjects. He often differed from other people, especially people in authority. Yet he was never for a moment bitter or conceited or anxious to contradict. There was no scorn about him; and his irrepressible sense of fun, so far from being unkind, had an element of positive affection in it.

In comparing him with other men who have fought and fallen in the war, I feel that one of his most marked characteristics was his instinct for understanding. In the midst of strong feeling and intense action his quiet, penetrating intelligence was always at work. Even at the front, where most men become absorbed in their immediate job, he was full of strategical problems, of the war as a whole. His courage was like that of the Brave Man in Aristotle, who knows that a danger is dangerous, and fears it, but goes through with it because he knows that he ought. He liked to understand what he was doing. He was ready, of course, to obey without question, but he would then know that he was obeying without question. He was ready to give his life and all the things that he valued in life, his reading and music and philosophy, but he liked to know what he was giving them for.

After his first wound: "Fear is a very odd thing. When I was up in the trenches about thirty yards from the enemy, I got over the parapet and crawled out to examine a mine-crater without anything worse than a certain amount of excitement. But when we are back here in Brigade Reserve and the shells start screaming over, I feel thoroughly afraid and there is no denying it."

He never groused about hardships, nor yet about the evils of war. The war was something he had to carry through, and he would make the best of it until it killed him.

On October 8, the end came. It was Heath's twenty-eighth birthday. The battalion held a series of trenches in front of Vermelles, across the Hulluch road, in that stretch of ghastly and shell-tortured black country which we now think of as the Loos Salient. For the whole day there had been an intense German bombardment, tearing and breaking the trenches, and presumably intended to lead up to a general infantry attack. It was decided, in order to prevent this plan developing, that the Sixth Battalion should attempt an attack on the enemy at "Gun Trench." This was a very difficult enterprise in itself, and doubly so to troops already worn by a long and fierce bombardment. The charge was made by "A" Company about 6:30 and beaten back. It was followed by a series of bombing attacks, for which a constant supply of bombs had to be kept up across the open. It was during this work that Arthur Heath fell, shot through the neck. He spoke once, to say "Don't trouble about me," and died almost immediately.

His platoon sergeant wrote to his parents: "It will console you to know that a braver man never existed."

One after another, a sacrifice greater than can be counted, they go; and will go until the due end is won.

At the close of the Michaelmas Term of 1914 there was a memorial service at New College, as in other colleges, for members who had fallen in the war. It seemed a long list even then, though it was scarcely at its beginning. And those who attended the service will not forget the sight of the white-haired warden, full of blameless years, kneeling before the altar on the bare stones, and praying that it might be granted to us, the survivors, to live such lives as these young men who had gone before us. His words interpreted, I think, the unconscious feeling of most of those who heard him. It certainly changes the whole aspect of the world, even to a man whose life is advanced and his character somewhat set, when the men who were his intimate friends are proved to have in them, not merely the ordinary virtues and pleasantnesses of common life, but something high and resplendent which one associates with the stories of old saints or heroes; still more when there is burned into him the unforgettable knowledge that men whom he loved have died for him.

From *Faith, War, and Policy*, by Gilbert Murray; Houghton Mifflin; Boston, 1917.

## *Eyes Lit with Risk*
—Jean Cocteau

How the Young Men Died in Hellas

Antigone went wailing to the dust
She reverenced not the face of Death like these
To who it came as no enfeebling peace
But a command relentless and august.

These grieved not the beauty of the morn,
Nor that the sun was on the ripening flower;
Smiling they faced the sacrificial hour,
Blithe nightingales against the fatal thorn.

They grieved not for the theatre's high-banked tiers,
Where restlessly the noisy crowd leans over,
With laughter and with jostling, to discover
The blue and green of chaffing charioteers.

Nor for the fluted shafts, the carven stones
Of that sole city, bright above the seas,
Where young men met to talk with Socrates

Or toss the ivory bones.
Their eyes were lit with tumult and with risk,
But when they felt Death touch their hands and pass
They followed, dropping on the garden grass
    The parchment and the disk.

It seemed no wrong to them that they just go.
They laid their lives down as the poet lays
On the white page the poem that shall praise
His memory when the hand that wrote is low.

Erect they stood and, festally arrayed,
Serenely waited the transforming hour,
Softly as Hyacinth slid from youth to flower,
Or the shade of Cyparis to a cypress shade.
They wept not for the lost Ionian days,
Nor liberty, nor household love and laughter,
Nor the long leaden slumber that comes after
    Life's little wakefulness.

Fearless they sought the land no sunsets see,
Whence our weak pride shrinks back, and would return,
Knowing a pinch of ashes in an urn
Henceforth our garden and our house shall be.

Young men, my brothers, you whose morning skies
I have seen the deathly lassitude invade,
Oh, how you suffered! How you were afraid!
What death-damp hands you locked about your eyes!

You, so insatiably athirst to spend
The young desires in your hearts abloom,
How could you think the desert was your doom,

The waterless fountain and the endless end?

You yearned not for the face of love, grown dim,
But only fought your anguished bones to wrest
From the Black Angel crouched upon your breast,
Who scanned you ere he led you down with him.

From *The Book of the Homeless*, edited by Edith Wharton; translated
by Edith Wharton; Charles Scribner's Sons; New York, 1916.

## *Drop Drop Drop of Blood*
### —Henry Beston

Montauville was the last habitable village of the region. The dirty,
mud-spattered village was caught between the leathery sweep of two
wooded ridges. Though less than a mile from the first German line, the
village, because of its protection from shells by a spur of the Bois-le-
Pretre, was in remarkably good condition; the only building to show
conspicuous damage being the church, whose steeple had been twice
struck. Here and there, among the uncultivated fields of those who
had fled, were the green fields of some one who had stayed. A woman
of seventy still kept open her grocery shop; it was extraordinarily dirty,
full of buzzing flies, and smelled of spilt wine.

"Why did you stay?" I asked her.

"Because I did not want to leave the village. Of course, my
daughter wanted me to come to Dijon. Imagine me in Dijon, I,
who have been to Nancy only once! A fine figure I should make in
Dijon in my sabots!"

"And you are not afraid of the shells?"

"Oh, I should be afraid of them if I ever went out in the street. But
I never leave my shop."

And so she stayed, selling the three staples of the French front,
Camembert cheese, Norwegian sardines, and cakes of chocolate.
But Montauville was far from safe. It was there that I first saw a

man killed. I had been talking to a sentry, a small young fellow of twenty-one or two, with yellow hair and gray-blue eyes full of weariness. He complained of a touch of jaundice, and wished heartily that the whole affair—meaning the war in general—was finished. He was very anxious to know if the Americans thought the Boches were going to win. Some vague idea of winning the war just to get even with the Boches seemed to be in his mind. I assured him that American opinion was optimistic in regard to the chances of the Allies, and strolled away.

Hardly had I gone ten feet, when a "seventy-seven" shell, arriving without warning, went Zip-bang, and, turning to crouch to the wall, I saw the sentry crumple up in the mud. It was as if he were a rubber effigy of a man blown up with air, and some one had suddenly ripped the envelope. His rifle fell from him, and he, bending from the waist, leaned faced down into the mud. I was the first to get to him. The young, discontented face was full of the gray street mud, there was mud in the hollows of the eyes, in the mouth, in the fluffy mustache. A chunk of the shell had ripped open the left breast to the heart. Down his sleeve, as down a pipe, flowed a hasty drop, drop, drop of blood that mixed with the mire.

From *A Volunteer Poilu*, by Henry Beston; Houghton Mifflin; Boston, 1916.

## *Of All the Days in My Life the Most Terrible*
### —Harry Lauder

I did not go to sleep for a long time. It was New Year's, and I lay thinking of my boy, and wondering what this year would bring him. It was early in the morning before I slept. And it seemed to me that I had scarce been asleep at all when there came a pounding at the door, loud enough to rouse the heaviest sleeper there ever was.

My heart almost stopped. There must be something serious indeed for them to be rousing me so early. I rushed to the door, and there was a porter, holding out a telegram. I took it and tore it open. And I knew why I had felt as I had the day before. I shall never forget what I read:

"Captain John Lauder killed in action, December 28. Official. War Office."

He had been killed four days before I knew it! And yet—I had known. Let no one ever tell me again that there is nothing in presentment. Why else had I been so sad and uneasy in my mind? Why else, all through that Sunday, had it been so impossible for me to take comfort in what was said to cheer me? Some warning had come to me, some sense that all was not well.

Realization came to me slowly. I sat and stared at that slip of paper, that had come to me like the breath of doom. Dead! Dead these four days! I was never to see the light of his eyes again. I was never to hear that laugh of his. I had looked on my boy for the last time. Could it be true? Ah, I knew it was! And it was for this moment that I had been waiting, that we had all been waiting, ever since we sent John away to fight for his country and do his part. I think we had all felt that it must come. We had all known that it was too much to hope that he should be one of those to be spared.

The black despair that had been hovering over me for hours closed down now and enveloped all my senses. Everything was unreal. For a time I was quite numb. For then, as I began to realize and to visualize what it was to mean in my life that my boy was dead there came a great pain. The iron of realization slowly seared every word of that curt telegram upon my heart. I said it to myself, over and over again. And I whispered to myself, as my thoughts took form, over and over, the one terrible word: "Dead!"

I felt that for me everything had come to an end with the reading of that dire message. It seemed to me that for me the board of life was black and blank. For me there was no past and there could be no future. Everything had been swept away, erased, by one sweep of the hand of a cruel fate. Oh, there was a past though! And it was in that past that I began to delve. It was made up of every memory I had of my boy. I fell at once to remembering him. I clutched at every memory, as if I must grasp them and make sure of them, lest they be taken from me as well as the hope of seeing him again that the telegram had forever snatched away.

I would have been destitute indeed then. It was as if I must fix in my mind the way he had been wont to look, and recall to my ears every tone of his voice, every trick of his speech. There was something left of him that I must keep, I knew, even then, at all costs, if I was to be able to bear his loss at all.

There was a vision of him before my eyes. My bonnie Highland laddie, brave and strong in his kilt and the uniform of his country, going out to his death with a smile on his face. And there was another vision that came up now, unbidden. It was a vision of him lying stark and cold upon the battlefield, the mud on his uniform. And when I saw that vision I was like a man gone mad.

But God came to me, and slowly His peace entered my soul. And He made me see, as in a vision, that some things that I had said and that I had believed, were not so. He made me know, and I learned, straight from Him, that our boy has not been taken from us forever as I had said to myself so often since that telegram had come.

He is gone from this life, but he is waiting for us beyond this life. He is waiting beyond this life and this world of wicked war and wanton cruelty and slaughter. And we shall come, some day, his mother and I, to the place where he is waiting for us, and we shall all be as happy there as we were on this earth in the happy days before the war.

My eyes will rest upon his face. I will hear his fresh young voice again as he sees me and cries out his greeting. I know what he will say. He will spy me, and his voice will ring out as it used to do. "Hello, Dad!" he will call, as he sees me. And I will feel the grip of his young, strong arms about me, just as in the happy days before that day that is of all the days in my life the most terrible and the most hateful in my memory—the day when they told me he had been killed.

From *A Minstrel in France*, by Harry Lauder; Hearst's International Library; New York, 1918.

# *He Wanted Me to Write*
## —Katherine Mansfield

*November, Bandol, France. Brother.* I think I have known for a long time that life was over for me, but I never realized it or acknowledged it until my brother died. Yes, though he is lying in the middle of a little wood in France and I am still walking upright and feeling the sun and the wind from the sea, I am just as much dead as he is. The only possible value that anything can have for me is that it should put me in mind of something that happened or was when he was alive.

"Do you remember, Katie?" I hear his voice in the trees and flowers, in scents and light and shadow. I feel I have a duty to perform to the lovely time when we were both alive. I want to write about it, and he wanted me to. We talked it over in my little top room in London. I said: I will put on the front page: To my brother, Leslie Heron Beauchamp. Very well: it shall be done . . .

*Wednesday. (December.)* To-day I am hardening my heart. I am walking all around my heart and building up the defences. I do not mean to leave a loophole even for a tuft of violets to grow in. Give me a hard heart, O Lord! Lord, harden thou my heart!

*February 14.* Dear brother, as I jot these notes, I am speaking to you. Yes, it is to you. Each time I take up my pen *you* are with me. You are mine. You are my playfellow, my brother, and we shall range all over our country together. You are more vividly with me now this moment than if you were alive and I were writing to you from a short distance away. As you speak my name, the name you call me by that I love so—"Katie!"—your lip lifts in a smile—you believe in me, you know. In every word I write and in every place I visit I carry you with me.

*February 15.* Love, I will not fail. If I write every day faithfully a little record of how I have kept faith with you—that is what I must do. Now you are back with me. You are stepping forward, one hand in your pocket. My brother, my little boy brother! He never, never must be unhappy. Now I will come quite close to you, take your hand, and we shall tell this story to each other.

From *Journal of Katherine Mansfield*, by Katherine Mansfield; Alfred A. Knopf, New York, 1926.

## *A Girl in a Pinafore*
### —H. G. Wells

And then as if it were something that every one in the Dower House had been waiting for, came the message that Hugh had been killed.

The telegram was brought up by a girl in a pinafore instead of the boy of the old dispensation, for boys now were doing the work of youths and youths the work of the men who had gone to the war.

Mr. Britling was standing at the front door; he had been surveying the late October foliage, touched by the warm light of the afternoon, when the messenger appeared. He opened the telegram, hoping as he had hoped when he opened any telegram since Hugh had gone to the front that it would not contain the exact words he read; that it would say wounded, that at the worst it would say "missing," that perhaps it might even tell of some pleasant surprise, a brief return to home such as the last letter had foreshadowed. He read the final, unqualified statement, the terse regrets. He stood quite still for a moment or so, staring at the words . . .

He had an absurd conviction that this ought to be a sixpenny telegram. The thing worried him. He wanted to give the brat sixpence, and he had only threepence and a shilling, and he didn't know what to do and his brain couldn't think. It would be a shocking thing to give her a shilling, and he couldn't somehow give just coppers for so important a thing as Hugh's death.

She stared at him, inquiring, incredulous. "Is there a reply, Sir, please?"

"No," he said, "that's for you. All of it . . . This is a peculiar sort of telegram . . . It's news of importance . . ."

As he said this he met her eyes, and had a sudden persuasion that she knew exactly what it was the telegram had told him, and that she was shocked at the gala-like treatment of such terrible news. He hesitated, feeling that he had to say something else, that he was socially inadequate, and then he decided that at any cost he must get his face away from her staring eyes. She made no movement to turn away. She seemed to be taking him in, recording him, for repetition, greedily, with every fibre of her being.

He stepped past her into the garden, and instantly forgot about her existence . . .

He had been thinking of this possibility for the last few weeks almost continuously, and yet now that it had come to him he felt that he had never thought about it before, that he must go off alone by himself to envisage this monstrous and terrible fact, without distraction or interruption.

He saw his wife coming down the alley between the roses.

He was wrenched by emotions as odd and unaccountable as the emotions of adolescence. He had exactly the same feeling now that he had had when in his boyhood some unpleasant admission had to be made to his parents. He felt he could not go through a scene with her yet, that he could not endure the task of telling her, of being observed. He turned abruptly to his left. He walked away as if he had not seen her, across his lawn toward the little summer-house upon a knoll that commanded a high road. She called to him, but he did not answer . . .

He would not look towards her, but for a time all his senses were alert to hear whether she followed him. Safe in the summer-house he could glance back.

It was all right. She was going into the house.

He drew the telegram from his pocket again furtively, almost guiltily, and re-read it. He turned it over and read it again . . .

*Killed.*

Then his own voice, hoarse and strange to his ears, spoke his thoughts.

"My God! how unutterably silly . . . Why did I let him go? Why did I let him go?"

Suddenly his boy was all about him, playing, climbing the cedars, twisting miraculously about the lawn on a bicycle, discoursing gravely upon his future, lying on the grass, breathing very hard and drawing preposterous caricatures. Once again they walked side by side up and down—it was athwart this very spot—talking gravely but rather shyly . . .

And here they had stood a little awkwardly, before the boy went in to say good-bye to his stepmother and go off with his father to the station . . .

"I will work to-morrow again," whispered Mr. Britling, "but to-night—to-night . . . To-night is yours . . . Can you hear me, can you hear? Your father . . . who had counted on you . . ."

He went into the far corner of the hockey paddock, and there he moved about for a while and then stood for a long time holding the fence with both hands and staring blankly into the darkness. At last he turned away, and went stumbling and blundering towards the rose garden. A spray of creeper tore his face and distressed him. He thrust it aside fretfully, and it scratched his hand. He made his way to the seat in the arbour, and sat down and whispered to himself, and then became very still with his arm upon the back of the seat and his head upon his arm.

From *Mr. Britling Sees It Through*, by H. G. Wells; Macmillan; New York, 1917.

## *Tears are Difficult for a Man to Shed*
### —Paul Claudel

#### The Precious Blood

Oh, what if Thou, that a cup of water promisest
The illimitable sea,
Thou, Lord, dost also thirst?
Hast Thou not said, our blood shall quench Thee best

And first
  Of any drink there be?

If then there be such virtue in it, Lord,
Ah, let us prove it now!
And, save by seeing it at Thy footstool poured,
  How, Lord—oh, how?

If it indeed be precious and like gold,
As Thou has taught,
Why hoard it? There's no wealth in gems unsold,
  Nor joy in gems unbought.

Our sins are great, we know it; and we know
We must redeem our guilt;
Even so.
But tears are difficult for a man to shed,
And here is our blood poured out for France instead
  To do with as Thou will!

Take it, O Lord! And make it Thine indeed,
Void of all lien and fee,
Nought else we ask of Thee;
But if Thou needst our Love as we Thy Justice need,
  Great must Thine hunger be!

From *The Book of the Homeless*, edited by Edith Wharton; translated by Edith Wharton; Charles Scribner's Sons; New York, 1916.

## *I Lay On that Brown Mound*
### —Harry Lauder

One of the officers at Albert was looking at me in a curiously intent fashion. I noticed that. And so on he came over to me.

"Where do you go next, Harry?" he asked me. His voice was keenly sympathetic, and his eyes and his manner were very grave.

"To a place called Ovilliers," I said.

"So I thought," he said. He put out his hand, and I gripped it hard. "I know, Harry. I know exactly where you are going, and I will send a man with you to act as your guide, who knows the spot you want to reach."

I couldn't answer him. I was too deeply moved. For Ovilliers is the spot where my son, Captain John Lauder, lies in his soldier's grave. That grave had been, of course, from the very first, the final, the ultimate object of my journey.

And so a private soldier joined our party as guide, and we took to the road again. The Bapaume road it was—a famous highway, bitterly contested, savagely fought for. There was no talking in our car. I certainly was not disposed to chat, and I suppose that sympathy for my feelings, and my glumness, stilled the tongues of my companions. And, at any rate, we had not traveled far when the car ahead of us stopped, and the soldier from Albert stepped into the road and waited for me.

"I will show you the place now, Mr. Lauder," he said, quietly. So we left the cars standing in the road, and set out across a field that, like all the fields in that vicinity, had been ripped and torn by shell-fire. All about us were little brown mounds, each with a white wooden cross upon it. June was out that day in full bloom. All over the valley, thickly sown with white crosses, wild flowers in rare profusion, and thickly matted, luxuriant grasses, and all the little shrubs that God Himself looks after were growing bravely in the sunlight.

It was a mournful journey, but, in some strange way, the peaceful beauty of the day brought comfort to me. And my own grief was altered by the vision of the grief that had come to so many others. Those crosses, stretching away as far as my eye could reach, attested to the fact that it was not I alone who had suffered and lost. And, in the presence of so many evidences of grief and desolation a private grief sank into its true proportions. It was no less keen, the agony of thought of my boy was as sharp as ever. But I knew that he was only one, and that I was only one father. And there were so many like him—and so many like me, God help us all!

I do not think we exchanged a word as we crossed that field. So we came, when we were, perhaps, half a mile from the Bapaume road, to a slight eminence, a tiny hill that rose from the field. A little military cemetery crowned it. Here the graves were set in ordered rows, and there was a fence around them, to keep them apart, and to mark that spot as holy ground, until the end of time. Five hundred British boys lie sleeping in that small acre of silence, and among them is my own laddie. There the fondest hopes of my life, the hopes that sustained and cheered me through many years, lie buried.

The soldier pointed to one brown mound in a row of brown mounds that looked alike, each like the other. Then he drew away. And so I went alone to my boy's grave, and flung myself down upon the warm, friendly earth. My memories of that moment are not very clear, but I think that for a few minutes I was utterly spent, that my collapse was complete.

He was such a good boy!

As I lay there on that brown mound, under the June sun, all that he had been, and all that he had meant to me and to his mother came rushing back afresh to my memory, opening anew my wounds of grief. I thought of him as a baby, and as a wee laddie, beginning to run around and talk to us. I thought of him in every phase and bit of his life, and of the friends that we had been, he and I!

And as I lay there, as I look back on it now, I can think of but the one desire that ruled and moved me. I wanted to reach my arms down into the dark grave, and clasp my boy tightly to my breast, and kiss him.

How long did I lie there? I do not know. And how I found the strength at last to drag myself to my feet and away from that spot, the dearest and the saddest spot on earth to me, God only knows. But I am going back to France to visit again and again that grave where he lies buried. And meanwhile the wild flowers and the long grasses and all the little shrubs will keep watch and ward over him there, and over all the other brave soldiers who lie hard by.

From *A Minstrel in France*, by Harry Lauder; Hearst's International Library; New York, 1918.

## *And I Will Murder Some German*
—H. G. Wells

Cissie and Letty had been sitting in silence before the fire. She had been knitting—she knitted very badly—and Cissie had been pretending to read, and had been watching her furtively. Cissie eyed the slow, toilsome growth of the slack woolwork for a time, and the touch of angry effort in every stroke of the knitting needles.

"Poor Letty!" she said very softly. "Suppose after all he is dead?"

Letty met her with a pitiless stare.

"He is a prisoner," she said. "Isn't that enough? Why do you jab at me by saying that? A wounded prisoner. Isn't that enough despicable trickery for God even to play on Teddy—our Teddy? To the very last moment he shall not be dead. Until the war is over. Until six months after the war . . .

"I will tell you why, Cissie . . ."

She leant across the table and pointed her remarks with her knitting needles, speaking in a tone of reasonable remonstrance. "You see," she said, "if people like Teddy are to be killed, then all our ideas that life is meant for honesty and sweetness and happiness are wrong, and this world is just a place of devils; just a dirty cruel hell. Getting born would be getting damned. And so one must not give way to that idea, however much it may seem likely that he is dead . . .

"You see, if he *is* dead, then Cruelty is the Law, and some one must pay me for his death . . . Some one must pay me . . . I shall wait for six months after the war, dear, and then I shall go off to Germany and learn my way about there. And I will murder some German. Not just a common German, but a German who belongs to the guilty kind. A sacrifice. It ought, for instance, to be comparatively easy to kill some of the children of the Crown Prince or some of the Bavarian princes. I shall prefer German children. I shall sacrifice them to Teddy. It ought not to be difficult to find people who can be made directly responsible, the people who invented the poison gas, for instance, and kill them, or to kill people who are dear to them. Or necessary to them . . . Women can do that so much more easily than men . . .

"That perhaps is the only way in which wars of this kind will ever be brought to an end. By women insisting on killing the kind of people who make them. Rooting them out. By a campaign of pursuit and assassination that will go on for years and years after the war itself is over . . . Murder is such a little gentle punishment for the crime of war . . . It would hardly be more than a reproach for what has happened. Falling like snow. Death after death. Flake by flake. This prince. That statesman. The count who writes so fiercely for war. The Kaiser and his sons and his sons' sons would know nothing but fear now for all their lives. Fear by sea, fear by land, for the vessel he sailed in, the train he traveled in, fear when he slept for the death in his dreams, fear when he walked for the death in every shadow; fear in every crowd, fear whenever he was alone. Fear would stalk him through the trees, hide in the corner of the staircase; make all his food taste perplexingly, so that he would want to spit it out . . . I shall get just as close to the particular Germans who made this war as I can, and I shall kill them and theirs . . .

"That is what I am going to do. If Teddy is really dead . . ."

From *Mr. Britling Sees It Through*, by H. G. Wells; Macmillan; New York, 1917.

# Chapter Eight:

# Entertain

For every Great War writer who agonized over the moral and existential issues raised by the war, there were a hundred who saw in the carnage the chance to make a quick buck. Hack writers, like farmers, machine tool operators, and munition makers, found that the war stimulated demand for their labor. In England alone, over 14,000 people listed their occupation on the most recent census returns (1911) as "author." Between wages doubling, book prices being halved, no competition yet from radio or talkies, and a rapidly expanding population of literate adults, the years 1914–18 were good ones for writers whose primary motives were commercial. The war provided them with an abundance of topical subject matter, and an audience, the vast majority of them seeking to be titillated rather than informed, soothed rather than challenged, entertained rather than depressed.

Most of the popular writers' work, judging by what survives in second-hand bookshops, was pure dreck—but evocative dreck that mirrors contemporary attitudes in the same way popular songs from the era can. The men and women who produced it, to give them their due, were being faithful to yet another time-honored responsibility of the writer: to divert, to beguile, to amuse. These tasks are all the more important, they might argue, in times like these, when war-weary people need help in simply carrying on. Yes, we'll include some morality here and there, but it will be the

simplest black-and-white kind: our side good, the other side bad—
and what's wrong with that, since it's true? The best hack writers,
then as now, believe with all sincerity in what they're writing.

Some of this entertainment was produced by authors who were
a long way from being hacks. John Buchan, taking time off from his
official propaganda duties, wrote one of his most successful "shock-
ers" in 1916, taking his hero Richard Hannay on a global chase that
includes, while he's disguised as an Anglophobic South African, an
interview with the Kaiser; *Greenmantle* was among the books read
most frequently in the trenches. Edith Wharton, capable of the highest literary art, could also turn out an unapologetic potboiler like
*The Marne,* though its fired-up American heroine, entertaining the
troops in a YMCA canteen near the front, says a lot about the spirit
in which America entered the war. Even a sober, no-nonsense writer
like Mildred Aldrich, still living near the front lines in France as the
tide of war swept back again in the *Kaiserschlacht,* the German's last-
ditch March 1918 offensive, could find some fun in the characters the
fighting brought to her doorstep.

After the war, poetry written to a very standard became one of its
leading literary legacies, but during the war itself people read verse,
rhymes, doggerel on themes of the most patriotic kind, written by
authors enjoying a celebrity and income that contemporary poets can
only dream of. The bitter antiwar poems of Siegfried Sassoon, published during the war, may have sold a thousand copies; the sentimental
flag-and-motherhood rhymes of Edgar Guest sold in the hundreds of
thousands. "We get the impression," the editor Harold Monro wrote
of the deluge of bad poetry, "of verse writers excitedly gathering to *do
something* for the flag, and as soon as they begin to rack their brains
how that something may be done in verse, a hundred old phrases for
patriotic moments float in their minds, which they reel into verse or
fit into sonnets—and the press is delighted to publish them."

Books for children also thrived—their authors saw the war as
a chance for their young heroes and heroines to have all kinds of

death-defying adventures, preferably in the air over France against German spies.

Some writers, brave or foolish, tried to pull off something that would seem, even in retrospect, to be nearly impossible: to make the Great War funny. Some of this, on the American side, plays off the innocents-abroad theme that goes back to Mark Twain; much of it, particularly on the English side, involves the roughest, most obvious kinds of stereotypes. Professor Gilbert Murray, looking down on this from his classical pedestal, tried to cut the Grub Streeters some slack.

> "All this callous cheerfulness, all this gay brutality, with which people write of bursting shells and the 'leg of a fat Hun performing circles in the air,' or of poking into dug-outs with bayonets and 'picking out the Boches like periwinkles on a pin' . . . all that loathsome stuff is to a great extent mere self protection. It is a kind of misplaced tact. Something more real, more near the truth, more undisguisedly horrible, is just round the corner of the writer's mind, and he is determined not to let it show itself. If it emerged, it would make every one feel awkward."

Of all the writers who tried mining humor out of the war, there is probably only one whose work is still, a hundred years later, authentically funny: Ring Lardner. The bestselling American humorist, with thousands of devoted readers, published three books on the war while it was still in progress, bringing his ironic, mordant sensibility to bear long before that kind of attitude became common. Writers of lesser talent thought fat Huns were laughable—Lardner knew there were funnier things out in "Nobody's Land" than that, starting with the big-talking American rubes he was a genius at capturing.

The establishment British writer and editor Edmund Gosse, writing at the start of the war in 1914, trying to understand what it would mean for literature, predicted, "The book which does not deal directly and crudely with the complexities of warfare and the various branches of strategy, will, from Christmas onwards, not be published at all."

He could not have been more wrong. Though hundreds of potboiler novels were written on war themes, the most popular books of the period had nothing to do with the war at all. The westerns of Zane Grey, the adventures of Tarzan or Dr. Fu Manchu—these topped the bestseller lists in America and England. Readers in the Great War, like readers in all eras, wanted escape more than they wanted involvement, and there were thousands of writers more than willing to provide it. The high moral and artistic purpose that writers like Conrad and Yeats brought to their work simply would not have occurred to them as having anything to do with their roles. As critic Harold Odell points out,

> "Most authors did not spend much time moralising about progress and civilization; they took for granted much that came into question during the Great War itself. And it is a nice question, calling for careful judgement, whether the unwillingness of the vast majority of them to treat the war directly, honestly and critically in their fiction constituted an evasion of authorial responsibility. At the time, they did not think so. Neither did their readers."

Florence Barclay, a rector's wife in her fifties, enjoyed huge popularity both in England and the States for her novels that combined sentimental religious themes with a touch of romance; each new volume sold in the hundreds of thousands. Judging by the blurbs included in the back of *My Heart's Right There,* even critics loved her, with reviews of her most famous book, *The Rosary,* gushing about "a perfect love story—one that justifies the publishing business, refreshes the heart of the reviewer, strengthens faith in the outcome of the great experiment of putting humanity on earth." Or, perhaps getting closer to the secret of her appeal: "The well-known author has not sought problems to solve nor social conditions to arraign, but has been satisfied to tell a sweet and appealing love-story in a wholesome simple way."

*My Heart's Right There* takes its title from a line in the enormously popular wartime song *Tipperary.* The novel consists almost entirely of the brave wounded soldier Jim addressing his brave passive wife Polly.

By 1914, Canadian Robert W. Service, "the Bard of the Yukon," was probably the world's most famous poet and one of its richest writers in any genre; his much-loved ballad of the Klondike gold rush, "The Shooting of Dan McGrew," was memorized and recited by millions. He was forty when the war broke out, and volunteered as an ambulance driver on the western front, though he soon had to resign due to poor health. His brother, Lieutenant Albert Service, died while serving with the Canadian infantry in France.

Service's *Rhymes of a Red Cross Man,* published in 1916 and dedicated to his brother, was one of the bestselling books of the year. He received three government decorations during the war for the effectiveness of his poems as propaganda.

His popularity continues today, with an Internet search of his name pulling down 206,000,000 results.

English paranoia about German spies provided bestselling novelist William Le Queux with the subject matter for several over-the-top espionage novels during the war—but at least his paranoia was genuine. Convinced that German special agents were out to assassinate him, he requested special protection from Scotland Yard, and fully believed in the treasonous machinations of high government officials, as depicted so melodramatically in *Number 70, Berlin: A Story of Britain's Peril.*

Le Queux, at fifty-four, was a protégé of the press baron Lord Northcliff, and an early popularizer of aviation and radio; he was said to have churned out over 150 novels, more than a few themed around a projected German invasion of England, which he greatly feared. His pamphlet, *German Atrocities: A Record of Shameless Deeds,* published in September 1914, was the first in the long series of similar "official" reports on alleged enemy dastardliness.

"Charles Amory Beach" was the made-up name for one or more of several "house writers" who created the "Air Service Boys" series published by the World Syndicate publishing company between 1918 and 1920, dealing with the adventures of two young American lads serving in France with the Lafayette Escadrille.

Children's books, during the war, were enlisted for propaganda purposes just as were books for adults—and not just books for boys. *The Camp Fire Girls Do Their Bit; or, Over the Top with the Winnebagos* by Hildegarde Gertrude Frey (most children's writers of the day seemed to favor three names) proved that adolescent girls could play an active role in the war as well.

Dorothy Canfield Fisher, thirty-nine, was one of those American novelists who occupied a position not quite in the first rank but a long way from the bottom; she enjoyed critical respect with wide popularity among readers of all types. Like Edith Wharton, she was involved in volunteer war work in France, founding a Braille press for blinded veterans in Paris, and running a convalescent center for refugee children. Her *Home Fires in France* is one of the relatively rare short-story collections themed on the war.

For many years after the war, Fisher served as an editorial board judge on the original Book-of-the-Month Club, and had an important role in guiding America's reading tastes; she was also an early influential proponent of both Montessori education and education for adults.

Edgar A. Guest, thirty-seven in 1917, was America's most popular poet, with his "rhymes" appearing in three hundred American newspapers.

"His rhymes—he never claimed for them the status of poetry—were of the simplest sort, full of folksy vernacular, friendship, and all the common virtues and verities. Guest was thoroughly realistic about his work, knowing it for doggerel and sentimental jingle, but it was, he explained, precisely what he liked and what, moreover, millions of other ordinary people liked, and the ridicule of unkind critics left him unscathed."

His collection of verses, *A Heap o' Livin'* ("It takes a heap o' livin' in a house t' make it a home") sold more than a million copies in 1916, and he followed it up with a collection grouped around war themes, *Over Here,* which became an immediate bestseller in 1918.

My copy of *Over Here,* a first edition from 1918 originally owned by a "Lois A. Antle," survives—and this is very rare—with its dust jacket intact. It shows a tall, handsome doughboy breaking ranks from a farewell parade to go to the curb to hug his adoring mother. The flap copy reads,

"Every father or mother who has a son 'over there' will find in *Over Here* a heartrending message of hope and good cheer, and a stirring appeal for a greater loyalty in the trying times ahead. If you are a true-blue American, you will enjoy *Over Here* with its glowing tribute to our soldier boys, and its ringing declaration of faith in the high destinies of our country and our flag."

Ring Lardner's reputation as a serious short-story writer would have to wait until the 1920s, when fans like F. Scott Fitzgerald and Hemingway praised his work. During the war, his popularity was already immense—but as a humorist and sportswriter, whose baseball-playing characters, hicks with huge self-regard, let him display his acidic genius with American slang. His most famous character is Jack Keefe, a semi-literate baseball pitcher who writes letters home to his pal Al that reveal a lot more than he intends. Keefe, the classic American rube, "has a mind as small as his ego was large."

When America entered the war in 1917, the thirty-two-year-old Lardner—his three young sons providing him with a draft defer-ment—had Keefe sign up in his place, and he features in two books: *Treat 'em Rough,* recounting his comic misadventures in stateside train-ing camps, and *The Real Dope,* where Keefe sails to France and serves in the trenches, ducking—despite his braggadocio—every dangerous situation he can.

Lardner wrote a third book on the war, the non-fiction *My Four Weeks in France,* about his comic attempts to get to the front line to actually report on something without being continuously hassled by officialdom.

> "Take me somewhere west of Ireland where they know I'm not a spy.
>> Where nobody gazes at me with a cold, suspicious eye.
>> To the good old U.S.A. where a gent can go his way
>> With no fear of being picked on forty thousand times a day."

Lardner's fans included Virginia Woolf.

> "Mr. Lardner has talents of a remarkable order. With extraordinary ease and aptitude, with the quickest strokes, the surest touch, the sharpest insight, he lets Jack Keefe the baseball player cut out his own outline, fill in his own depths, until the figure of the foolish, boastful innocent lives before us."

# Lips Under Sod
## —Florence L. Barclay

My dear Wife—wrote Jim—

Now don't you be startled, my girl, to find that I am on the same side of the English Channel as yourself and Tiny, and Home. It's the right side of it, I can tell you!

I'm in a Red Cross hospital in London. I'm wounded—but nothing to matter; so don't you worry. A German ran his bayonet into my shoulder, and a bullet found a billet in the muscle of my leg. But the steel made a good clean wound, which is healing quickly, and they moved on the bullet, before they brought me over.

My dear, this is no end of a grand place, and I feel like the King, in fine pyjamas, full of pockets, and lots of ladies—tip-top ladies, mind you, for all they wear caps and aprons—to wait on me.

They *do* make a lot of me. And yet I know quite well it is not because it's *me* and *my* wounds; it's because I stand to them for what they feel for the whole great glorious British Army. While they're doing me, they're thinking of all the other chaps, still fighting in the trenches, or lying helpless and wounded on the battlefields. Ay, and some of them are thinking of quiet graves, left behind, lying silent and alone, where the thunder of battle has passed on; of lips under the sod, they'll never kiss again; or tumbled hair they would like just to have smoothed at the last.

It gives me a lonely kind of feeling, and makes me downright hungry to get to the one woman who'll nurse me for myself, and want me to get well, because I'm *her* man and she can't do without me. Well, please God, it won't be many days before I walk up the little path; and we'll get best part of a month together—you, and I, and Tiny.

I can't close without telling you the best thing of all; a sort of *crowning* thing—not that they had 'em on. Oh, no!

Well, the very day I was brought here, the King and Queen came to see the hospital, walked through all the wards, and spoke to the men.

I heard afterwards that as soon as they knew the visit was going to be, everybody was getting out their Ps and Qs, and brushing themselves up. But I was too dead beat by the journey, to know much about it. Oh, nothing to matter; don't you worry; just, so to say, sleepy.

But, by and by, something sort o' made me open my eyes, and there, by my bed, stood the King and Queen, looking down at me. I knew them at once, by their pictures—as I naturally would, seeing we have them framed in the parlour. It made it seem very homelike to see them standing there; which was perhaps why, when the King asked me what I wanted most, I up and said to see my little village home again, and my wife. Polly—I thought you'd like to be named to the King—and my baby girl we call Tiny, though her name is Mary, after her mother. At that, the King smiled, and looked at the Queen. And I knew I hadn't been quite honest, because it *was* in Coronation Year we named her. So I up and said: "And after the Queen, Sir, if I may make so bold as to say so."

Then the sweetest kindest voice I ever heard, said: "I am glad your little Tiny is called after me, as well as after her mother." And I looked up; and the Queen was smiling down at me with a kind of glisten in her eyes, like very gentle tears.

I lay there, calm and proud; answered all questions about my wounds and how I got 'em; and about our little home. You might have thought there was nobody else in the hospital—nobody else in the whole army—wounded but me, for just those few minutes while They stood beside my bed. And the King told me to make haste and get well, because *I* was the sort of chap he wanted.

Polly—it's one thing to read in print on a placard, YOUR KING AND COUNTRY WANT YOU; and quite another thing to hear it from himself, as man to man, so to speak—straight from him to you.

After They had gone, though I hadn't been able before to do much more than whisper, I felt as if I must lie and shout "God save the King" right through, from beginning to end. And I wanted to be up and out at the Front again, to start "scattering his enemies," right away. Then, all of a sudden, I found myself up on my elbow, laughing and cheering and singing, in a shaky kind of voice, "See how they run! See how they run!"

And the next thing that happened, was that I felt tears running down my cheeks. I couldn't think where they came from. Sister wiped them away with a very soft handkerchief.

This war, Polly, is more than a fight for earthly crowns and kingdoms; ay, more even than a struggle to keep our homes safe, and our wives and little children free from perils worse than shot and shell. We're fighting for right and justice, against treachery and wrong.

It's a righteous war, my girl; and every man who fears God and honours the King should be up, and out, and ready to do his share; and every woman who loves her home must be willing bravely to do her part, by letting her man go. And if she has to hear that he has given his life, she must stand up, brave and true—as a soldier's wife or a soldier's mother—and say: "God save the King!"

From *My Heart's Right There*, by Florence L. Barclay; G.P. Putnam's Sons; New York, 1915.

## *Thoughts Rode Him like a Nightmare*
### —John Buchan

The door opened and Stumm entered. There was a proud light in his eye.

"Brandt," he said, "you are about to receive the greatest privilege that ever fell to one of your race. His Imperial Majesty is passing through here, and has halted for a few minutes. He has done me the honour to receive me, and when he heard my story he expressed a wish to see you. You will follow me to his presence. Do not be afraid. The All-Highest is all merciful and gracious. Answer his questions like a man."

I followed him with a quickened pulse. Here was a bit of luck I had never dreamed of. At the far side of the station a train had drawn up, a train consisting of three big coaches, chocolate-coloured and picked out with gold. On the platform beside it stood a small group of officers, tall men in long grey-blue cloaks. They seemed to be mostly elderly, and one or two of the faces I thought I remembered from photographs in the picture papers.

As we approached they drew apart, and left me face to face with one man. He was a little below middle height, and all muffled in a thick coat with a fur collar. He wore a silver helmet with an eagle atop it, and kept his left hand resting on his sword. Below the helmet was a face the colour of grey paper, from which shone curious sombre restless eyes with dark pouches beneath them. There was no fear of my mistaking him. These were the features which, since Napoleon, have been best known to the world.

I stood as stiff as a ramrod and saluted. I was perfectly cool and most desperately interested. For such a moment I would have gone through fire and water.

"Majesty, this is the Dutchman I spoke of," I heard Stumm say.

"What language does he speak?" the Emperor asked.

"Dutch," was the reply, "but being a South African he also talks English."

A spasm of pain seemed to flit over the face before me. Then he addressed me in English.

"You have come from a land which will yet be our ally to offer your sword to our service? I accept the gift and hail it as a good omen. I would have given your race its freedom, but there were fools and trailers among you who misjudged me. But that freedom I shall yet give you in spite of yourselves. Are there many like you in your country?"

"There are thousands, sir," I said, lying cheerfully. "I am one of many who think that my race's life lies in your victory. And I think that the victory must be won not in Europe alone. In South Africa for the moment there is no chance, so we look to other parts of the continent. You will win in Europe. You have won in the East, and it now remains to strike the English where they cannot fend the blow. If we take Uganda, Egypt will fall. By your permission I go there to make trouble for your enemies."

A flicker of a smile passed over the worn face. It was the face of one who slept little and whose thoughts rode him like a nightmare.

"That is well," he said. "Some Englishman once said that he would call in the New World to redress the balance of the Old. We Germans will summon the whole earth to suppress the infamies of England. Serve us well and you will not be forgotten."

Then he broke out fiercely.

"I did not seek the war . . . It was forced on me . . . I laboured for peace . . . The blood of millions is on the heads of England and Russia, but England most of all. God will yet avenge it. He that takes the sword will perish by the sword. Mine was forced from the scabbard in self-defence, and I am guiltless. Do they know that among your people?"

"All the world knows it, sire," I said.

He gave his hand to Stumm and turned away. The last I saw of him was a figure moving like a sleep-walker, with no spring in his step, amid his tall suite. I felt that I was looking on at a far bigger tragedy than any I had seen in action. Here was one that had loosed Hell, and the furies of Hell had got hold of him. He was no common man, but in his presence I felt an attraction which was not merely the mastery of one used to command. That would not have impressed me, for I had never owned a master. But here was a human being who, unlike Stumm and his kind, had the power of laying himself alongside other men. This was the irony of it. Stumm would not have cared a tinker's curse for all the massacres in history. But this man, the chief of a nation of Stumms, paid the price in war for the gifts that had made him successful in peace. He had imagination and nerves, and the one was white hot and the others were quivering. I would not have been in his shoes for the throne of the Universe.

From *Greenmantle*, by John Buchan; Thomas Nelson and Sons; London, 1916.

## *I Brag of Bear and Beaver*
### —Robert W. Service

### The Man from Athabaska

Oh the wife she tried to tell me that 'twas nothing but the thrumming
　　Of a woodpecker a-rapping on the hollow of a tree;
　　And she thought that I was fooling when I said it was the drumming
　　Of the mustering of legions, and 'twas calling unto me;
　　'Twas calling me to pull my freight and hop across the sea.

And a-mending of my fish-nets sure I started up in wonder
　　For I heard a savage roaring and 'twas coming from afar;
　　Oh the wife she tried to tell me 'twas only summer thunder,
　　And she laughed a bit sarcastic when I told her it was War;
　　'Twas the chariots of battle where the mighty armies are.

Then down the lake came Half-Breed Tom with russet sail a-flying,
　　And the word he said was "War" again, so what was I to do?
　　Oh the dogs they took to howling, and the missis took to crying,
　　As I flung my silver foxes in the little birch canoe;
　　Yes, the old girl stood a-blubbering till an island hid the view.

Says the factor: "Mike, you're crazy! They have soldier men a-plenty.
　　You're as grizzled as a badger, and you're sixty year or so."
　　"But I haven't missed a scrap," says I, "since I was one and twenty.
　　And shall I miss the biggest? You can bet your whiskers—no!"
　　So I sold my furs and started . . . and that's eighteen months ago.

For I joined the Foreign Legion, and they put me for a starter
In the trenches of the Argonne with the Boche a step away;
And the partner on my right hand was an *apache* from Montmartre;
On my left there was a millionaire from Pittsburgh, U.S.A.
(Poor fellow! They collected him in bits the other day.)

But I'm sprier than a chipmunk, save a touch of the lumbago,
And they calls me Old Methoosalah, and *blagues* me all the day.
I'm their exhibition sniper, and they work me like a Dago,
And laugh to see me plug a Boche a half a mile away.
Oh I hold the highest record in the regiment, they say.

And at night they gather round me, and I tell them of my roaming
In the Country of the Crepuscule beside the Frozen Sea;
Where the musk ox runs unchallenged, and the cariboo goes homing,
And they sit like little children, just as quiet as can be:
Men of every crime and colour, how they harken unto me!

And I tell them of the Furland, of the tumpline and the paddle,
Of secret rivers loitering, that no one will explore;
And I tell them of the ranges of the pack-strap and the saddle,
And they fill their pipes in silence, and their eyes beseech for more;
While above the star-shells fizzle and the high explosives roar.

And I tell them of lakes fish-haunted, where the big bull moose are calling,
And forests still as sepulchres with never trail or track;
And valleys packed with purple gloom and mountain peaks appalling,
And I tell them of my cabin on the shore at Fond du Lac;
And I find myself a-thinking: Sure I wish that I was back.

So I brag of bear and beaver, while the batteries are roaring,
And the fellows on the firing steps are blazing at the foe;
And I yarn of fur and feather when the *marmites* are a-soaring,
And they listen to my stories, seven *poilus* in a row,
Seven lean and lousy *poilus* with their cigarettes aglow.

And I tell them when it's over how I'll hike for Athabaska;
And those seven greasy *poilus* they are crazy to go, too.
And I'll give the wife the "pickle-tub" I promised and I'll ask her
The price of mink and marten, and the run of the cariboo,
And I'll get my traps in order, and I'll start to work anew.

For I've had my fill of fighting, and I've seen a nation scattered,
And an army swung to slaughter, and a river red with gore,
And a city all a-smoulder, and . . . as if it really mattered,
For the lake is yonder dreaming, and my cabin's on the shore;
And the dogs are leaping madly, and the wife is singing gladly,
And I'll rest in Athabaska, and I'll leave it nevermore.

From *Rhymes of a Red Cross Man*, by Robert W. Service; Barse &
Hopkins; New York, 1916.

## *Settling Down to His Dastardly Work*
### —William Le Queux

True, the British public will never be able to realise one hundredth
part of what Germany has done by her spy-system, or of the great
diplomatic and military successes which she has achieved by it. Yet
we know enough to realise that for years no country and no walk of
life—from the highest to the lowest—has been free from the ubiq-
uitous, unscrupulous and unsuspected secret agents of whom Lewin
Rodwell was a type.

In Germany's long and patient preparation for the world-war,
nothing in the way of espionage was too large, or too small for atten-

tion. The activity of her secret agents in Berlin had surely been an object-lesson to the world. Her spies swarmed in all cities, and in every village; her agents ranked among the leaders of social and commercial life, and among the sweepings and outcasts of great communities. The wealthiest of commercial men did not shrink from acting as her secret agents. She was not above employing beside them the very dregs of the community. No such system has ever been seen in the world. Yet the benefits which our enemies were deriving from it, now that we were at war, were incalculable.

By every subtle and underhand means in her power, Germany had prepared her supreme effort to conquer us, and, as a result of this it was that Lewin Rodwell that night sat at the telegraph-key of the Berlin spy-bureau actually established on British soil.

He waited until the call had been repeated three times with the secret code number of the Koeniger-gratzerstrasse, namely: "Number 70 Berlin."

Then, putting out his cigarette, he drew his chair forward until his elbows rested upon the table, and spreading out the closely-written document before him, tapped out a signal in code.

The letters were "F.B.S.M."

To this kind of pass-word, which was frequently altered from time to time, he received a reply: "G.L.G.S." and then he added his own number, "0740."

The signals were quite strong, and he drew a long breath of relief and satisfaction.

Then, settling down to his dastardly work, he began to tap out rapidly the following in German:

"British Naval Dispositions: Urgent to Q.S.R.

"Sources of information H.238. To-night, off the Outer Skerries, Shetlands, are battleships *King Charles, Mole, Wey, Welland, Teign, Yare, Queen Boadicea, Emperor of India, King Henry VIII;* with first-class cruisers *Hogue, Stamford, Petworth, Lichfield, Dorchester;* second-class cruisers *Rockingham, Guildford, Driffield, Verlam, Donnington,*

*Pirbright, Tremayne* and *Blackpool;* destroyers *Viking, Serpent, Chameleon, Adder, Batswing, Study* and *Havoc,* with eight submarines, the aircraft-ship *Flyer,* and repair-ship *Vulcan.* Another strong division left Girdle Ness at 4 p.m. coming south. The division in Moray Firth remains the same. *Trusty, Dragon, Norfolk* and *Shadower* left Portsmouth this evening going east. British Naval war-code to be altered at midnight to 106-13."

The figures he spelt out very carefully, repeating them three times so that there could be no mistake. Again he paused, until, from Berlin, they were repeated for confirmation. Then Rodwell glanced again at the closely-written sheet spread before him, and began to tap out the following secret message in German to the very heart of the Imperial war-machine.

"Official information just gained from a fresh and most reliable source—confirmed by H.238, M.605, and also B. 1928—shows that British Admiralty have conceived a clever plan for entrapping the German Grand Fleet. Roughly, the scheme is to make attack with inferior force upon Heligoland early on Wednesday morning, the 16th, together with corresponding attack upon German division in the estuary of the Eider and thus draw out the German ships northwards toward the Shetlands, behind which British Grand Fleet are concealed in readiness. This concentration of forces northward will, according to the scheme of which I have learned full details, leave the East coast of England from the Tyne to the Humber unprotected for a full twelve hours on the 16th, thus full advantage could be taken for bombardment. Inform Grand Admiral immediately."

Having thus betrayed the well-laid plans of the British Admiralty to entice the German fleet out of the Kiel canal and the other harbours in which barnacles were growing on their keels, Lewin Rodwell, the popular British "patriot," paused once more.

But not for long, because, in less than a minute, he received again the signal of acknowledgement that his highly interesting message to the German Admiralty had been received.

He gave the signal that he had ended his message, and, with a low laugh of satisfaction, rose from the rickety old chair and lit another cigarette.

Thus had England been foully betrayed by one of the men whom her deluded public most confidently trusted and so greatly admired.

From *Number 70, Berlin*, by William Le Queux; Hodder and Stoughton; London, 1916.

## *Far Too Young to Assist*
—Charles Amory Beach

That night Tom and Jack preferred the quiet of their own apartment to the general sitting room, where the tired pilots gathered to smoke, talk, play games, sing, and give their opinions on every topic imaginable, including scraps of news received in late letters from home towns across the sea.

"Do you know, Tom," Jack said unexpectedly, "I'd give something to know where Bessie Gleason is just at this time. It's strange how often I think about that young girl. It's just as if something that people call intuition told me she might be in serious trouble through that hard-looking guardian of hers, Carl Potzfeldt."

Tom smiled.

Bessie Gleason was a very pretty and winsome girl of about twelve years of age, with whom Jack in particular had been quite "chummy" on the voyage across the Atlantic, and through the submarine zone, as related in "Air Service Boys Flying for France." The last he had seen of her was when she waved her hand to him when leaving the steamer at its English port. Her stern guardian had contracted a violent dislike for Jack, so that the two had latterly been compelled to meet only in secret for little confidential chats.

"Oh, you've taken to imagining all sorts of terrible things in connection with pretty Bessie and her cruel guardian. He claimed to be a native of Alsace-Lorraine."

Bessie Gleason was a little American girl, a child of moods, fairylike in appearance and of a maturity of manner that invariably attracted those with whom she came into contact.

Her mother had been lost at sea, and by Mrs. Gleason's will the girl and her property were left in Potzfeldt's care. Mr. Potzfeldt was taking her to Europe, and on the steamship she and Jack Parmly had been friends, and as Potzfeldt's actions were suspicious and, moreover, the girl did not seem happy with him Jack had been troubled about her.

"I'm afraid you think too much about Bessie and her troubles, Jack; and get yourself worked up about things that may never happen to her," Tom went on after a pause.

"She's a queer girl, you know, and intensely patriotic."

"Yes, I noticed that, even if you did monopolize most of her time," chuckled Tom.

"How she does hate the Germans! And that's what will get her into trouble, I'm afraid, if she and her guardian have managed to get through the lines in any way, and back to his home town, wherever that may be."

"Why should she feel so bitter toward the Kaiser and his people, Jack?"

"I'll tell you. Her mother was drowned. She was aboard the *Lusitania* and was never seen after the sinking. Mr. Potzfeldt was there, too, it seems, but couldn't save Mrs. Gleason, he claims, though he tried in every way to do so."

"Then if Bessie knows about her mother's death," Tom went on to say, "I don't wonder she feels that way toward everything German. I'd hate the entire race if my mother had been murdered, as those women and children were, when the torpedo was launched against the great passenger steamer without any warning."

"She told me she felt heart-broken because she was far too young to do anything to assist in the drive against the central empires. You see, Bessie had great hopes of some day growing tall enough to become a war nurse. She is deeply interested in the Red Cross; and

Tom, would you believe it, the midget practices regular United States Army standing exercises in the hope of hastening her growth."

"I honor the little girl for her ambition," Tom said. "But I'm inclined to think this war will be long past before she has grown to a suitable size to enlist among the nurses of the Paris hospitals. And if that Carl Potzfeldt entertains the sentiments we suspected him of, and is secretly in sympathy with the Huns, although passing for a neutral, her task will be rendered doubly hard."

"I'm sure that dark-faced man is a bad egg," expostulated Jack. "If only we could prove that Potzfeldt was in the pay of the German government, don't you see he could be stood up against a wall and fixed."

"Still, we can't do the least thing about it, Jack. If fortune should ever bring us in contact with that pair again, why then we could perhaps think up some sort of scheme to help Bessie. Now, I've got something important to tell you."

"Something the captain must have said when he was chatting with you in the mess-room immediately after supper, I guess. At the time I thought he might be asking you about our adventures of to-day, but then I noticed that he was doing pretty much all the talking. What is on the carpet for us now?"

"We're going to be given our chance at last, Jack!"

"Do you mean to fly with the fighting escadrille and meet German pilots in a life and death battle up among the clouds?" asked Jack, in a voice that had a tinge of awe about it; for he had often dreamed of such honors coming to him.

"That is what we are promised," his chum assured him. "Of course our education is not yet complete; but we have shown such progress that, as there is need of additional pilots able to meet the Fokker planes while a raid is in progress, we are to be given a showing."

"I'll not sleep much to-night for thinking of it," declared Jack.

From *Air Service Boys Over the Enemy's Lines*, by Charles Amory Beach; World Syndicate Publishing; New York, 1919.

## *To Die is Easier*
—Edgar A. Guest

### The Mother on the Sidewalk

The mother on the sidewalk as the troops are marching by
Is the mother of Old Glory that is waving in the sky.
Men have fought to keep it splendid, men have died to keep it
bright.
But that flag was born of woman and her sufferings day and night;
'Tis her sacrifice has made it, and once more we ought to pray
For the brave and loyal mother of the boy that goes away.

There are days of grief before her, there are hours that she will
weep,
There are nights of anxious waiting when her fear will banish sleep;
She has heard her country calling and has risen to the test,
And has placed upon the altar of the nation's need, her best.
And no man shall ever suffer in the turmoil of the gray
The anguish of the mother of the boy who goes away.

You may boast men's deeds of glory, you may tell their courage
great,
But to die is easier service than alone to sit and wait,
And I hail the little mother, with the tear-stained face and grave
Who has given the Flag a soldier—she's the bravest of the brave.
And that banner we are proud of, with its red and blue and white
Is a lasting tribute holy to all mother's love of right.

### A Patriot

It's funny when a feller wants to do his little bit,
And wants to wear a uniform and lug a soldier's kit,

And ain't afraid of submarines nor mines that fill the sea,
They will not let him go along to fight for liberty.
They make him stay at home and be his mother's darling pet,
But you can bet there'll come a time when they will want me yet.

I want to serve the Stars and Stripes, I want to go and fight,
I want to lick the Kaiser good, and do the job up right.
I know the way to use a gun and I can dig a trench
And I would like to go and help the English and the French.
But no, they say, you cannot march away to stirring drums;
Be mother's angel boy at home; stay there and twirl your thumbs.

I've read about the daring boys that fight up in the sky;
It seems to me that must be a splendid way to die.
I'd like to drive an aeroplane and prove my courage grim
And get above a German there and drop a bomb on him,
But they won't let me go along to help the latest drive;
They say my mother needs me here because I'm only five.

From *Over Here*, by Edgar A. Guest; Reilly & Lee; Chicago, 1918.

## *That Dumb, Backwoods, Pie-faced Stenographer*
### —Dorothy Canfield Fisher

Ellen, plain, rather sallow, very serious, was a sort of office manager in the firm of Walker and Pennypacker, the big wholesale hardware merchants of Marshallton, Kansas. She was there at twenty-seven, on the day in August, 1914, when she opened the paper and saw that Belgium had been invaded by the Germans. She read with attention what was printed about the treaty obligations involved, though she found it hard to understand. At noon she stopped before the desk of Mr. Pennypacker, the senior member of the firm, for whom she had great respect, and asked him if she had made out correctly the import of the editorial. "*Had* the Germans promised they wouldn't ever go into Belgium in a war?"

"Looks that way," said Mr. Pennypacker, nodding, and searching for a lost paper. The moment after, he had forgotten the question and the questioner.

Ellen had always rather regretted not having been able to "go on with her education," and this gave her certain little habits of mind which differentiated her somewhat from the other stenographers and typewriters in the office with her, and from her cousin, with whom she shared a small bedroom in Mrs. Wilson's boarding-house. For instance, she looked up words in the dictionary when she did not understand them, and she had kept all her old schoolbooks on the shelf of the boarding-house bedroom. Finding that she had only a dim recollection of where Belgium was, she took down her old geography and located it. The relation between the size of the little country and the bulk of Germany made an impression on her. "My! It looks as though they could just make one mouthful of it," she remarked. "It's *awfully* little."

In the days which followed, the office-manager of the wholesale hardware house more and more justified the accusation of looking "queer." It came to be so noticeable that one day her employer, Mr. Pennypacker, asked her if she didn't feel well. "You've been looking sort of under the weather," he said.

She answered, "I'm just *sick* because the United States won't do anything to help Belgium and France."

Mr. Pennypacker had never received a more violent shock of pure astonishment. "Great Scotland!" he ejaculated, "what's that to *you.*"

"Well, I live in the United States," she advanced, as though it were an argument.

Mr. Pennybacker looked at her hard. It was the same plain, serious, rather sallow face he had seen for years bent over his typewriter and his letter files. But the eyes were different—anxious, troubled.

"It makes me sick," she repeated, "to see a great big nation picking on a little one that was only keeping its promise."

Her employer cast around for a conceivable reason for the aberration. "Any of your folks come here from there?" he ventured.

"Gracious, *no!*" cried Ellen, shocked at the idea that there might be "foreigners" in her family. She added: "But you don't have to be related to a little boy, do you, to get mad at a man that's beating him up, especially if that boy hasn't done anything he oughtn't to?"

Mr. Pennypacker stared. "I don't know that I ever looked at it that way." He added: "I've been so taken up with that lost shipment of nails that I haven't read much about the war. There's always *some* sort of war going on over there in Europe seems to me."

On the 8th of May, 1915, when Ellen went down to breakfast, the boarding-house dining-room was excited. Ellen heard the sinking of the *Lusitania* read out loud by the young reporter. To every one's surprise, she added nothing to the exclamations of horror with which the others greeted the news. She looked very white and left the room without touching her breakfast. She went directly down to the office and when Mr. Pennypacker came in at nine o'clock she asked him for a leave of absence, "maybe three months, maybe more," depending on how long her money held out. She explained that she had in the savings-bank five hundred dollars, the entire savings of a lifetime, which she intended to use now.

It was the first time in eleven years that she had ever asked for more than her regular yearly fortnight, but Mr. Pennypacker was not surprised. "You've been looking awfully run-down lately. It'll do you good to get a real rest. But it won't cost you all *that!* Where are you going? To Battle Creek?"

"I'm not going to rest," said Miss Boardman, in a queer voice. "I'm going to work in France."

The first among among the clashing and violent ideas which this announcement aroused in Mr. Pennypacker's mind was the instant certainty that she could not have seen the morning paper. "Great Scotland—not much you're not! This is no time to be taking ocean trips. The submarines have just gotten one of the big ocean ships, hundreds of women and children drowned."

"I heard about that," she said, looking at him very earnestly, with a dumb emotion in her eyes. "That's why I'm going."

Then she went back to the boarding-house and began to pack two-thirds of her things into her trunk, and put the other third into her satchel, all she intended to take with her.

At noon her cousin Maggie came back from her work, found her thus, and burst into shocked and horrified tears. At two o'clock Maggie went to find the young reporter, and, her eyes swollen, her face between anger and alarm, she begged him to come and "talk to Ellen. She's gone off her head."

The reporter asked her what form her mania took.

"She's going to France to work for the French and Belgians as long as her money holds out . . . all the money she's saved in her life!"

The first among the clashing ideas which this awakened in the reporter's mind was the most heartfelt and gorgeous amusement. The idea of that dumb, backwoods, pie-faced stenographer carrying her valuable services to the war in Europe seemed to him the richest thing that had happened in years! He burst into laughter. "Yes, sure, I'll come and talk to her," he agreed.

He found her lifting a tray into her trunk. "See here, Miss Boardman," he remarked reasonably, "do you know what you need? You need a sense of humor! You take things too much in dead earnest. The sense of humor keeps you from doing ridiculous things, don't you know it does?"

Ellen faced him, seriously considering this. "Do you think all ridiculous things are bad?" she asked him, not as an argument, but as a genuine question.

He evaded this and went on. "Just look at yourself now . . . just look at what you're planning to do. Here is the biggest war in the history of the world; all the great nations involved; millions and millions of dollars being poured out; the United States sending hundreds and thousands of packages and hospital supplies by the million, and nurses and doctors and Lord knows how many trained people . . . and, look! who comes here?—a stenographer from Walker and Pennypacker's in Marshallton, Kansas, setting out to the war!"

Ellen looked at this picture of herself, and while she considered it the young man looked long at her. As he looked, he stopped laughing. She said finally, very simply, in a declarative sentence devoid of any but its obvious meaning. "No, I can't see that this is so very funny."

From *Home Fires in France*, by Dorothy Canfield Fisher; Henry Holt and Company; New York, 1918.

## *The Azure Gaze of Miss Hinda Warlick*
### —Edith Wharton

It was a big cellar, but brown uniforms and ruddy faces crowded it from wall to wall. In one corner the men were sitting on packing boxes at a long table made of boards laid across barrels, the smoky light of little oil-lamps reddening their cheeks and deepening the furrows in their white foreheads as they laboured over their correspondence. Others were playing checkers, or looking at the illustrated papers.

It was the first time that Troy had ever seen a large group of his compatriots so close to the fighting front, and in an hour of ease, and he was struck by the gravity of the young faces, and the low tones of their talk. Everything was in a minor key. No one was laughing or singing or larking; the note was that which might have prevailed in a club of quiet elderly men, or in a drawing room where the guests did not know each other well.

Troy and Jack perched on a packing box, and talked a little with their neighbors; but suddenly they were interrupted by the noise of a motor stopping outside. There was a stir at the mouth of the cavern, and a girl said eagerly: "Here she comes!"

Instantly the cellar woke up. The soldiers' faces grew young again, they flattened themselves laughingly against the walls of the entrance, the door above was cautiously opened, and a girl in a long blue cloak appeared at the head of the stairs.

"Well, boys—you see I managed it!" she cried; and Tony instantly recognized the piercing accents and azure gaze of Miss Hinda Warlick.

"*She* managed it!" the whole cellar roared as one man, drowning her answer in a cheer: and "Of course I did!" she continued, laughing and nodding right and left as she made her triumphant way down the line of khaki to what, at her appearance, had somehow instantly become the stage at the further end of a packed theatre. The elderly Y.M.C.A. official who accompanied her puffed out his chest like a general, and blinked knowingly behind his gold eye-glasses.

Troy's first movement had been one of impatience. He hated all that Miss Warlick personified, and hated it most of all on this sacred soil, and at this fateful moment, with the iron wings of doom clanging so close above their heads. But it would have been almost impossible to fight his way out through the crowd that had closed in behind her—and he stayed.

The cheering subsided, she gained her improvised platform—a door laid on some biscuit-boxes—and the recitation began.

She gave them all sorts of things, ranging from grave to gay, and extracting from the sentimental numbers a peculiarly piercing effect that hurt Troy like the twinge of a dental instrument. And her audience loved it all, indiscriminately and voraciously, with souls hungry for the home-flavour and long nurtured on what Troy called "cereal-fiction." One had to admit that Miss Warlick knew her public, and could play on every chord.

It might have been funny, if it had not been so infinitely touching. They were all so young, so serious, so far from home, and bound on a quest so glorious! And there overhead, just above them, brooded and clanged the black wings of their doom . . . Troy's mockery was softened to tenderness, and he felt, under the hard shell of his youthful omniscience, the stir of all the things to which the others were unconsciously responding.

"And now, by special request, Miss Warlick is going to say a few words,"—the elderly eye-glassed officer importantly announced.

Ah, what a pity! If only she had ended on that last jolly chorus, so full of artless laughter and tears! Troy remembered her dissertations on the steamer, and winced at a fresh display of such fatuity, in such a scene.

She had let the cloak slip from her shoulders, and stepped to the edge of the unsteady stage. Her eyes burned large in a face grown suddenly grave. "Only a few words, really," she began, apologetically; and the cellar started a cheer of protest.

"No—not that kind. Something different . . ."

She paused long enough to let the silence prepare them; sharp little artist that she was! Then she leaned forward. "This is what I want to say; I've come from the French front—pretty near the edge. They're dying there, boys—dying by thousands, *now,* this minute . . . But that's not it. I know: you want me to cut it out—and I'm going to . . . But this is why I began that way: because it was my first sight of—things of that sort. And I had to tell you—"

She stopped, pale, her pretty mouth twitching.

"What I really wanted to say is this: Since I came to Europe, nearly a year ago, I've got to know the country they're dying for—and I understand why they mean to go on and on dying—if they have to—till there isn't one of them left. Boys—I know France now—and she's worth it! Don't you make any mistake! I have to laugh now when I remember what I thought of France when I landed. My! How d'you suppose she got on so long without us? Done a few things too—poor little toddler! Well—it was time we took her by the hand, and showed her how to behave. And I wasn't the only one either. I guess most of us thought we'd have to teach her her letters. Maybe some of you boys right here felt that way too?"

A guilty laugh, and loud applause.

"Thought so," said Miss Warlick smiling.

"Well," she continued, "there wasn't hardly anything I wasn't ready to teach them. On the steamer coming out with us there was a lot of those Amb'lance boys. My! How I gassed them. I said the French had got to be taught how to love their mothers—I said they hadn't any home-feeling—and didn't love children the way we do. I've been round among them some since then, in the hospitals, and I've seen fellows lying there shot 'most to death, and their little old mothers in white caps arriving from 'way off at the other end of France. Well, those fellows know how to see their mothers coming even if they're blind, and how to hug 'em even if their arms are off . . . And the children—the way they go on about children! Ever seen a French soldier yet that didn't have a photograph of a baby stowed away somewhere in his dirty uniform? *I* never have. I tell you, they're *white!* And they're fighting as only people can who feel that way about mothers and babies. The way we're going to fight; and maybe we'll prove it to 'em sooner than any of us think . . .

"Anyhow, I wanted to get this off my chest tonight; not for *you,* only for myself. I didn't want to have a shell get me before I'd said 'Veever la France!' before all of you.

"See here, boys—the Marsellaze!"

She snatched a flag from the wall, drawing herself up to heroic height; and the whole cellar joined her in a roar.

From *The Marne*, by Edith Wharton; D. Appleton and Co.; New York, 1918.

## *My God, Lady!*
### —Mildred Aldrich

March 1, 1917

Well, I have been very busy for some time now receiving the famous 118th regiment, and all on account of the flag. It had been going up in the "dawn's early light," and coming down "with the twilight's last gleaming" for some weeks when the regiment marched past the gate again. I must tell you the truth—the first man who attempted to cry "*Vivent les Etats-Unis*" was hushed by a cry of *"Attendez-pa-*

*tience—pas encore,"* and the line swung by. That was all right. I could afford to smile,—and, at this stage of the game, to wait. You are always telling me what a "patient man" Wilson is. I don't deny it. Still, there are others.

The very next day I got the most delicious type of all—the French-American—very French to look at him, but with New York stamped all over him—especially the speech. Of all these boys, this is the one I wish you could see.

When I opened the door for him, he stared at me, and then he threw up both hands and simply shouted, "My God it is true! My God, it is an American!"

Then he thrust out his hand and gave me a hearty shake, simply yelling, "My God, lady, I'm glad to see you. My God, lady, the sight is good for sore eyes."

Then he turned to his comrade and explained, *"J'ai dit a la dame,"* and in the same breath he turned back to me and continued.

"My God, lady, when I saw them Stars and Stripes floating out there, I said to my comrade, 'If there is an American man or an American lady here, my God, I am going to look at them,' and my God, lady, I'm glad I did. Well, how do you do, anyway?"

I told him that I was very well, and asked him if he wouldn't like to come in.

"My God, lady, you bet your life I do," and he shook my hand again, and came in, remarking, "I'm an American myself—from New York—great city, New York—can't be beat. I wish all my comrades could see Broadway—that would amaze them," and then he turned away to his companion to explain, *"J'ai dit a Madame que je voudrais bien que tous les copains pouvaient voir Broadway—c'est la plus belle rue de New York—ils seront epates—tous,"* and then he turned to me to ask, *"N'est-ce pas, Madame?"*

I laughed. It did not seem worth while to tell him I did not live in New York, so I said "Boston," and he declared it a "nice, pretty slow town," he knew it, and, of course, he added, "But my god, lady, give

me New York every time. I've lived there sixteen years—got a nice little wife there—here's her picture—and see here, this is the name," and
he laid an envelope before me with a New York postmark.

"Well," I said, "if you are an American citizen, what are you doing
here in a French uniform? The States are not in the war."

His eyes simply snapped.

"My God, lady, I'm a Frenchman just the same. My God, lady,
you don't think I'd see France attacked by Germany and not take a
hand in the fight, do you? Not on your life!"

I asked him, when I got a chance to put in a word, what he did
in New York, and he told me he was a chauffeur, and that he had a
sister who lived on Riverside Drive up by 76th Street. He launched
into an enthusiastic description of Riverside Drive, and immediately put it all into French for the benefit of his *copain*, who stood
by with his mouth open in amazement at the spirited English of
his friend.

When he went away, he shook me again violently by the hand,
exclaiming: "Well, lady, of course you'll soon be going back to the
States. So shall I. I can't live away from New York. No one ever could
who had lived there. Great country the States. I'm a voter—I'm a
Democrat—always vote the Democratic ticket—voted for Wilson.
Well, goodbye, lady."

As he shook me by the hand again, it seemed suddenly to occur
to him that he had forgotten something. He struck a blow on his
forehead with his fist, and cried: "My God, lady, did I understand
that you have been here ever since the war began? Then you were here
during the battle out there? My God, lady, I'm an American, too, and
my God, lady, I'm proud of you!"And he went off down the road
explaining to his companion, "*J'ai dit a madame,*" etc.

From *On the Edge of the War Zone,* by Mildred Aldrich; Small, Maynard
and Co.; Boston, 1917.

# *Nobody's Land*
## —Ring Lardner

Camp Grant, Sept. 24.

FRIEND AL: Well Al they give us some work out today and I am pretty tired but they's no use going to bed until 9 o'clock which is the time they blow the buggle for the men to shut up their noise. They do everything by buggles here. And we had to tell our family history to a personal officer that writes down all about you on a card and what kind of work you done before so if the General or somebody tears their pants they won't have to chase all over the camp and page a taylor because they can look at the cards and find out who use to be a taylor and send for them to sew him up.

The officer asked me my name and age and etc. and what I had done in civil life so I said "I guess you don't read the sporting page." So he says "Oh are you a fighter or something?" So I said "I am a fighter now but I use to pitch for the White Sox." So then he asked me what I done before that so I told him I was with Terre Haute in the Central League and Comiskey heard about me and bought me and then he sent me out to Frisco for a while and I stood that league on their head and he got me back and I been with him about 3 years.

So the officer asked me if I ever done anything besides pitch so I told him about the day I played the outfield in Terre Haute when Burns and Stewart shut their eyes going after a fly ball and their skulls came together and it sounded like a freight wreck.

So then the officer says "Yes but didn't you do something when you wasn't playing ball?" so I told him a pitcher doesn't have to do nothing only set on the bench or hit fungos once in a while or warm up when it looks like the guy in there is beginning to wobble. So he says "Well I guess I will put you down as a pitcher and when we need one in a hurry we will know where to find one." But I don't know when they would need a pitcher Al unless it was to throw one of them bombs and believe me when it comes to doing that I will make a sucker out of the rest of these birds because if my arm feels O.K. they's nobody got better control and if they tell me to stick one in a German's right eye that is where I will put it and not in their stomach or miss them altogether like I was a left hander or something.

For dinner we had roast chicken and sweet potatoes and cream corn and biscuits and coffee and for supper there was bake beans with tomato sauce and bread and pudding and cake and coffee and the grub is pretty fair only a man can't enjoy it because you got to eat to fast because if theys anything left on your plate when the rest of them birds get through you got to fight to keep it from going to the wrong address. Well Al its pretty near time for the tattoo buggle which means the men has got to shut up and keep quiet so I am going to get ready for bed but I don't know if I would rather have them keep quiet or not because when they are keeping quiet you don't know what they are up to and maybe they are snooping a round somewheres waiting for a man to go to sleep so they can cut your throat. Some of them has been use to doing it all their life Al and they are beginning to miss it. But I don't know if I wouldn't just as leave die that way as from those upsetting exercises.

Your pal,

Jack

On the Ship Board, Jan.15.

FRIEND AL: Well Al I suppose it is kind of foolish to be writeing you a letter now when they won't be no chance to mail it till we get across the old pond but still and all a man has got to do something to keep busy and I know you will be glad to hear all about our trip so I might as well write you a letter when ever I get a chance and I can mail them to you all at once when we get across the old pond and you will think I have wrote a book or something.

Jokeing a side Al you are lucky to have an old pal thats going to see all the fun and write to you about it because its a different thing haveing a person write to you about what they see themself then getting the dope out of a newspaper or something because you will now that what I tell you is the real dope that I seen myself where if you read it in a newspaper you know its guest work because in the 1rst. place they don't leave the reporters get nowheres near the front and besides that they wouldn't go there if they had a leave because they would be to scared like baseball reporters that sets a mile from the game because they haven't got the nerve to get down on the field where a man can take a punch at them and even when they are a mile away with a screen in front of them they duck when somebody hits a pop foul.

Well Al it is against the rules to tell you when we left the old U.S. or where we come away from because the pro Germany spy might get hold of a man's letters some way and then it would be good night because he would send a telegram to where the submarines is located at and they wouldn't send no 1 or 2 submarines after us but the whole German navy would get after us because they would figure that if they ever got us it would be a rich hall.

But we will get there some time and when we do you can bet we will show them something and I am tickled to death I am going and if I lay down my life I will feel like it wasn't throwed away for nothing like you would die of tyford fever or something.

Your pal,
Jack
Somewheres in France, Jan. 26

FRIEND AL: Well old pal here we are and its against the rules to tell you where we are at but of course it doesn't take no Shylock to find out because all you would have to do is look at the post mark that they will put on this letter.

Any way you couldn't pronounce what the town's name is if you see it spelled out because it isn't nothing like how its spelled out and you won't catch me trying to pronounce none of these names or talk French because I am off of languages for a while and good old American is good enough for me eh Al?

Well Al now that its all over I guess we was pretty lucky to get across the old pond without no trouble because between you and I Al I heard just a little while ago from one of the boys that three nights ago we was attacked and our ship just missed getting hit by a periscope and the destroyers went after the subs and they was a whole flock of them and the reason we didn't hear nothing is that the death bombs don't go off till they are way under water so you can't hear them but between you and I Al the navy men say they was nine subs sank.

Well any way its all over now and here we are and you ought to of heard the people in the town here cheer us when we come in and you ought to see how the girls look at us and believe me Al they are some girls. Its a good thing I am an old married man or I believe I would be pretty near tempted to flirt back with some of the ones that's been trying to get my eye but the way it is I just give them a smile and pass on and they's no harm in that and I figure a man always ought to give other people as much pleasure as you can as long as it don't harm nobody.

Well Al everybody's busier than a chicken with their head cut off and I haven't got no more time to write. But when we get to where we are going I will have time maybe and tell you how we are getting along and if you want to drop me a line and I wish you would send me the Chi papers once in a while especially when the baseball training trips starts but maybe they won't be no Jack Keefe to send them to by that time but if they do get me I will die fighting. You know me Al.

Your friend,
Jack
Somewheres in France, March 13.

FRIEND AL: Well Al I bet you will pretty near fall over in a swoon when you read what I have got to tell you. Somebody must have sent a coppy of the paper I told you about to Gen. Pershing and marked up what I wrote up so as he would be sure and see it and probably one of the officers done it. Well that's either here or there but this afternoon when we come in they was a letter for me and who do you think it was from Al. Well you can't never even begin to guess so I will tell you. It was from Gen. Pershing Al and it comes from Paris where he is and I have got it here laying on the table but they's nothing to prevent me from copping down the letter so as you can read what it says and here it is.

PRIVATE KEEFE,

*Dear Sir:* My attention was called yesterday to an article written by you in your regimental paper under the title War and Baseball: Two Games Where Brains Wins. In this article you state that our generals would be better able to accomplish their task if they had enjoyed the benefits of strategic training in baseball. I have always been a great admirer of the national game of baseball and I heartily agree with what you say. But unfortunately only a few of us ever possessed the ability to play your game and few never were proficient enough to play it professionally. Therefore the general staff is obliged to blunder along without that capacity for quick thinking which is acquired only on the baseball field.

But I believe in making use of all the talent in my army, even among the rank and file. Therefore I respectfully ask whether you think some of your baseball secrets would be of strategic value to us in the prosecution of this war, either offensive or defensive, and if so whether you would be willing to provide us with the same.

By the way I note with pleasure that our first names are the same. It makes a sort of bond between us which I trust will be further cemented if you can be of assistance to me in my task.

I shall eagerly await your reply. Sincerely,

Black Jack Pershing
Follies Bergere, Paris, France.

That is the letter I got from him Al and I'll say its some letter and I bet if some of these smart alex officers seen it it would reduce some of the swelling in their chest but I consider the letter confidential Al and I haven't showed it to nobody only 3 or 4 of my buddies and I showed it to Johnny Alcock and he popped his eyes out so far you could of snipped them off with a shears. And he said it was a cinch that Pershing realy wrote it on acct. of him signing it Black Jack Pershing and they wouldn't nobody else sign it that way because it was a private nickname between he and some of his friends and they wouldn't nobody else know about it.

So then he asked was I going to answer the letter and I said of course I was and he says well I better take a whole lot of pains with my answer and study up the situation before I wrote it and put some good idears in it and if my letters made a hit with Gen. Pershing the next thing you know he would probably summons me to Paris and maybe stick me on the war board so all I would half to do would be figure up plans of attacks and etc. and not half to go up in the trenchs and wrist my life and probably get splattered all over France.

I would go if Black Jack wanted me and after all Al I am here to give Uncle Sam the best I have got and if I can serve the stars and stripes better by sticking pins in a map then getting in the trenches why all right and it takes more than common soldiers to win a war and if I am more use to them as a kind of adviser instead of carrying a bayonet why I will sacrifice my own feelings for the good of the cause like I often done in baseball.

Your pal,
Jack
In the trenchs, May 18.


FRIEND AL: Well Al if I am still alive yet its not because I laid back and didn't take no chances and I wished some of the baseball boys that use to call me yellow when I was in there pitching had of seen me last night and I guess they would of sang a different song only in the 1rst. Place I was where they couldn't nobody see me and secondly they would of been so scared they would of choked to death if they tried to talk let alone sing.

Well yesterday P.M. Sargent Crane asked me how I liked life in the trenchs and I said O.K. only I got tired on acct. of they not being no excitement or nothing to do and he says oh they's plenty to do and I could go out and help the boys fix up the bob wire in Nobodys Land. So I said I didn't see how they could be any fixing needed as they hadn't nothing happened on this section since the war started you might say and the birds that was here before us had plenty of time to fix it if it needed fixing. So he says "Well any ways they's no excitement to fixing the wire but if you was looking for excitement why didn't you go out with that patrol the other night?" So I said "Because I didn't see no sence to trying to find out who was in the other trenchs when we know they are Germans and that's all we need to know. Wait till they's a real job and you won't see me hideing behind nobody." So he says "Ive got a real job for you tonight and you can go along with Ted Phillips to the listening post."

Well Al a listening post is what they call a little place they got dug out way over near the German trenchs and its so close you can hear them talk sometimes and you are supposed to hear if they are getting ready to pull something and report back here so they won't catch us asleep. Well I was wild to go just for something to do but I been haveing trouble with my ears lately probably on acct. of the noise from so much shell fire but any ways I have thought a couple times that I was getting a little deef so I thought I better tell him the truth so I said "I would be tickled to death to go only I don't know if I ought to or not because I don't hear very good even in English and of course Jerry would be telling their plans in German and suppose I didn't catch on to it and I would feel like a murder if they started a big drive and I hand't gave my pals no warning." So he says "Don't worry about that as Phillips has got good ears and understands German and he has been there before only in a job like that a man wants company and you are going along for company."

Well Al it finely come time for us to go and we went and if anybody asks you how to spend a pleasant evening don't steer them up against a listening post with a crazy man. There was the bosh trench about 20 yrds. from us but not a sound out of them and a man couldn't help from thinking what if they had of heard us out there and they was getting ready to snoop up on us and that's why they was keeping so still and it got so as I could feel 1 of their bayonets burrowing into me and I am no quitter Al when it comes to fighting somebody you can see but when you have got a idear that somebody is cralling up on you and you haven't no chance to fight back I would like to see the bird that could enjoy himself and besides suppose my ears had went back on me worse than I thought and the Dutchmens was really making a he—ll of a racket but I couldn't hear them and maybe they was getting ready to come over the top and I wouldn't know the differents and all of a sudden they would lay a garage and dash out behind it and if they didn't kill us we would be up in front of the court's marshall for not warning our pals.

Well when this here Phillips finely opened his clam and spoke I would of jumped a mile if they had of been any room to jump anywhere. Well the sargent had told us not to say nothing but all of a sudden right out loud this bird says this is a he—ll of a war. Well I motioned back at him to shut up but of course he couldn't see me and thought I hadn't heard what he said so he said it over again so then I thought maybe he hadn't heard the sargent's orders so I whispered to him that he wasn't supposed to talk. Well Al they wasn't no way of keeping him quite and he says "That's all bunk because I been out here before and talked my head off and nothing happened." So I says well if you have to talk you don't half to yell it. So then he tried to whisper Al but his whisper sounded like a jazz record with a crack in it.

So he shut up for a while but pretty soon he busted out again and this time he was louder than ever and he asked me could I sing and I said no so then he says well you can holler can't you so I said I suppose I could so he says "Well I know how we could play a big joke on them square heads. Lets the both of us begin yelling like a Indian and they will hear us here and they will begin bombing us or something and think they are going to kill a whole crowd of Americans but it will only be us 2 and we can give them the laugh for waisting their ammunitions."

Well Al I seen then that I was parked there with a crazy man and for a while I didn't say nothing because I was scared that I might say something that would encourage him some way so I just shut up and finely he says what is the matter ain't you going to join me? So I said I will join you in the jaw in a minute if you don't shut your mouth and then he quited down a little, but every few minutes he would have another swell idear and once he asked me could I imitate animals and I said no so he says he could mew like a cow and he had heard the boshs were so hard up for food and they would rush out here thinking they was going to find a cow but it wouldn't be no cow but it would be a horse on them.

Well you can imagine what I went through out there with a bird like that and I thought more then once I would catch it from him and go nuts myself but I managed to keep a hold of myself and the happiest minute of my life was when it was time for us to crall back to our dug outs through Nobodys Land but at that I can't remember how we got back here.

This A.M. Sargent Crane asked me what kind of a time did we have and I told him and I told him this here Phillips was squirrel meat and he says Phillips is just as sane as anybody usualy only everybody that went out on the listening post was effected that way by the quite and it's a wonder I didn't go nuts to.

Well its a wonder I didn't Al and its a good thing I kept my head and kept him from playing 1 of those tricks as god knows what would of happened and the entire regt. might of wipped out. But I hope they don't wish no more listening post on me but if they do you can bet I will pick my own pardner and it won't be no nut.

Your pal,
Jack


From *Treat 'em Rough*, by Ring Lardner; Bobbs-Merrill; Indianapolis, 1918, and *The Real Dope*, Bobbs-Merrill; Indianapolis, 1919.

# Epilogue:

# Guide

The killing and the irony lasted until the very end. On the morning of November 11, 1918, with the armies knowing in advance that firing on the western front would cease at 11:00 a.m., there were still over ten thousand casualties, including 2,738 dead—a one-day butcher's bill comparable to D-Day's in the next war. Ambitious officers wanted to burnish their war record while they still could, old scores were yet to be settled, and some units either didn't get the message about the armistice or chose to ignore it; a good many died when gunners celebrated by firing off a last round. Among the casualties were Private George Ellison, shot by a sniper just east of Mons at two minutes before 11:00, the last official British fatality of the war, and Private Henry Gunther, killed by German machine gunners as he charged a roadblock near Ville-devant-Chaumont at 10:59, the last official American fatality of the war.

November 11, 1918, is usually thought of as a time of wild celebration across the victorious Allied nations, but it's clear that this mood was far from universal. Too many families mourned too many sons for them to feel anything but sorrow. Writers picked up on this sense of loss (George Bernard Shaw: "Every promising young man I know has been blown to bits") and, looking toward the future, added many somber warnings.

Here is D. H. Lawrence voicing his opinion at an Armistice night party in London.

"I suppose you think the war is over and that we shall go back to the kind of world you lived in before. But the war isn't over. The hate and evil are greater now than ever. Very soon war will break out again and overwhelm you. It makes me sick to see you rejoicing like a butterfly in the last rays of sun before the winter. The war isn't over. The evil will be worse because the hate will be dammed up in men's hearts and will show itself in all sorts of ways which will be worse than war."

No writer was more unlike Lawrence than H. Rider Haggard, the adventure novelist known for *King Solomon's Mines,* but he shared the same foreboding.

"The Germans will neither forgive nor forget. They have been beaten by England and they will live and die to smash England—she will never have a more deadly enemy than the new Germany. In future years the easy-going, self-centered English will forget that just across the sea there is a mighty, cold-hearted and remorseless people waiting to strike her through the heart. For strike they will someday."

Thomas Hardy, at seventy-eight, found a more nuanced way to express the 11/11/18 mood.

Calm fell. From heaven distilled a clemency;
There was peace on earth, and silence in the sky;
Some could, some could not, shake off misery:
The Sinister Spirit sneered, "It had to be!"
And again the Spirit of Pity whispered, "Why?"

The moment the war ended thousands of people—"pilgrims," as the press called them—began spontaneously making their way to the western front battlefields to see for themselves where the fighting had taken place. Many of these first visitors were parents who had lost sons and wives who had lost husbands; they needed to find what we now call "closure," seeking the graves of their soldiers or, if they were among the huge numbers of missing, at least their names on a monument or plaque.

The killing fields hadn't been prettied up yet—the devastation was plain to be seen—and a careless pilgrim, straying across the trenches, could easily blow herself up on a buried shell (as, a hundred years later, a careless Belgian farmer occasionally still does). Mildred Aldrich, from her little village of Huiry, writes movingly of her own pilgrimage to the nearby American battlefield at Chateau-Thierry in the excerpt included on page 308.

Along with the mourners came thousands of well-heeled tourists, curious to explore the famous battlefields. As early as 1917, the Michelin Tire Company had begun issuing guidebooks to the western front, meticulously researched and heavily illustrated with maps and evocative photos of French villages before the fighting and their ruins afterwards. Included—and this was very rare in books published during the war—were photographs of dead soldiers lying where they fell. These early guides, published while the war was still on, may have given ordinary people, fed nothing but propaganda, their first look at a truthful depiction of the carnage.

The Michelin editors set out their intentions in a brief forward.

> "For the benefit of tourists who wish to visit the battle-fields and mutilated towns of France we have tried to produce a work combining a practical guide and a history . . . Such a visit should be a pilgrimage, not merely a journey across the ravaged land. Seeing is not enough, one must understand; a ruin is more moving when one knows what has caused it; a stretch of country which might seem dull and uninteresting to the

unenlightened eye becomes transformed at the thought
of the battles that have been fought there . . . Our
readers will not find any attempt at literary effect in
these pages; the truth is too beautiful and tragic to be
altered for the sake of embellishing the story."

The anonymous compilers of these guides took great pains to
include even small sites of interest, so after directing tourists to where
three elderly hostages were shot by the Germans outside the village
of Varreddes during the Battle of the Marne, they lead them on, with
great specificity, to another landmark.

"*After having traversed Varreddes and before re-crossing
the canal* a tree will be noticed on the left of the road
(the 38th on the way out) which has been pierced by
a 75 shell as by a punching press."

Enough of these guidebooks were published that they form a
Great War genre of their own, one that remains surprisingly moving and evocative a hundred years later; there is no better way to
understand what the ravaged western front looked like than by
perusing the Michelin battlefield guides published immediately
after the war ended.

Closely linked to these was another style of postwar book: the visit
to the old western front by soldier-writers who had once served there.
Almost all of these are thoughtful, well-written, and moving, and they
form a bridge to the harder, more disillusioned novels and memoirs
that were published in the 1920s, which came to form *the* canon of
World War I literature. C. E. Montague called his own account of
this mood *Disenchantment*, one of the earliest to be published—the
extract included in this section points the way to the familiar literature
of the war, the books whose power and impact still determine how we
remember it.

A hundred years after the fighting ended, it should be possible, if it ever will be possible, to gain some perspective on the years 1914–18, to write of what happened with the Olympian kind of detachment a century can bring. Measured against the long history of mankind, four years in the early twentieth century shouldn't matter very much. A continent of nation-states fell out with each other, the conflict spread across the world, and a rough equivalence between the armies engaged and various technological improvements in military defense (as well as an old one: digging holes) meant that millions of young men would needlessly die. The original reasons for fighting, no matter what revisionist historians might claim, now seem like a form of inexplicable insanity. Alberto Moravia, the Italian novelist, might not have been exaggerating as much as he thought when he termed World War I "an outbreak of collective madness, the reasons for which should be studied by the psychoanalyst rather than the historian."

If we want to apply even more hindsight to the war, we can see it as another form of collective madness: environmental madness. The Great War (though the thought would not have occurred to a single one of its participants) was a carbon war, releasing huge amounts of fossil fuels into the atmosphere; indeed, access to Arab oil was one of the strategic prizes the war was fought over.

Environmental scientists now understand that the world's temperatures and $CO_2$ levels were beginning to rise even by 1914. If statesmen and generals had been granted superhuman powers of foresight, they would have worried about their armies' carbon footprint and not the gain or loss of a few yards of mud. If civilization in the twenty-first century is heading toward environmental suicide, then surely we must look back on the twentieth with an eye toward those events that contributed to our doom—and, looked at that way, World War I was a senseless distraction that, along with World War II, kept us from understanding where the real existential danger to mankind's future lay.

In the same way, though with less exaggeration, it's now possible to draw back from the literature of the period, to see it in perspective—and the first thing that hits you, taking this long view, is that literature not only *existed* but *thrived.* Back before computers, before television and radio, before talkies, before color photos, before all the marvels and doodads of the last hundred years, people seeking to understand the world turned automatically to books, novels, poems, essays, and plays as the best means available to understand the world—often, as the *only* means possible.

It's plausible to assume that in 1914 there were more serious writers at work and more serious readers willing to read them than at any time before or since; writers never had such power and influence over the minds of men. Simultaneously, the Western world approached the worst catastrophe it had ever known, so these writers and readers were faced with their hardest challenge ever. This is why World War I is the most "literary" war; there was simply no better way for a thinking person to try to come to terms with it than by reading books.

Just as no Great War general ever worried about climate change, no World War I writer worried about the dawning visual age, let alone the future digital age, nor about a future that could very well see the extinction of books as physical objects and the subsuming of what was rather quaintly termed "literature" under the avalanche of mass culture.

But you can focus back on the past too far; lofty detachment sometimes obscures as well as sharpens. The soldier-critic Samuel Hynes found just the right distance when he wrote his 1990 study of Great War culture, *A War Imagined.* His introduction explains in one pithy paragraph why, even a hundred years later, we still need to care about what the writers of that era had to say.

> "The First World War was the great military and political event of its time, but it was also the great *imaginative* event. It altered the ways in which men and women thought not only about war but about the world, and about culture and its expression. No one

after the war—no thinker or planner, no politician or
labor leader, no writer or painter—could ignore its historical importance or frame his thought as though the
war had not occurred, or had been simply another war."

It's through this understanding that the neglected war literature
collected in this volume should be approached. World War I, if nothing else, presented writers with a challenging literary experiment few
of them would have wished for. Faced with the collapse of civilization,
how, as a writer, do you respond?

We've seen the answers.

Some respond by giving up their writing and enlisting in the
armies. Some respond by getting killed. Some respond by using their
words to get other men to enlist and be killed. Some argue about
politics, strategy, who's to blame. A small number—a *very* small number—protest. Some—Yeats, Pound, Forester, Strachey, Frost—ignore
the war entirely. Some try to ameliorate its worst features, to fight
toward a better future. Some swallow every lie the government hands
them; some intuitively spit them out. Some seek to increase the hatred,
others to reduce it. Some try to make money. Some attempt to understand the larger tragedy. Every one of them believes in the permanence
of literature, the supremacy of the written word, the primacy of books.

The forgotten literature of the war written by civilians is vaster than
one volume can do justice to. If space permitted, it would be good
to quote from Hermann Hesse's heartfelt appeals for peace, or from
the pacifist playwright Miles Malleson, or novelist Stephen McKenna,
whose *Sonia* was a bestseller in 1917, or Rose Allatini, whose 1918
novel *Despised and Rejected,* about a homosexual pacifist, brought her
prosecution under the Defence of the Realm Act and the destruction
of all copies, or Francis Meynell, among the first pacifist writers in any
Allied country. And it would be good to include the antiwar satire of
the brave Austrian writer Karl Krauss.

For that matter, it would be good to include those forgotten writers on the war whose best work appeared years afterwards, like American Humphrey Cobb, whose *Paths of Glory*, published in 1935, remains one of the best Great War novels (and, directed by Stanley Kubrick, one of the best films about the Great War), and the remarkable Mary Borden, whose experimental *The Forbidden Zone,* published in 1929, is one of the most original of the war's memoirs. And there's another: C. S. Forester's novel *The General,* published in 1936, which shows how when fate needs hard men to do its dirty work, hard men come to the fore.

Most of these men and women were middle-aged or older; the younger generation of writers, the ones who had actually experienced the fighting, would not have their turn until the 1920s, when their voices, so authentic and "modern," would help cause much of the writing from 1914–18 to be immediately forgotten.

This book has tried to restore the imbalance. "An ignorant, middle-aged civilian will not write about the war in the way that a young subaltern will," Hynes reminds us, "but he may write movingly nonetheless."

To me, it's their *trying* that I find moving, a hundred years later. A novelist myself, an "aging non-combatant," I know what it's like to sit down at your desk to attempt to comprehend a world that seems engaged in perpetual war. I know, in other words, what H. G. Wells's Mr. Britling feels as he sits down at the conclusion of the novel, his son dead, his civilization in ruins, with nothing to fight back with but his puny ability with words . . . and for that reason, it's with Britling at his desk, speaking for all writers in all times, that these excerpts will end.

This book concerns the past, so perhaps it's appropriate to take a moment and look toward the future. Specifically, to the future of the books I've drawn from here. For the past twenty years, almost accidentally at first, then eventually with more purpose, they have been accumulating on the bookshelves in my office, to the point that they take up almost an entire wall. They look good there. For reasons of economy, most of the books published 1914–18 were small, so they match each other, forming neat rows. Most are brown—chocolate brown, reddish brown, khaki brown, trench brown. For the past two years, as I've stitched together this book, they were taken down often from their perches, opened and closed, read and perused, and they've held up to the usage quite well. Some have bindings that are crumbling, and others, when you turn the pages, flake into rough paper bits, but I'm gentle with them, and they respond by hanging tough; having survived two world wars and a murderous century, they will not mind continuing to fulfill their original purpose: being handled, being read. They are a long way yet from dust.

So they're survivors, these books—but for how much longer? I'll keep them for a while, enjoying if nothing else the stolid, knowing way they sit there on my shelves. But when I'm gone, it's hard to see them surviving me more than a few years. These are, after all, books that have already been discarded, some discarded many times. No library wants them, no collectors. My heirs, with no other recourse, will empty them into a dumpster along with the other life's accumulations they won't have use for.

A few of these titles, by then, will have been digitized; if students in the future want to consult them, some will be waiting in the Internet cloud. That's survival, of sorts, though for some of us, the quaintly old-fashioned physicality is still important, and digital books, whatever else they are, are not the books these writers created, nor the books that people alive in 1918 held in their hands.

But they've made their mark, done their job, reminding us, in an age where literature is dying, how writers at the height of their powers faced a catastrophe armed with nothing more powerful than words—and how, against all odds, they did this so successfully that their words, even now, are the best way to understand what mankind suffered in those four fated years.

*A Guide to the American Battle Fields in Europe* was prepared by the American Battle Monuments Commission and printed by the United States Government Printing Office in Washington. My sturdily bound copy is stamped with the name "A. R. Farless" in the front, of "San Mateo, California." Mr. Farless, or another reader, tore out a 1919 *National Geographic* article and folded it in the pages; it's about Gold Star Mothers—mothers who lost a son in the fighting—traveling to France on organized visits to see where their sons were killed. The photo shows them posed on a liner in mid-ocean, overdressed, hundreds of them, staring up at the photographer on the bridge.

This guide was a quality production, with copious photographs, maps so detailed and beautifully printed they could be hung in a museum, and an informative, no-nonsense text. The preface states, "The publication of this book was expedited in order to have it available for the large number of ex-service men who intend to go to Europe in the fall of 1927"—a pilgrimage to mark the tenth anniversary of America's entrance into the war.

Henry Williamson served in the war as a twenty-year-old, and went on to a long career as an author; he became famous for his nature books, including the bestselling *Tarka the Otter*. Later, he wrote a series of fifteen novels based on the war, *A Chronicle of Ancient Sunlight*. Despite a later flirtation with fascism, he's still read and admired today—a Henry Williamson Society is dedicated to perpetuating his memory. If you go online, you can watch him interviewed, an old man now, in the 1964 BBC series *The Great War*. It is fascinating, particularly his description of taking part, as a young man, in the famous Christmas Truce in the middle of No Man's Land in 1914.

"It is sad to think," he wrote in 1934, "that in a few years the literature of the war of 1914–18 will be forgotten, like that of other wars, in a European war arising not because the last war was forgotten, but because its origins and contributing causes in each one of us were never clearly perceived by ourselves."

Michelin Tires traces its history back to 1889, when the company patented the first pneumatic bicycle tire; it continues to be one of the world's largest tire companies today, famous for its emblem, the tire-chested "Michelin Man," and its Red Guides to European restaurants and the bestowal of the coveted Michelin stars for the world's best chefs.

*Ypres and the Battle of Ypres* was published in 1920 in the "Michelin Illustrated Guides to the Battlefields" series. No other book from that era is more evocative, with its photos, maps, and matter-of-fact descriptions of what the devastated western front looked like just after the fighting stopped. I came across a copy in an old bookstore in Vermont—and found it so moving it was one of the inspirations for my own World War I novel, *A Century of November.*

It's a small book, designed to be easily carried, with only a single advertisement for Michelin there in the front: a drawing of a woman helping her daughter into an elegant touring car while the chauffeur patiently waits. "The Best & Cheapest Wheel," the caption reads, "is the Michelin wheel. Elegant Strong Simple Practical."

On the title page is the dedication.

"In Memory of the Michelin Workmen and Employees Who Died Gloriously For Their Country."

Stephen Graham, at thirty, already had a reputation as a travel writer when he enlisted in the Scots Guards, thanks to his books on prewar Russia. He wrote two books on the war, *A Private in the Guards* and *The Challenge of the Dead,* with its subtitle "A vision of the War and the life of the common soldier in France, seen two years afterwards between August and November 1920."

John Masefield served as Britain's Poet Laureate for almost fifty years; I'm old enough to remember having to memorize his "Sea Fever" in school. Thirty-six when the war broke out, he volunteered at a military hospital in France, went to Gallipoli to report on the battle, then spent weeks walking over the Somme trenches after the front line had temporarily moved eastward.

Very much a traditional Georgian poet, "believing that poetry is made out of natural beauty, and plain, traditional words," he found the war made writing poetry impossible; rather than write "false" war poetry, he spent the war writing prose.

Forty-seven was old to enlist in the British army, so C. E. Montague, an editorial writer for the *Manchester Guardian,* dyed his white hair black in order to pass the medical. He served as a captain at General Headquarters—responsible for, among other duties, escorting VIP writers like Shaw and Wells around the trenches—before being invalided back to civilian life. His *Disenchantment* of 1922, "a book about how England turned, and betrayed herself, her soldiers, and her values," was one of the first books to capture—and perpetuate—the bitter postwar mood.

## *The Pilgrimage*
### —Mildred Aldrich

The expected news came early Monday morning. As we anticipated, the order had been given to cease firing at eleven. We had known it would come, but the fact that the order had been given rather stunned us. To realize that it was over! How could one in a minute?

I was up early to wait for the papers. It was a perfect white day. The whole world was covered with the first hoar frost and wrapped in an impenetrable white fog, as if the huge flag of truce were wound around it. I went out on the lawn and turned my eyes toward the invisible north. Standing beside my little house I was as isolated as if I were all alone in the world, with all the memories of these years since that terrible day in August 1914. I could not see as far as the hedge. Yet out there I knew the guns were still firing, and between them and me lay such devastation as even the imagination cannot exaggerate, and such suffering and pain as the human understanding can but partly conceive. Against the white sheet which encircled me I seemed to see the back water of the war which touched here. Four years and four months—and how much is still before us? The future has its job laid out for it. Is ordinary man capable of putting it over?

I had expected that at eleven, when they ceased firing at the front, our bells would ring out the victory. We had our flags all ready to run up. I was standing on the lawn listening, flags ready at the gate, and Amelie stood in the window at her house, ready to hang out hers. All along the road, though I could not see them for the fog, I knew that women and children were listening with me. The silence was oppressive. Not a sound reached me, except now and then the passing of a train over the Marne. Then Amelie came down to say that lunch was ready, and that I might as well eat whether I had any appetite or not, and that perhaps something had happened, and that after lunch she would go over to Quincy and find out what it was.

So, reluctantly, I went into the house.

It was just quarter past twelve when I heard someone running along the terrace, and a child's voice called, "*Ecoutez, Madame, ecoutez! Les carillons de Meaux!*"

Far off, faint through the white sheet of mist, I could hear the bells of the cathedral, like fairy music, but nothing more. I waited expecting any moment to hear the bells from Couilly or Quincy or Conde, and the guns from the forts. But all was silent. There were no longer any groups on the roads. I knew that every one had gone home to eat. Somewhere things were happening, I was sure of that. But I might have been alone on a desert island.

I was too nervous to keep still any longer, so I walked up to the corner of the Chemin Madame, thinking I might hear the bells from there. As I stood at the corner I heard footsteps running toward me on the frozen ground, and out of the fog came Marin, the town crier, with his drum on his back and a *cocarde* in his cap. He waved his drumsticks at me as he ran, and cried, "I am coming as fast as I can,

Madame. We are ringing up at four—at the same time the Tiger reads the terms in the Chamber of Deputies and Lloyd George reads them in London," and as he reached the corner just above my gate he swung his drum around and beat it up like mad.

It did not take two minutes for all our little hamlet to gather about him, while in a loud, clear voice he read solemnly the *ordre de jour* which officially announced that the war had ended at eleven o'clock, and the inhabitants of the *commune* were authorized to hang out all their flags, light up their windows, and join in a dignified and seemly celebration of the liberation of France. Then he slowly lifted his cap in his hand as he read the concluding phrases, which begged them not to forget to pray for the brave men who had given their lives that this day might be, nor to be unmindful that to many among us this day of rejoicing was also a day of mourning.

There was not a cheer.

Morin swung the drum over his shoulder, saluted his audience, and marched solemnly down the hill. In dead silence the little group broke up.

The run out to Chateau-Thierry from here took less than an hour in a little Ford car. It was not an ideal day for the trip. It was gray and windy, and there was a fine drizzle of rain now and then. A sunny day would have been less sad, but I doubt it would have suited my mood any better.

Over the line where the first battle of the Marne passed in the fall of 1914 time has effaced almost every trace, so it was not until we neared Bouresches and Belleau that we began to realize that here battles had been fought. These three little hamlets are so tiny that, although they feature on road maps for the guidance of ardent auto-mobilists, you will find no mention made of them in any guide-books. Even by name they were, until June of last year, unknown to every one outside the immediate vicinity. Now, ruined as they all are, each bears at either end a board sign, with the name of the town painted in black letters.

With the ruins of what was once a tiny hamlet on one hand, across a shell-torn field rises the small, densely wooded height whose name is known today to every American—the tragic Belleau Wood. The little hamlet is just a mass of fallen or falling walls, as deserted as Pompeii and already looking centuries old.

The road approaching it is still screaming with reminiscences of the war four months after the last gun was fired. All along the way are heaps of salvaged stuff of all sorts—mountains of empty shell cases of all sizes, piles of wicker baskets containing unused German shell, thrown down and often broken shell racks, all sorts of telegraphic materials, cases of machine-gun belts, broken kitchens, smashed buckets, tangles of wire and rolls of new barbed wire—in fact all the debris of modern warfare plus any quantity of German artillery material left in their retreat—everything, in fact, except guns and corpses.

Across the fields still zigzag barbed-wire entanglements in many places, while in others the old wire is rolled up by the roadside. Here and there is still a trench, while a line of freshly turned soil in the green fields shows where the trenches have been filled in.

In the banks along the road are the German dugouts, with broken drinking cups, tin boxes, dented casques, strewn about the entrances, which are often broken down, while every little way are the "foxholes" in the banks marking the places where the American boys tried to dig in. The ground before the town which the Germans had shelled so furiously, as the Americans were pushing through to cross the fields and clean out the wooded hill opposite, has been swept and ploughed by the artillery on both sides. The American Captain whose guest I was could say, from a glance at the shell holes: "That is one of ours." "That was one of theirs." "That is a 75." "That is an 88." "That is a 240." "This place was rushed." "That place was shelled."

Nature is doing her best to heal the scarred landscape, but Belleau Wood, across the field from the ruined hamlets, is a sinister sight still. It is a ghastly sort of place to fight in—a thickly wooded slope, a tangle of uncleared brush on the outskirts ideal for masking machine guns; the clearing of it called for a terrible loss of life.

Today the whole hill is shell-shot. The trees hang dead, dried and broken. The ground looks as though verdure could never clothe it again. Everywhere else Nature has already laid her soothing hands, but she has yet to touch that tragic wood. On the gray, rainwashed walls of the little hamlets, green things already trail and wild flowers are beginning to grow. Even the shell-holes in the fields are gay with dandelions and field primroses, *paquerettes* and *boutons d'or*. But Belleau Wood, as seen from the ruined hamlet, is an open grief on the face of Nature.

The roads are absolutely deserted—except for Americans. Across the broken fields toward the dark forests, groups of boys in khaki or women in the uniforms of the various relief units, were constantly passing as we sat in the road between the ruins and the woods. At every corner stood an American *camion* or a *camionette,* and we passed no other sort of automobile on the road, and no other pedestrians, as we slowly ran over the sacred ground into Chateau-Thierry. Along the quiet roadsides lie buried the American lads who fell here in the long battle which ended the war.

All the little cemeteries are alike—rectangular spaces, enclosed in a wire fence. Usually there are three or four guns stacked in the centre, often surmounted by a "tin hat," as the boys call their helmets. There are always several lines of graves, each with a wooden cross at the head with a small American flag set in a round disk under isinglass, surrounded by a green metal frame representing a wreath to which is attached a small card-shaped plaque with the name and number.

None of these cemeteries about Chateau-Thierry is large. They are all on the banks on the side of the road, and I can't tell you how I felt as we approached our first, and stopped the car beside it, and crawled out into the mud. Just now the well-ordered graves are not sodded. I suppose it was the idea of seeing so many graves—we saw at least a dozen of these little cemeteries—and remembering how young they were who slept there that impressed me. Later, I imagine, when the graves are all properly tended, the scene would lose its look of sadness.

An American woman who has been going back and forward over that devastated country said to me the other day, as she stopped at my gate: "Terrible as it all is it gets less terrible every day."

From *When Johnny Comes Marching Home*, by Mildred Aldrich; Small, Maynard and Company; Boston, 1919.

## *Turn Right at Cemetery Gate*
—American Battle Monuments Commission

The Oise-Aisne American Cemetery contains 5,962 graves. The majority of the battle dead who sleep here are from the divisions that fought in the vicinity of the Ourcq River and in the territory from there to the north as far as the Oise River. In 1922, the American soldiers then buried in France in the general area west of the line Tours-Romorantin-Paris-LeHavre were removed to this cemetery.

The Cemetery is under direct charge of the American Graves Registration Service, Quartermaster Corps, United States Army, whose offices at this time are at 20 rue Molitor, Paris. An information bureau is maintained at that office, which can be consulted by those who wish to known in which cemetery a particular grave is located.

It is about 18 miles by road from Chateau-Thierry, and slightly more from Reims. Good train service is available to each of these places, where hotel accommodations can be obtained and automobiles hired.

*After the cemetery chapel is built, a good view of the surrounding battle fields may be had from its tower.*

This point is the most advanced line reached by the 2d Division. The series of attacks which carried that division forward to this line were invariably accompanied by fighting of the most desperate character. BELLEAU WOOD, at the edge of which the observer is standing, in particular lent itself admirably to defensive fighting on account of its rocky character and tangled undergrowth. The wood was the scene of bitter fighting, extending over 21 days, and in honor of its capture by the Marine Brigade of the 2d Division the French changed its official name to the Bois de la Brigade de Marine.

The splendid conduct of the 2d Division in taking Belleau Wood and other difficult positions along its front in spite of a casualty list of approximately 8,000 officers and men, was enthusiastically proclaimed by the French Army and people.

*Turn right at cemetery gate. At road fork just beyond, take road to left.* This road, from the point where it crosses the railroad to the top of the next hill, was in "no-man's-land" during the afternoon and evening of July 20. *At kilometer post 21.9,* by looking back, a good view is obtained of the cemetery and Belleau Wood.

*Cross highway (at kilometer post 25.8), taking road straight ahead. STOP at end of road at site selected for American monument on Hill 204.*

*Information concerning this monument is given in Chapter XI.*

The large town, a mile away, lying on both sides of the Marne River, is Chateau-Thierry. On the left, just before reaching the bridge, there is a building of a Methodist institution, established by Americans as a war memorial, and a monument erected by the 3d American Division. The building contains a small museum of war relics . . . .

From *A Guide to the American Battle Fields of Europe*, prepared by the American Battle Monuments Commission; United States Government Printing Office; Washington, 1927.

## *Peasants Go There to Dig*
### —Henry Williamson

Hill 60 is one of the show places of the Ypres Salient to-day. Every morning about a dozen peasants go there to dig. You see the "souvenirs" they have dug up lying on sacks or lengths of cloth at the edge of the pits in which they are working. There are wooden pipes, both British and German shapes, well preserved in the light sandy soil, fragments of rifles, bayonets, picklehaube eagle-badges, English county and London regimental badges, buttons, straps, bully-beef tins, pistols, bombs, revolvers, boots. Imagine an ant-hill, fifty yards across its base, thrown up a few dozen times by subterranean heavings, and dropping again after each mine-explosion more or less in the same place; always being pocked and repocked with shells; and now set with a small memorial to the 9th London Regiment, and dug over, and strolled over by 10,000 people every week.

All day long charabancs stop in the road opposite Hill 60, and tourists file past the melancholy little group of men and children standing, collecting-box in hand, by the footpath entrance, and hoping to take half a franc off each visitor. By their sad faces they do not own the heap of earth, originally piled there when the railway cutting was made; yet by the occasional gleams of hate in those eyes we deduce that they have stood there with their boxes long enough to believe that they ought to own it.

Along the footpath the pitches of the souvenir-sellers begin. Prices range from 50 centimes for a brass button to 20 francs for a Smith and Wesson revolver.

From *The Wet Flanders Plain*, by Henry Williamson; E. P. Dutton & Co.; New York, 1929.

## *Visit to the Battlefield*
### —Michelin & Cie.

A visit to Ypres Town and Salient requires two days, and may be made most conveniently by taking Lille as the starting point.

Starting point: The Grand Place, Lille.

*Take Rue Nationale to the end, go round Place Tourcoing, take Rue de La Basse on the left, then the first turning on the right. At Canteleu follow the tram-lines leading to Lomme. At the end of the village, cross the railway. Go through Lomme by Rue Thiers, leaving the church on the right* (transept greatly damaged).

On the left are the burnt ruins of a large spinning mill. In the fields: numerous small forts of reinforced concrete, which commanded all the roads into Lille. The road passes through a small wood, in the right-hand part of which are the ruins of Premesques Chateau, of which only the facade remains. Further on, to the left, is Wez Macquart, whose church was badly damaged. Trenches lead to the road, while in the fields traces of violent shelling are still visible.

*Pass through Chapelle d'Armentieres (completely destroyed). After crossing the railway, a British cemetery is seen on the right. ARMENTIERES lies on the other side of the next level crossing.*

Belfry, churches and houses are all in ruins.

In everything connected with the spinning and weaving of linen Armentieres was considerably in advance of Germany. Consequently, the Germans destroyed all the mills, factories and metallurgical works, and what machinery could not be taken to pieces and sent to Germany they ruthlessly smashed.

*Cross the Cloth Market, then follow the tram-lines along Rue de Flandre and Rue Bizet. Go through Bizet Village* (badly damaged houses). *Leaving the ruins of the church on the right, turn first to the right, then to the left. Cross the frontier into Belgium a few yards further off. Leaving on the right the road to the gasworks* (of which nothing is left but a wrecked gasometer) *the first hours of Ploegsteert are reached. The village lay west of the first lines in May, 1918, and was captured by the Germans on April 12.*

British cemetery No. 53 lies at the entrance to the village. *Go straight through the village* (in ruins). *On leaving it,* Cemetery No. 54 is seen on the right, then beyond a large concrete shelter, Cemetery No. 55. Cemetery No. 56 is on the left, beyond the level-crossing.

*Cross Ploegsteert Wood, leaving the road to Petit-Pont Farm on the left. Here the road rises.* To the left, on the slopes of Hill 63, are seen the ruins of La Hutte Chateau. On the crest opposite stand the ruins of Messines. In June, 1919, it was not possible to go direct to Messines, the road being cut at the Petite Douve stream.

Stop the car at Rossignol terre-plain and walk a few yards into the little wood on the right; numerous concrete shelters, from the top of which there is a very fine view over the Hills Kemmel, Rouge, Noir and Cats. The last-named can be recognized by its abby, which stands out against the sky.

*Return to the car. The road now descends past the "tank cemetery" containing fourteen broke-down tanks. Passing by a few ruined houses—all that remain of the hamlet of Habourdin—a fork is reached, where take the Neuve-Eglise-Messines road on the right.* British cemetery on the right. *Turn to the right at the first ruins of Wulverghem, then go through the village, passing in front of the cemetery. Next cross the Steenbeck, by the St. Quentin Bridge. The road now rises sharply to the crest on which Messines used to stand.* Numerous small forts are seen to the right and left. These machine-gun nests are all that now mark the site of the village.

At the entrance to the village leave the car at the junction of the Ypres-Armentieres road and visit these pathetic ruins on foot.

From *Ypres and the Battles of Ypres*, by Michelin & Cie; Clermont-Ferrand, 1920.

## *Cemeteries Become Unremarkable*
—Stephen Graham

You make for what was once a wood; it afforded cover. What is it now—thrice thrashed and riven, the abode of rats, lizards, weasels, a calamitous and precipitous abyss covered with wreckage. Unexploded stick-bombs, rusty grog-bottles, helmets, lie there in plenty. Weather-beaten ammunition baskets with shells intact where they fell off the ammunition wagons or where men dropped them. There are broken rifles, there are graves. There is all but the blood.

On the vast waste you come upon houses built of salvage. Duck-boards have been gathered in, old bits of rusty corrugated iron which sheltered trenches and kept out rain have been collected by the returned Flemish—what a return!—and they have made shacks of shreds and patches. Fierce dogs on chains bark from them; no children venture forth—there are no children there. Heaps of the jetsam of the battlefields are in the yards. The uncouth workers are not too pleased to see any stranger, and look suspiciously at you. They have pistols ready at need. For these oases in the wilderness are not unvisited by robbers, and thieves lurk in old holes in the ground. One comes to a road, and there is what was Zonnebeke resurrected in a tail of diminutive cabins each roofed with corrugated iron, each numbered as a claim for reparation. Not a few of the houses are named thus:—"In den Niewen wereld." Half of them seem to be estaminets. It is the same at Becelaere. The people earn a living drinking beer in one another's estaminets.

Cemeteries soon become all too frequent and unremarkable. At Klein Zillebeke there is an Englishwoman going from grave to grave diligently examining the aluminum ribbons on which the names are fixed to the wooden crosses—looking perhaps for her husband's grave.

Death and the ruins completely outweigh the living. One is tilted out of time by the huge weight on the other end of the plank, and it would be easy to imagine someone who had no insoluble ties killing himself here, drawn by the lodestone of death.

From *The Challenge of the Dead,* by Stephen Graham; Cassel and Co.; New York, 1921.

## *Back to the Somme*
—John Masefield
All the way up the hill the road is steep, rather deep and bad. It is worn into the chalk and shows up very white in sunny weather.

Before the battle it lay about midway between the lines, but it was always patrolled at night by our men. The ground on both sides of it is almost more killed and awful than anywhere in the field. On the English or south side of it, distant from one hundred to two hundred yards, is the shattered wood, burnt, dead, and desolate. On the enemy side, at about the same distance, is the usual black enemy wire, much tossed and bunched by our shells, covering a tossed and tumbled chalky and filthy parapet. Our own old line is an array of rotted sand-bags, filled with chalkflint, covering the burnt wood. One need only look at the ground to know that the fighting here was very grim, and to the death. Near the road and up the slope to the enemy ground is littered with relics of our charges, mouldy packs, old shattered scabbards, rifles, bayonets, helmets curled, torn, rolled, and starred, clips of cartridges, and very many graves. Many of the graves are marked with strips of wood torn from packing cases, with penciled inscriptions, "An unknown British Hero;" "In loving memory of Pte.—;" "Two unknown British heroes;" "An unknown British soldier;" "A dead Fritz." That gentle slope to the Schwaben Redoubt is covered with such things.

Where the crown of the work once reared itself aloft over the hill, the heaps of mud are all blurred and pounded together, so that there is no design, no trace, no visible plan of any fortress, only a mess of mud bedevilled and bewildered. All this mess of heaps and hillocks is strung and filthied over with broken bodies and ruined gear.

Once in a lull of the firing a woman appeared upon the enemy parapet and started to walk along it. Our men held their fire and watched her. She walked steadily along the whole front of the Schwaben and then jumped down into her trench. Many thought at the time that she was a man masquerading for a bet, but long afterwards, when our men took the Schwaben, they found her lying in the ruins dead. They buried her there, up on the top of the hill. God alone knows who she was and what she was doing there.

From *The Old Front Line*, by John Masefield; The Macmillan Company; New York, 1918.

## *Whose Credulous Hearts the Maggots Were Now Eating*
### —C. E. Montague

The senior generals need not have feared. The generous youth of the war was pretty well gone. The authentic flame might still flicker on in the minds of a few tired soldiers and disregarded civilians. Otherwise it was as dead as the half-million of good fellows who it had fired four years ago, whose credulous hearts the maggots were now eating under so many shining and streaming square miles of wet Flanders and Picardy. They gone, their war had lived into a kind of dotage ruled by mean fears and desires. At home our places of honour were brown with shirkers masquerading in the dead men's clothes and licensed by careless authorities to shelter themselves from all danger under the titles of Colonel, Major, and Captain. Nimble politicians were rushing already to coin into votes for themselves—"the men who won the war"—the golden memory of the dead before the living could come home and make themselves heard.

"This way, gents, for the right sort of whip to give Germans!" "Rats, gentlemen, rats! Don't listen to *him*. Leave it to me and I'll chastise 'em with scorpions." "I'll devise brave punishments for them." "Ah, but I'll sweat you more money out of the swine." Each little demagogue got his little pots of pitch and sulphur on sale for the proper giving of hell to the enemy whom he had not faced.

"The freedom of Europe," "The war to end war," "The overthrow of militarism," "The cause of civilization"—most people believe so little now in anything or anyone that they would find it hard to understand the simplicity and intensity of faith with which these phrases were once taken among our troops, or the certitude felt by hundreds of thousands of men who are now dead that if they were killed their monument would be a new Europe now soured or soiled with the hates and greeds of the old. That the old spirit of Prussia might not infest our world any more; that they, or, if not they, their sons might breathe a new, cleaner air they had willingly hung themselves up to rot on the uncut wire at Loos or wriggled to death, slow hour by hour, in the cold filth at Broodseinde. Now all was done that man could do, and all was done in vain.

So we had failed—had won the fight and lost the prize; the garland of the war was withered before it was gained. The lost years, the broken youth, the dead friends, the women's overshadowed lives at home, the agony and bloody sweat—all had gone to darken the stains which most of us had thought to scour out of the world that our children would live in. Many men felt, and said to each other, that they had been fooled. So we come home draggle-tailed, sick of the mess that we were unwittingly helping to make when we tried to do so well.

From *Disenchantment*, by C. E. Montague; Chatto and Windus; London, 1922.

## *The Most Tragic and Dreadful Thing that Has Ever Happened to Mankind*
### —H. G. Wells

It was now the middle of November, and Mr. Britling, very warmly wrapped in his thick dressing-gown and his thick llama wool pyjamas, was sitting at his night desk and working ever and again at an essay, an essay of preposterous ambitions, for the title of it was "The Better Government of the World."

Latterly he had much sleepless misery. In the day life was tolerable, but in the night—unless he defended himself by working, the losses and cruelties of the war came and grimaced at him, insufferably. Now he would be haunted by long processions of refugees, now he would think of the dead lying stiff and twisted in a thousand dreadful attitudes. Then again he would be overwhelmed with anticipations of the frightful economic and social dissolution that might lie ahead . . . At other times he thought of wounds and the deformities of body and spirit produced by injuries. And sometimes he would think of the triumph of evil. Stupid and triumphant persons went about a world that stupidity had desolated, with swaggering gestures, with a smiling consciousness of enhanced importance, with their scornful hatred of all measured and temperate and kindly things turned now to scornful contempt. And mingling with the soil they walked on lay the dead body of Hugh, face downward. At the back of the boy's head, rimmed by blood-stiffened hair—the hair that had once been "as soft as the down of a bird"—was a big red hole. That hole was always pitilessly distinct. They stepped on him—heedlessly. They heeled the scattered stuff of his exquisite brain into the clay . . .

From all such moods of horror Mr. Britling's circle of lamplight was his sole refuge. His work could conjure up visions, like opium visions, of a world of order and justice. Amidst the gloom of world bankruptcy he stuck to the prospectus of a braver enterprise—reckless of his chances of subscribers . . .

But this night even this circle of lamplight would not hold his mind. Doubt had crept into this last fastness. He pulled the papers towards him, and turned over the portion he had planned.

His purpose in the book he was beginning to write was to reason out the possible methods of government that would give a stabler, saner control to the world. He believed still in democracy, but he was realising more and more that democracy had yet to discover its method. It had to take hold of the consciences of men, it had to equip itself with still unformed organisations. Endless years of patient thinking, of experimenting, of discussion lay before mankind ere this great idea could become reality, and right, the proven right things, could rule the earth.

Meanwhile the world must still remain a scene of blood-stained melodramas, or deafening noise, contagious follies, vast irrational destructions. One fine life after another went down from study and university and laboratory to be slain and silenced . . .

Was it conceivable that this mad monster of mankind would ever be caught and held in the thin-spun webs of thought?

Was it, after all, anything but pretension and folly for a man to work out plans for the better government of the world?—was it any better than the ambitious scheming of some fly upon the wheel of the romantic gods?

Man has come, floundering and wounding and suffering, out of the breeding darkness of Time, that will presently crush and consume him again. Why not flounder with the rest, why not eat, drink, fight, scream, weep and pray, forget Hugh, stop brooding upon Hugh, banish all these priggish dreams of "The Better Government of the World" and turn to the brighter aspects, the funny and adventurous aspects of the war, the Chestertonian jolliness, *Punch* side of things? Think you because your sons are dead that there will be no more cakes and ale? Let mankind blunder out of the mud and blood as mankind has blundered in . . .

Let us at any rate keep our precious Sense of Humour . . .

He pulled the manuscript towards him. For a time he sat decorating the lettering of his title, "The Better Government of the World," with little grinning gnomes' heads and waggish tails . . .

Mr. Britling's pen stopped.

There was perfect stillness in the study bedroom.

"The tinpot style," said Mr. Britling at last in a voice of extreme bitterness.

He fell into an extraordinary quarrel with his style—at his exasperation about his own inexpressiveness, at his incomplete control of these rebel words and phrases that came trailing each its own associations and suggestions to hamper his purpose with it. He read over the offending sentence.

"The point is that it is true," he whispered. "It is exactly what I want to say" . . .

Exactly? . . .

His mind stuck on that "exactly" . . . When one has much to say style is troublesome. It is as if one fussed with one's uniform before a battle . . . but that is just what one ought to do before a battle . . . One ought to have everything in order.

He took a fresh sheet and made three trial beginnings.

*"War is like a black fabric."* . . .

*"War is a curtain of black fabric across the pathway."*

*"War is a curtain of dense black fabric across all the hopes and kind-liness of mankind. Yet always it has let through some gleams of light, and now—I am not dreaming—it grows threadbare, and here and there and at a thousand points the light is breaking through. We owe it to all these dear youths—"*

His pen stopped again.

"I must work on a rough draft," said Mr. Britling.

From *Mr. Britling Sees It Through*, by H. G. Wells; The Macmillan Company; New York, 1917.

# Works and Writers Selected, Per Chapter

**Chapter One: Argue**

*The most desperately earnest thing*, Arthur Conan Doyle; *They must be destroyed*, Maurice Maeterlinck; *The most sincere war*, G. K. Chesterton; *The moral energy of nations*, Henri Bergson; *I do not hold my tongue easily*, George Bernard Shaw; *Mere wordmonger to shame*, Christabel Pankhurst; *The god of force*, John Galsworthy; *I am a professional observer*, Arnold Bennett; *The children of Attila*, Romain Rolland; *Are we barbarians?*, Gerhart Hauptmann; *The man who does his fighting with his mouth*, Jerome K. Jerome; *All normal Americans*, Booth Tarkington.

**Chapter Two: Moralize**

*The big guns at work*, Joseph Conrad; *The abyss of our past delusion*, Henry James; *The unfurling of the future*, Thomas Hardy; *Let loose these evil powers*, Gilbert Murray; *The will to power*, Thomas Mann; *Wordsworth's Valley in War-Time*, Mrs. Humphrey Ward; *Men whispered together*, H. G. Wells; *Scientific Barbarism*, Havelock Ellis; *Keep our mouths shut*, W. B. Yeats.

**Chapter Three: Witness**

*A calamity unheard of in human annals*, Edith Wharton; *I shall stay*, Mildred Aldrich; *Its purpose is death*, Richard Harding Davis; *Stench of the battlefield*, Frances Wilson Huard; *The swathe of stillness*, Henry Beston; *Little household gods shiver and blink*, Edith Wharton; *The Gothas*, Mildred Aldrich; *It is no pleasure to tell what I saw*, Richard Harding Davis; *The War Capital of Serbia*, John Reed; *That sepia waste*, Winston Churchill.

## Chapter Four: Lie

*Babies on bayonets*, Arnold J. Toynbee; *Hymn of Hate*, Ernest Lissauer; *Mother is the name of the gun*, Arthur Conan Doyle; *The master spirit of hell*, W. D. Howells; *Vandal guns of dull intent*, Edmond Rostand; *These terrific symbols*, Rudyard Kipling; *Few wished themselves elsewhere*, John Buchan; *Nearer than any other woman*, Mrs. Humphrey Ward; *The world has a right to know*, Richard Harding Davis; *Old men don't go*, H. G. Wells.

## Chapter Five: Pity

*All that this war has annihilated*, May Sinclair; *A bit of metal turned them for home*, Enid Bagnold; *The very flower of the human race*, Henry James; *With the wounded I was at home*, Hugh Walpole; *The Boche bread is bad*, Henry Beston; *The Return of the Soldier*, Rebecca West; *On Leave*, H. M. Tomlinson; *Andiamo a casa*, G. M. Trevelyan; *What manner of man*, John Dos Passos; *Smashed in some complicated manner*, H. G. Wells.

## Chapter Six: Protest

*This war is trivial*, Bertrand Russell; *The last great carouse*, G. F. Nicolai; *Courage there is no room for*, Jane Addams; *This unspeakably inhuman outrage*, W. E. B. Du Bois; *A war made deliberately by intellectuals*, Randolph Bourne; *Women who dared*, Emily G. Balch; *The bitterness of gall*, Scott Nearing; *Crime against the individual*, Reinhold Niebuhr; *This saturnalia of massacre*, E. D. Morel.

## Chapter Seven: Mourn

*And the bullet won*, Richard Harding Davis; *He loved his youth*, John Buchan; *Demons of the whirlwind*, George Santayana; *All four lie buried on the Western Front*, Gilbert Murray; *Eyes lit with risk*, Jean Cocteau; *Drop drop drop of blood*, Henry Beston; *Of all the days in my life the most terrible*, Harry

Lauder; *He wanted me to write*, Katherine Mansfield; *A girl in a pinafore*, H. G. Wells; *Tears are difficult for a man to shed*, Paul Claudel; *I lay on that brown mound*, Harry Lauder; *And I will murder some German*, H. G. Wells.

## Chapter Eight: Entertain

*Lips under sod*, Florence L. Barclay; *Thoughts rode him like a nightmare*, John Buchan; *I brag of bear and beaver*, Robert W. Service; *Settling down to his dastardly work*, William Le Queux; *Far too young to assist*, Charles Amory Beach; *To die is easier*, Edgar A. Guest; *That dumb, backwoods, pie-faced stenographer*, Dorothy Canfield Fisher; *The azure gaze of Miss Hinda Warlick*, Edith Wharton; *My God, lady!*, Mildred Aldrich; *Nobody's Land*, Ring Lardner.

## Epilogue: Guide

*The pilgrimage*, Mildred Aldrich; *Turn right at cemetery gate*, American Battle Monuments Commission; *Peasants go there to dig*, Henry Williamson; *Visit to the Battlefield*, Michelin & Cie.; *Cemeteries become unremarkable*, Stephen Graham; *Back to the Somme*, John Masefield; *Whose credulous hearts the maggots were now eating*, C. E. Montague; *The most tragic and dreadful thing that has ever happened to mankind*, H. G. Wells.

# Notes

INTRODUCTION: The quote from Cyril Connolly appears in *Enemies of Promise* (Persea, 1983). The Doyle, Murray, Montague, Maeterlinck, Kipling, Davis, Wharton, Wells, and Ellis quotes are taken from their books cited in the text. Barbara Tuchman's comment on the changes caused by the war is from *Promise of Greatness* edited by George A. Panichas (John Day, 1968), as are L. P. Hartley's and Vera Brittain's. The famous benediction, "We will remember them," comes from Laurence Binyon's poem "For the Fallen." You can watch a fascinating interview with survivor Harry Patch, filmed when he was 109, on YouTube.

CHAPTER ONE: The story of the first two soldiers killed in the war comes from Gene Smith's small classic, *Still Quiet on the Western Front* (Morrow, 1965). Wells's and Doyle's quotes are from their books cited in the text. Much of the information on Maeterlinck comes from *Cyclopedia of World Authors* edited by Frank N. Magill (Harper, 1958), which is a good source for writers who are now almost forgotten. *20th Century Culture, a biographical companion* edited by Bullock and Woodings (Harper, 1983) also proved useful, as did the ever-reliable *Webster's American Biographies*, edited by Charles Van Doren (Merriam, 1974). The American Chesterton Society website is www.chesterton.org. The quote about Shaw's belligerence is from Jonathan Wisenthal and Daniel O'Leary. John Galsworthy's quote on propaganda is from the *History News Network* website.

CHAPTER TWO: The statistics about casualties and the trench system are taken from John Keegan's *The First World War* (Vintage, 2003), and *Fields of Memory* by Ann Rose (Seven Dials, 2000). Kipling's quote is from his book cited in the text. Rolland's quote on intellectual cowardice is found in Vera Brittain's *Testa-*

*ment of Experience* (Wideview, 1970). Conrad's complaint about what the war has done to his writing is drawn from *Joseph Conrad* by Jeffrey Meyers (Scribner, 1991), as is his pessimistic forecast at the war's end. Leon Edel's biography *Henry James* (Harper and Row, 1985) is the source of the quote from James's letters. Connolly's put-down of the late James style is from his book listed above. Quotations from Thomas Hardy are in *Thomas Hardy* by Michael Millgate (Random House, 1982). Russell on Murray is found in *The Autobiography of Bertrand Russell* (Atlantic Monthly Press, 1968). The Mann quotation comes from a Walter D. Morris translation; Richard Strauss's rejoinder is found in *The Rest is Noise* by Alex Ross (Farrar Straus and Giroux, 2007), while Rolland's is from his *Above the Battle* cited in the text. David C. Smith's *H. G. Wells* (Yale University Press, 1986) was very helpful on Wells's war years. Yeats's comment on war is from *W. B. Yeats* by R. F. Foster (Oxford University Press, 1991).

CHAPTER THREE: H. L. Mencken was accused of being pro-German—which he almost certainly was, believing the United States had joined the wrong side. Camus's brave quote is from *Resistance, Rebellion and Death* (Knopf, 1960). Hermione Lee's *Edith Wharton* (Knopf, 2007) is the source of the quote on her Francophile sensibilities, as well as the Wharton letter to her American friend. Mildred Aldrich's friendship with Gertrude Stein is described in *Gertrude and Alice* by Diana Souhami (I. B. Tauris, 2013). It's worth going back to the old books of Van Wyck Brooks to learn about the American writers of the 1914–18 era; his summary of Richard Harding Davis's enormous influence on young American writers is from *The Confident Years* (E. P. Dutton, 1952). The Henry Beston quote about courage in nature is from his little-known classic *Northern Farm* (Rinehart & Co., 1948). Upton Sinclair's description of John Reed is taken from the Brooks book cited above.

CHAPTER FOUR: Kipling's quote, "Because our fathers lied," is sometimes interpreted as a bitter rant at arms manufacturers not producing enough artillery shells, not at war in general, though it's come to be remembered as the latter. Montague's quote comes from his book cited in the text; Shaw's is from *The New York Times History of the War* cited there also. Martin Middlebrook's *The First Day on the Somme* (Norton, 1972) has a justifiably high reputation. The quote on the Somme's effect on English optimism is from

Keegan cited above. Rich Atkinson's *The Guns at Last Light* (Henry Holt, 2013) is the source for the poll on British public opinion regarding concentration camps. John Buchan briefing the king is quoted in *John Buchan* by Andrew Lownie (McArthur, 1995), as is the Peter Buitenhuis quote criticizing Buchan's omissions. J. C. Squire, when he wasn't writing ironic light verse, was a powerful right-wing editor in London; Virginia Woolf liked dismissing his circle of like-minded writers as the "Squirearchy."

CHAPTER FIVE: The quote from Samuel Hynes is from his introduction to West's novel (Penguin, 198), while Vera Brittain's are from *Testament of Youth* (Wideview, 1980). Sinclair's quote is taken from her book cited in the text. Arthur Miller's review of Bagnold's play appears in *Echoes Down the Corridor* (Viking Penguin, 2000). James's appreciation of Walpole is from Leon Edel's biography cited above. The West-Wells affair is detailed in *Rebecca West* (Fawcett Columbine, 1987) by Victoria Glendinning. The Tomlison quote on nobodies is from *Old Junk* cited in the text. Dos Passos's summation of the war is from his introduction to the reprinting of *One Man's Initiation* (under a new title: *First Encounter*) published by the Philosophical Library at the start of World War II.

CHAPTER SIX: The statistics on war deaths comes from Keegan's history cited above, as well as Hew Strachan's *The First World War* (Penguin, 2003). *Conscience* by Louis Thomas (Viking, 2013) gives a good idea of what antiwar protestors suffered in the United States. Romain Rolland's tribute to the protestors is from his book cited in the text. The chaplain's screed is from *The Great War in Europe* by Thomas H. Russell (J. Peper, 1914). Bertrand Russell's explanation of his motives for protesting are taken from his autobiography cited above. W. E. B. Du Bois's reversal in opinion on the war is described in *W. E. B. Du Bois* by David Levering (Henry Holt, 1993). Dos Passos's summary of Randolph Bourne appears in his novel *Nineteen Nineteen* (Modern Library, 1937).

CHAPTER SEVEN: Strachan and Keegan were the sources for the casualty statistics; the Beatrice Webb quote comes from Strachan. Wharton's quote is from her book cited in the text. Emile Verhaeren's quote is taken from *The Book of the Homeless*. Russell's snarky comment on Santayana is taken from the former's autobiography cited above. Lauder's description of firing a revenge cannon shot is taken from his book cited in the text. "Charlie Chaplin meets Harry Lauder" is a must-view on YouTube. W. H. Auden's poem "In Memory of W. B. Yeats" includes the reference to Paul Claudel.

CHAPTER EIGHT: The information on the book business is from Harold Orel's interesting *Popular Fiction in England 1914–18* (University Press of Kentucky, 1992). Murray's quote on humor is from his book cited in the text. The quote about most authors not wasting their time on moralizing is from Odel. Virginia Woolf's praise of Ring Lardner is taken from *Ring* by Jonathan Yardley (Random House, 1977). Lardner's non-fiction book *My Four Weeks in France,* while less interesting than his wartime fiction, contains Wallace Morgan's charming illustrations; Lardner's bitter little doggerel appears there.

EPILOGUE: The names of the last ones to die in the war comes from Nicholas Best's *The Greatest Day in History* (Public Affairs, 2008), as does Shaw's bitter lament. D. H. Lawrence's dark forecast is described in Samuel Hynes's indispensable *A War Imagined* (Atheneum, 1991). Hynes was a fighter pilot in World War II, then went on to a long career (still in progress as of 2015) as a professor and writer, with many thoughtful books to his credit. Hynes is also the source for the stanza by Thomas Hardy. The Michelin guide is cited in the text. Albert Moravia's quote is found in *Promise of Greatness* cited above. Hynes's summation of the war and literature is from his book cited above, as is his quote on middle-aged civilians. I have a first edition of Cobb's classic (Viking, 1935); thanks to Nicola Smith of the *Valley News* for steering me to Mary Borden's little-known book. Henry Williamson's lament is in Hynes. If you do an Internet search for "BBC Great War Interviews Henry Williamson" you'll find the TV interview referred to. The quotes on Masefield and Montague are from Hynes.